Auctorem House
276 5th Ave, Ste 704-2591
New York, NY 10001
www.auctoremhouse.com
Phone: 1 888-332-7718

Published by Auctorem House: 01/30/2025

ISBN: 978-1-965687-28-4(sc)
ISBN: 978-1-965687-29-1(e)

Library of Congress Control Number: 2024922629

The
Puzzled
Preacher

A Pastoral Exposition of Ecclesiastes

David A. Balsley, M.Div.

Dedicated to
my dear wife,
Janice - who helped
by proofreading the text,
and whose partnership has done
so much to contribute to the
rich sense of meaning in my life;
and to my children,
Stephen and Alissa,
who are responding to
Solomon's challenge to
"remember [their] Creator
in the days of [their] youth."

Table of Contents

4

5

6

The **Puzzled** Preacher
A Pastoral Exposition of Ecclesiastes

Preface

What is life all about? People have pondered the question down through the ages. The varied religious views and philosophical speculations of mankind bear witness to the multiplicity of ideas which people have come up with in regard to life's meaning.

There is no better place to go for answers to our questions regarding the meaning of life than to the Word of God Himself. As the creator of all life, the Lord has revealed that there is nothing more important for a human being than to walk in faith and obedience with His Maker. And the revelation of the Scriptures progressively fills in the finer points of what the Lord is looking for in human behavior.

For Adam and Eve the will of God was summed up in a single command. They were not to eat the fruit of the tree of the knowledge of good and evil. It is evident from the Biblical record that Cain and Able, though we don't have the details of God's revelation to them, were aware of the importance of sacrifice in maintaining a healthy relationship with the Lord.   Additional clarification regarding the will of God was given to Noah following the great flood. The Lord's promises called for a response of faith from Abraham who, because he believed what he was told, was credited with righteousness. And, of course, a major step forward in the revelation of God's will for mankind took place in the giving of the Law at Mount Sinai - a revelation which was clarified with additional detail during the wanderings of Israel in the desert.

By the time of Israel's early kings (Saul and David and Solomon), there was more than enough truth revealed to guide the trusting soul in a deep and fulfilling walk with the Lord. When, centuries later, the Lord Jesus was asked by a testy lawyer which was the greatest commandment of the Law, Jesus went (without hesitation) to the instruction of Moses in Deuteronomy 6:4-5: "Hear, O Israel! The Lord is our God, the Lord is one! [5] You shall love the Lord your God with all your heart and with all your soul and with all your might." So, well acquainted as he was with the Law of the Lord, it is not surprising that King David could challenge his people centuries after Moses, as he did in Psalm 31:23-24:

> [23] "O love the Lord, all you His godly ones!
> The Lord preserves the faithful
> And fully recompenses the proud doer.
> [24] Be strong and let your heart take courage,
> All you who hope in the Lord."

Many millions of earth's citizens have discovered that life, at its best, will be found in a love

7

for the Lord. Such love results in hope in the Lord and in faithfulness to the will of the Lord, which David wrote about. And one who made that discovery was King David's son Solomon. He authored the wisdom-sayings of the Proverbs, with their wealth of revelation regarding life's meaning. But another of Solomon's writings, the book of Ecclesiastes, reveals that Solomon did not manage to stay focused on life at its best throughout the whole of his earthly pilgrimage. He obviously became distracted for a time, with the result that he spent a great deal of time and resources and energy searching "under the sun" for the source of meaning in life, to rediscover at last that life at its best does not find its source "under the sun."

It is my hope that the pages which follow will help us to better understand where Solomon's search took him and, what is more important, where it finally ended for the man I have chosen to describe as "the puzzled preacher."

Section One:
Solomon's Introduction
to Life's Futility

1:1-18

Life "Under the Sun"
Ecclesiastes 1:1-11

In recent decades something called "suicidology" has flourished in the United States and in other parts of the western world. Many studies have arisen, as a result, and thousands of books have been written - some of them explaining how to go about successfully committing suicide.

For many people in our world life is viewed as not worth living. In addition to the hundreds of thousands who commit suicide each year, there are many more who attempt it, or who would attempt it if they could muster the courage. They have decided, for one reason or another, that their lives are no longer worth living.

What is it that gives meaning to human existence? There are many things, of course, which contribute to satisfaction in life. Among them are the satisfactions which are found in family relations, education, careers, material possessions, physical achievements, love of the arts, and humanitarian efforts. But, when all is said and done, none of these things are fully and finally satisfying. Though there are many things to enjoy on earth, life's meaning in its fullest dimensions will never be found by those who look only on the face of the earth. Mankind was created by an omniscient God for reasons that reach beyond the earth, and it is only when a person takes God and His will into consideration in living that he will find life at its best.

Many centuries ago a well-educated and wealthy man set about to examine life in search of its meaning. He had the time, the mind, and the resources to go much farther in his search than most people will ever go. So we can be thankful that he recorded his findings in a book for our advantage - though many others have discovered what he discovered. One of his early discoveries was that life "under the sun" (i.e., apart from God) is full of emptiness.

I. Introduction to Ecclesiastes

A. The Author 1:1

"The words of the Preacher, the son of David, king in Jerusalem."

The word translated "preacher" is the Hebrew title for the book of Ecclesiastes. The Hebrew word *qohelet* means "one who convenes and speaks at an assembly" (according to Charles

10

Ryrie),[1] or "speaker," or "preacher." The word occurs only in the book of Ecclesiastes, whose title in our English Bibles comes from the Greek version of the Old Testament (the Septuagint).

Centuries of tradition have maintained that the "preacher" of Ecclesiastes is Solomon. Some modern scholars have followed the lead of Martin Luther, who believed that the book was written after the time of the exile by someone who was writing from Solomon's viewpoint, but there are good reasons for staying with the traditional view that Solomon is the author.

1. The author identifies himself as the "Son of David" (which Solomon was).

2. The author claims to have been "King in Jerusalem" (which Solomon was as well).

3. The author claims unusual wisdom (1:16), which Solomon had.

4. The author possessed unusual wealth (which Solomon did).

Writing the book of Ecclesiastes, Solomon spoke from the viewpoint of a man who had taken a careful look at life and who now summoned and spoke to his people to let them know what he had found - and it wasn't very encouraging!

B. The Assertion 1:2

"Vanity of vanities," says the Preacher,
"Vanity of vanities! All is vanity."

"Vanity" is well illustrated by another good translation of the word which Solomon used: "breath" or "breeze." Like a breath or a breeze which cannot be seen, but is breathed or blown only to be breathed or blown again, this earthly life is a transitory thing which (when you add it all up) hardly amounts to much.

The Bible shows us that God created us for more worthwhile things than we spend much of our time engaged in. But, with the entrance of sin, much of life took on a futility and a brevity which might make a man, in his more thoughtful moments, wonder why he has to be bothered!

It is interesting that Solomon's word for "vanity" is the word which was used as the name of the fourth human being on earth, Abel (*Hebel* in Hebrew). Eve gave birth to her second son as the effects of the curse began to impress her with the truth that Solomon discovered many centuries later. It was the truth that life is fleeting and full of meaningless activity - especially if God is left out of the picture.

---

[1] Charles Caldwell Ryrie, *Ryrie Study Bible,* Expanded Edition, (Chicago, IL: Moody Press, 1995), p. 1018.

11

Ecclesiastes is the only book in the Bible which pursues the theme of life's emptiness at any great length, but it isn't the only book which says what it says about the futility and the brevity of life! The apostle Paul wrote about the futility of life on a sin-cursed earth in Romans 8:18-21:

> "For I consider that the sufferings of this present time are not worthy to be compared with the glory that is to be revealed to us. [19] For the anxious longing of the creation waits eagerly for the revealing of the sons of God. [20] For the creation was subjected to futility, not willingly, but because of Him who subjected it, in hope [21] that the creation itself also will be set free from its slavery to corruption into the freedom of the glory of the children of God."

And Jesus' half-brother James addressed the same issue in James 4:13-14:

> "Come now, you who say, 'Today or tomorrow we will go to such and such a city, and spend a year there and engage in business and make a profit.' [14] Yet you do not know what your life will be like tomorrow. You are just a vapor that appears for a little while and then vanishes away."

Solomon wasn't, as he might sound here, an incurable pessimist. But he was a determined realist; a man who observed and announced that life as we know it on our sin-cursed earth (and even more so, perhaps, in his age prior to Christ) is just full of things that don't make a lot of sense!

You have noticed that about life, haven't you? If you haven't, stick around! We all eventually have occasion to wonder why life isn't adding up to all we think it should!

II. The Message of Ecclesiastes

A. Solomon's Question 1:3

"What advantage does man have in all his work
Which he does under the sun?"

Before anyone can adequately understand this question or understand the book of Ecclesiastes, he has to understand the meaning of the frequently recurring phrase "under the sun."

An enlightened Christian in our age would have a reasonable response to Solomon's question ("What advantage does man have in all his work?"). He would observe that God has provided many satisfactions on earth which make life worth living, in spite of life's numerous and obvious problems. And he would observe that God is going to reward men in the kingdom age, and in the eternal ages to follow, for the works they perform in this life on earth. But Solomon's phrase, "under the sun," eliminates any consideration of God or of the rewards which are planned in the

12

ages to come.

By the phrase "under the sun" Solomon leaves God completely out of the picture. His question is addressed to earthly life as we now know it - apart from God! What he asks is this: If you leave God completely out of the picture, what reason does a man have for living and what reward does he have for laboring all his life on the face of a sin-cursed earth?

Solomon's viewpoint in Ecclesiastes is the viewpoint of the crude and pessimistic bumper sticker you may have seen: "Life is a bitch - and then you die!" With this understanding of his question, Solomon is going to proceed to show us that the answer is this: There **isn't** much reason for living and there **isn't** much reward for laboring on earth if you think only in terms of what is "under the sun."

B. Solomon's Observations 1:4-7

Wherever you look on the face of the earth, you will find an endless series of circles!

1. The Passing of Generations 1:4

"A generation goes and a generation comes,
But the earth remains forever."

There is nothing quite as fresh as a brand-new baby, but what is it that happens to brand-new babies? As we all know, they grow up (if their life is "normal") and they grow old and they die! So why do we still have people on earth? Because old and dying people are always being replaced by brand-new babies - who grow up and grow old and die, and are replaced by brand-new babies - who grow up and grow old and die, and are replaced by brand-new babies - and on and on it goes!

Do you see the futility of it all? People are born to die, and be replaced by people who are born to die! And, meanwhile, the earth abides and watches this seemingly endless parade of people who are born to die, but who are replaced with people who are born to die! Is there any great profit in being one of an ongoing procession of people who are born to die? Perhaps, instead, you would like to be the sun!

2. The Circuit of the Sun 1:5

"Also, the sun rises and the sun sets;
And hastening to its place it rises there again."

We see the sun rise in the east - when it can be seen - every morning [and it rises in the east every morning even when it can't be seen], and then we watch it set in the west every evening. And what is the sun doing during the night when it can't be seen? It is "hastening" to its place!

13

Solomon graphically portrays the scene by saying, literally, that the sun comes "panting" (*shaaph*) to its place!

But why all this hurried motion? So that it can rise in the east and set in the west, and then hurry back to the east so it can set in the west! What an exciting adventure! How would you like to be the sun? Or perhaps you would prefer to be the wind!

3. The Circles of the Wind 1:6

"Blowing toward the south,
 Then turning toward the north,
The wind continues swirling along;
And on its circular courses the wind returns."

The wind doesn't travel such a predictable course as the sun appears to travel, but it still travels in circles! Solomon observed what modern science confirms, that wind currents travel in regular, circular patterns - blowing north and south, east and west, up some and down some - but never really "going" anywhere!

If blowing with the wind doesn't sound too rewarding, how about falling with the rain or flowing with a river or rising and falling with the sea?

4. The Cycles of the Waters 1:7

"All the rivers flow into the sea,
Yet the sea is not full.
To the place where the rivers flow,
There they flow again."

Rivers are still flowing to the sea today just as they were yesterday and last week and last year and a century ago and a millennium ago and in Solomon's day (three millennia ago). And in Solomon's day they had already been flowing for millennia to the sea!

So what has come of all this flowing? Has the sea filled up and overflowed? No, it hasn't. And it won't. For all their flowing, there isn't a great deal of evidence that the rivers have gotten anywhere or accomplished anything (apart from some sculpting of the surface of the land) - but that is pretty much a picture of all of life!

C. Solomon's Conclusions 1:8-11

1. Life Is Wearisome 1:8

"All things are wearisome;

14

Man is not able to tell it.
The eye is not satisfied with seeing,
Nor is the ear filled with hearing."

If you take a long and careful look at life, leaving God out of the picture, you will get tired of looking, but you may not be able to say exactly what you saw. Though the scenes keep changing, it isn't very certain that they are going anywhere. It is something like standing in the busyness of one of earth's cities and watching endless motion without knowing where it all leads.

You can watch and watch and watch the world and the people around you, but there will still be more to see - and you may not even be certain what you have seen! You can listen and listen and listen again to the sounds that fill your life, but there will still be more to hear - no matter how long you have already been listening - and all the listening you can do won't bring you to conclude that you have heard enough to understand what it all means.

You will literally wear yourself out seeing and listening and still never be able to say that you have seen it all or heard it all, or that what you have seen and what you have heard has gotten you where you feel you ought to be!

2. Life Is Relative 1:9-10

"That which has been is that which will be,
And that which has been done is that which will be done.
So there is nothing new under the sun.
[10] Is there anything of which one might say,
'See this, it is new'?
Already it has existed for ages
Which were before us."

You walk and walk and walk until you are sure you have arrived where no other man has ever been - then you stop for lunch and sit down on a rusty coke can! You study and study and write and write and produce a new, exciting book on a subject no one has ever addressed before - only to be told that you will have to change your title because someone has already used it for another book on the same subject!

Every once in a while someone introduces something which seems to be brand-new, but if you will carefully look around, you will find something like it somewhere else - often something that has been around for years.

3. Life Is Forgetful 1:11

"There is no remembrance of earlier things;
And also of the later things which will occur,

15

There will be for them no remembrance
Among those who will come later still."

Library shelves are filled with volumes and volumes of "Who's Who" books, all full of the names of people whom almost nobody knows and about whom almost nobody cares. There are a few people who have become well enough known that most people in their sphere of influence know of them. In the United States that would include such national figures as George Washington and Abraham Lincoln. But, as a general rule, when a man dies he will soon be forgotten by almost everyone!

If you are hoping to be remembered long past your time on earth, your chances are very slim. In fact, they are almost nonexistent! There are millions of people in the world who have never even heard of the city where you live, let alone anyone in it. And those who have heard of your city or some of its residents won't last long or remember long having heard of it or having heard of them.

Most people who become famous are remembered for only a short time. But most of us will never become famous, or anything like it! Most people are fortunate if they are even known, let alone remembered. Solomon's message was reflected in the song which many people were familiar with in the second half of twentieth century America - "Do You Know the Way to San Jose?"

Do you know the way to San Jose?
I've been away so long, I may go wrong and lose my way.

Do you know the way to San Jose?
I'm going back to find some peace of mind in San Jose.

L.A. is a great big freeway!
Put a hundred down and buy a car!
In a week - maybe two - they'll make you a star!

Weeks turn into years - how quick they pass -
And all the stars that never were are parking cars and pumping gas.[2]

We are no more likely to be remembered than the millions and billions of nameless people who have gone before us, because no one has the capacity or will have the longevity to remember us for long. And, quite frankly, most of them don't care! Life is forgetful!

Life "under the sun" (i.e. apart from God) is full of emptiness. So don't go looking for a meaningful life if you are planning to leave God out of the picture.

---

[2] Burt Bacharach and Hal David, "Do You Know the Way to San Jose?"

16

Why Bother?
Ecclesiastes 1:12-18

Do you ever come to the end of a day and wonder what all of the time and energy you have invested during the day has really amounted to? You get out of bed in time to have breakfast, and the first thing you know you are getting hungry for lunch! Or you get out of bed in time to **make** breakfast and clean up the kitchen when it is time to start **making** lunch!

Many, if not most, of the things we do in a day are things we have also done the day before or the week before - with some minor variations - and we will do again in another day or few days or week or month. Life can be - and often is - very repetitious. So any thinking person can't help stopping from time to time to wonder if he is really making any progress, or just going around and around in circles, and creating deeper and deeper ruts.

For the Christian, of course, life **is** going somewhere. Salvation is a process - beginning with our new birth in Christ. It then continues (ideally) with steps of growth which take us higher and higher in this life (in terms of our knowledge of truth and our likeness to Christ). And it is leading us ultimately to eternal joy in heaven.

The apostle Paul expressed his satisfaction in following Christ in Philippine 3:13-14: "Brethren, I do not regard myself as having laid hold of it yet; but one thing I do: forgetting what lies behind and reaching forward to what lies ahead, [14] I press on toward the goal for the prize of the upward call of God in Christ Jesus."

Even though the Christian experiences many of the same circles which the world experiences, there is a sense of **progress** in knowing that our circles have some meaning in the process of salvation in this life, and an eternity of meaning projected forward into the life to come!

How we arrive at the breakfast table is important in Christ! It isn't just a matter of getting there. Our actions and our attitudes are all very important in the Christian life - even on the way to the breakfast table!

But just imagine how empty life could be if it weren't seen in view of eternity! Imagine how frustrating it would be going through some of life's circular patterns if this life were all there is. Maybe you don't have to imagine! Maybe you have been there recently enough to remember how it is - or maybe you are still there!

17

In his search for purpose and meaning in life "under the sun," Solomon came to the realization that all the works and wisdom of man, apart from God, are "vanity."

I. Solomon's Search of Man's Works 1:12-15

A. His Position 1:12

"I, the Preacher, have been king over Israel in Jerusalem."

The word "preacher" (*qoheleth*) refers to a "speaker" in some kind of an assembly. Either in fact or in his imagination, Solomon gathered before him the assembly of Israel to speak to them about the meaning of life.

His more familiar role to us is that of king over Israel in its capital city Jerusalem, a position he still held when he wrote the book of Ecclesiastes. There are many questions as to when and why the experiences of the book of Ecclesiastes took place in Solomon's life, but the suggestion that it wasn't really Solomon who wrote the book raises more questions than it answers. The "preacher" was "king over Israel in Jerusalem" (v. 12) and he "magnified and increased wisdom more than all who were over Jerusalem before him " (v. 16) - and that is a description of Solomon if it is a description of any Bible person we know!

Now it might seem that a king as wise and wealthy as Solomon was would have the pieces of life's puzzle pretty well sorted out. But there appears to have been a time in his life when this was not the case - as he acknowledges for all to read.

B. His Search 1:13

"And I set my mind to seek and explore by wisdom concerning all that has been done under heaven. It is a grievous task which God has given to the sons of men to be afflicted with."

We know that Solomon received from God a gift of wisdom (*chokmah*) like no other man has ever had. He was given the skill (*chokmah*) to understand and apply the facts of life to practical matters. So Solomon decided to use his wisdom in a research project - which he describes for us in two phrases in 1:13.

1. "to seek . . . all that has been done under heaven."

Solomon went looking to see what kinds of things men were accomplishing - apart from divine direction. "Under heaven," like "under the sun," tells us that Solomon's search involved man's works apart from God's direction. So Solomon was looking for things like building projects, learning institutions, the latest inventions, and so forth.

2. "To explore by wisdom concerning all that has been done under heaven."

18

Solomon wanted not only to see what men were doing by their own ability, but to investigate what they were doing. He applied his skillful mind to understanding not only the "what" but the "why" of human activity and accomplishment.

So Solomon wanted answers to questions like these: What makes one building better than another? How does one learning institution compare with another? What are its strengths and weaknesses? What makes the latest invention work? Why is it needed? How will it improve things?

By his God-given gift of wisdom Solomon was better equipped to enumerate and evaluate all the things he found men doing than any other mere human has ever been. But his findings weren't very encouraging, because he summed up his findings: "It is a grievous task which God has given to the sons of men to be afflicted with." Literally, what he said was "it is a work of (ra) evil" ("evil" in the sense of noxious, hurtful, unpleasant).

Looking at it realistically, Solomon concluded that life on earth is hard and, in many respects, unrewarding. Knowing what the Bible tells us about the Lord's unusual gifting in his life, we have to wonder how he could arrive at such a pessimistic conclusion. His explanation continues.

C. His Summary 1:14

"I have seen all the works which have been done under the sun, and behold, all is vanity and striving after wind."

Solomon, of course, did not tour the whole world and look into every work that man was doing anywhere, or had ever done at any time - you can be sure! But he searched and investigated thoroughly enough that he was satisfied he had seen every activity man was involved in, at least in representative fashion. Though he didn't see every building, he saw buildings. Though he didn't see every school, he saw schools. And though he didn't see every new invention or innovation, he saw inventions and innovations until he was satisfied that he had seen enough!

In his extensive investigation, Solomon left God out of the picture - whether intentionally or not, we can't be sure. His investigation concerned that which was "under the sun" - that which man does on his own initiative and in his own energy and with his own resources (to the extent that such is possible, of course). Solomon's viewpoint in the book of Ecclesiastes was essentially the same as that of the humanist in our day: the view that man is the measure of all things.

Now, if you push, to its limits, the thinking that man is the measure of all things, what will you finally conclude? The discovery of man's fallibility and finiteness eventually leads to the conclusion Solomon arrived at, that "All is vanity and striving after the wind."

19

What happens to all of the construction projects which man engages in? They all require extensive maintenance to keep them from disintegrating and disappearing - so building buildings ultimately becomes an exercise in futility, like chasing the wind. And what happens to all that mankind has learned? His learning becomes outdated. So it has to be constantly updated, or it becomes obsolete. Some fields of knowledge are moving so rapidly in our day that a few months can make your learning obsolete. So pursuing learning is like chasing the wind. And what happens to man's latest inventions? They are soon replaced by a newer invention. Obsolescence is the name of the game. In our day we even have planned obsolescence (as if it needed any planning), so trying to keep up with the latest invention is like chasing the wind.

D. His Illustration 1:15

"What is crooked cannot be straightened and what is lacking cannot be counted."

There are many things about life as we know it which are "crooked" and aren't capable of being "straightened." For example, there are, since Adam's sin in the Garden of Eden, flaws in man himself which cannot be straightened out in this life. Mankind is flawed by sin. And there are flaws in man's workmanship, and there always will be such flaws in this life, because man is a fallible creature. There are also flaws in man's learning, and in some cases they are getting bigger rather than smaller (as in the case of evolutionary thinking in our age). Try as you might, you will not be able to remove all of these flaws!

There are many things lacking in this life as we know it - so many that they can't be counted. Consider, for example, the problem of injustice. How many instances of injustice do you suppose we might be talking about from the beginning of time until now? How about the love that is lacking in our world? How about the humility? How about the peace? How about the happiness? How about the self-control? And the list could go on and on.

If you survey the works of man, leaving God entirely out of the picture, you will find that man has done a very thorough job of scuffing up God's earth, and that he doesn't have anything that is worth dedicating your existence to. Man has done some great things, make no mistake about it, but nothing worth living for, because everything man produces (using I Peter 1:4's description of heaven - in reverse) is corruptible, defiled and fading away.

If you are "putting all your stock" in what you can accomplish in this life, leaving the Lord out of the picture of your life, you are going to discover that it will all self-destruct, leaving you in the end with nothing to show for all your labors in life.

And what is true of man's works is also true of man's wisdom.

II. Solomon's Search of Man's Wisdom 1:16-19

A. His Achievement 1:16

20

"I said to myself, 'Behold, I have magnified and increased wisdom more than all who were over Jerusalem before me; and my mind has observed a wealth of wisdom and knowledge.'"

If there was ever any mere man who was qualified to appraise the value and importance of man's wisdom and knowledge it was Solomon, because God gave Solomon His Own wisdom in greater measure than He has ever given it to any other man (except the God/man, Jesus).

Recall how Solomon received his gift of wisdom. I Kings 3:3-12 reports that, while he was sacrificing to the Lord at Gibeon, Solomon was asked by God in a dream what he would like God to give him. His reply was "an understanding heart to judge your people and discern between good and evil." So God said: "Behold, I have given you a wise and discerning heart, so that there has been no one like you before you, nor shall one like you arise after you."

And recall how Solomon's wisdom and understanding made themselves evident in his life. He produced brilliant judgments - like the I Kings 3:16-18 decision regarding the two harlots and their babies. He demonstrated administrative genius, overseeing the construction of the Jerusalem temple, as well as the many other construction projects he will report about in chapter two. He accumulated incredible wealth - with an annual income in gold alone at 83,250 pounds. He was a prolific author, writing (among other things) 3,000 proverbs and 1,005 songs. And he demonstrated a vast knowledge of nature - speaking "of trees, from the cedar that is in Lebanon even to the hyssop that grows on the wall; he spoke also of animals and birds and creeping things and fish" (I Kings 4:33).

Solomon isn't bragging in this verse when he describes, in general terms, his wisdom and knowledge. He is just telling it like it was - the sober truth.

B. His Realization 1:17

"And I set my mind to know wisdom and to know madness and folly; I realized that this also is striving after wind."

Solomon understood by his wisdom how things should be done, as revealed by the many positive proverbs he wrote, challenging his readers to fear and follow the Lord. And he understood by his wisdom things which should not be done, as revealed in the warnings of his negative proverbs, such as his warnings about harlots and drunkenness and slothfulness and surety.

It is certainly a good thing to have a lot of knowledge about a lot of things if you have the mind for it. And it is even better to know how to skillfully apply the knowledge you have to everyday situations. But if you accumulate knowledge only for the sake of knowledge and wisdom only for the sake of wisdom, you will find that they aren't enough to provide you with a reason for living. If wisdom and knowledge are all there is, then death is the end of all there is.

21

Dead men don't know anything and dead men can't apply knowledge any longer. So if there is no God to bring man back to life, then wisdom and knowledge are of value only during this very short stay on earth we know as life. Beyond that they won't do you any good.

They too are like chasing the wind because just when you think you have them they are gone forever if there is only life "under the sun." In fact, there is a sense in which you are better off without them if this life is all there is.

C. His Illustration 1:18

"Because in much wisdom there is much grief, and increasing knowledge results in increasing pain."

The better you understand how things should be done - how the facts of life could be turned to every man's advantage - the more grief you are bound to experience over all the things that aren't being done as they should be done. If a poorly constructed building is evident to me, it is far more evident and troublesome to a knowledgeable builder. If poorly performed music is not to my liking, it is far more distressing to a skilled musician.

The more you know, the more bad news you know, because much of what there is to know on this sin-cursed earth is bad news. All you have to do is turn on a news broadcast or sit down with the newspaper and you will be reminded again that there isn't much good news available in our world. So the more you know, the more you have to be pained about.

If there were no God, we would be in a much bigger mess than we are in already, because all of the work and all of the wisdom we can muster in our lives would ultimately be for no lasting purpose whatsoever. All the works and wisdom of man, leaving God out of the picture, are vanity. So why bother?

How encouraging to know that life on earth does not have to be lived only "under the sun," and that this life is not all there is. As the apostle Paul stated it, "For to me to live is Christ and to die is gain" (Philippians 1:21). Regrettably, Solomon lived years of his life in frustration because he failed to look above the sun. Let's be careful not to make the same mistake!

Section Two: Solomon's Investigation of Life's Futility

2:1-26

23

Going Nowhere Fast
Ecclesiastes 2:1-11

It isn't exactly encouraging, but it is true that most people in the world are heading in the wrong direction. Jesus addressed the problem, as recorded in Matthew 7:13-14: "Enter through the narrow gate; for the gate is wide and the way is broad that leads to destruction, and there are many who enter through it. [14] For the gate is small and the way is narrow that leads to life, and there are few who find it."

For all of their speed and all of their busyness, most of the people who are rushing by us each day in the hectic pace of modern American society are "going nowhere fast." Though, like people in all times and in every place, they are looking for deep and lasting satisfaction, they aren't finding it, and they aren't going to find it because they are looking in the wrong places, and they are pursuing the wrong pursuits.

We have all experienced the fact that the things we think will really bring us satisfaction in this life seldom do. Benjamin Franklin is reported to have said "Who is rich? He that is content. Who is that? Nobody."[3]

It might not be so bad if only earth's unbelieving people, for looking in the wrong places and for pursuing the wrong things, were dissatisfied with their lot in life. But it is not only earth's unbelieving people who fail to find what they are looking for. God's people too are often guilty of "chasing pretty rainbows." There are believers who want more than they have - in many areas of life - and who keep looking to the world in hope that their longings will be satisfied, only to find (again and again) that the world isn't capable of providing satisfaction in ultimate dimensions.

Will we ever really learn that worldly aims and accomplishments will never provide soul satisfaction? We may come to see this truth. Many already have. But there isn't much hope that many people will ever really learn this truth to the extent that they will stop turning to the world to provide what it isn't capable of providing.

Solomon finally saw this truth, but only after he had spent much of his life searching for satisfaction in the things of the world without finding it.

---

[3] Paul Lee Tan, *Encyclopedia of 7,700 Illustrations* (Rockville, MD: Assurance Publishers, 1979), p. 273, #839.

24

I. Solomon's Decision 2:1-2

A. His Search 2:1

"I said to myself, 'Come now, I will test you with pleasure. So enjoy yourself.' And behold, it too was futility."

As we saw in the opening chapter of Ecclesiastes, Solomon was trying to discover what life is all about - what life's purpose is. He sought to know which direction a person should take to find a feeling of fulfillment in this life. His search was being conducted - as he says again in this chapter (2:3,11) - "under the sun" (or "under heaven"). He was seeking satisfaction at a time in his life when he was failing to take God and eternal issues into consideration.

In his search Solomon decided to try pleasure. There are many people in our day who are trying the same approach to life, so what Solomon has to say to us from his experience is extremely relevant to our age.

For his pleasure, Solomon tried anything and everything his heart desired - literally (because he could afford it). His pleasure didn't consist only of lightheartedness and leisure; it also included industrious accomplishment. It included anything he thought he might find enjoyable. Interestingly, though, it didn't yield what he thought it would yield, because he sums up his search with the now familiar sounding "and behold, it too was futility."

B. His Summary 2:2

"I said of laughter, 'It is madness,' and of pleasure, 'What does it accomplish?'"

We all enjoy a good time and a good laugh - but Solomon concluded that you would be "mad" to try to laugh your life away.

There are times when I have laughed so hard that my ribs ached, and I have enjoyed every minute of it. But I am well aware that such fun times will, sooner or later, be followed by times which aren't the least bit funny. Laughter is appropriate in its place, but it is neither fulfilling nor realistic as a way of life. Consider the experience of Ralph Barton.

Ralph Barton, who made his life as a cartoonist making people laugh, wrote in his suicide note: "I have had few difficulties, many friends, great successes; I have gone from wife to wife, and from house to house, visited great countries of the world, but I am fed up with inventing devices to fill up 24 hours of the day."[4]

---

[4] Josh McDowell, *The Resurrection Factor* (San Bernardino, CA.: Here's Life Publishers, 1981), p. 1.

And what is true of laughter is also true of pleasure. It is good to do things you enjoy doing from time to time, but most of the things people enjoy doing aren't very productive things as life pursuits. Besides that, the things we enjoy most lose their pleasure if they are pursued too hotly. For example, the man who becomes a professional basketball player because he likes basketball soon comes to see the game as work, not as play, and it loses some of its pleasure in his thinking.

Solomon concluded that "doing your own thing" is not a fulfilling way to live - and he ought to know better than anybody what is fulfilling and what is not because he tried more things than most anyone else has ever been able to afford.

II. Solomon's Direction 2:3-10

A. He Tried Wine 2:3

"I explored with my mind how to stimulate my body with wine while my mind was guiding me wisely . . ."

Solomon was not the typical "drunk" in his exploration of the stimulation which comes by wine. His drinking was carried on at the highest level of respectability at which such an experiment can be carried on - "while [his] mind was guiding [him] wisely."

Interestingly, though, he also did some things which he now describes as "folly" in his attempt to understand what would be best for a man to do. Because he doesn't elaborate, we can't be sure exactly what Solomon had in mind but, since "folly" is normally a description of irresponsible behavior, or even of ungodliness, it appears that Solomon's search for satisfaction wasn't always conducted on the highest plane of wisdom.

"I explored . . . how to take hold of folly, until I could see what good there is for the sons of men to do under heaven the few years of their lives."

We all know that we most appreciate life's best when we have had a glimpse of life's worst - though, fortunately, we don't have to personally experience life's worst to see the other side in better perspective.

Whatever Solomon did, both in his use of wine and in his pursuit of folly, he now knew that it didn't bring him the satisfaction he was seeking. It certainly wasn't worth giving his life to.

B. He Tried Work Projects 2:4-6

"I enlarged my works . . ."

_____

26

Many people have tried this avenue of seeking to satisfy themselves in life - though perhaps no one else has done it with the extravagance of Solomon.

1. He Built Houses 2:4a

"I built houses for myself."

One of Solomon's house building projects, the house he and his Egyptian wife occupied, is described for us in Scripture (I Kings 7:1-12). That it was no simple structure is evident by the fact that it took thirteen years to complete; it was 150 feet in length, 75 feet in width, and 45 feet in height; it included rows of cedar pillars, topped with cedar beams - all imported from Lebanon; its windows and doors were artistically framed; and it included large and costly cut stones - some with twelve and fifteen foot dimensions.

2. He Planted Vineyards (2:4b)

"I planted vineyards for myself."

Many people find a lot of satisfaction in growing plants. Solomon decided to multiply his satisfaction by growing many of them - not just a vineyard but vineyards. And that was not all he planted!

3. He Planted Gardens and Parks 2:5

"I made gardens and parks for myself and I planted in them all kinds of fruit trees."

Solomon did not restrict his horticultural pursuits to the growing of grapes. His gardens included many varieties of plants. And his plants were not restricted to gardens, but were grown in displays massive enough to fill parks, and in displays varied enough to create orchards.

4. He Created Water Projects 2:6

"I made ponds of water for myself from which to irrigate a forest of growing trees."

Solomon's interest in plants became so extensive that he had to arrange for the storage of water in ponds in order to have the water he needed to sustain gardens and parks and orchards and even forests. If all of this sounds overly ambitious, it was actually only a small part of the projects undertaken by Solomon. The Scriptural record tells us that Solomon's building projects included entire cities (II Chronicles 8:1-6)!

Now it came about at the end of the twenty years in which Solomon had built the house of the Lord and his own house [2] that he built the cities which Huram had given to him, and settled the sons of Israel there.

[3] Then Solomon went to Hamath-zobah and captured it. [4] He built Tadmor in the wilderness and all the storage cities which he had built in Hamath. [5] He also built upper Beth-horon and lower Beth-horon, fortified cities with walls, gates and bars; [6] and Baalath and all the storage cities that Solomon had, and all the cities for his chariots and cities for his horsemen, and all that it pleased Solomon to build in Jerusalem, in Lebanon, and in all the land under his rule.

C. He Tried Wealth 2:7-8a

Solomon's experimentation with wealth was a highly diversified "portfolio."

1. He Accumulated Slaves 2:7a

"I bought male and female slaves and I had homeborn slaves."

Slaves were the "labor-saving" devices of Solomon's day. But they were also a form of wealth, because it took money to buy them, and they had resale value. In addition, they were an indication of wealth, because it required wealth to maintain them with food and clothing and housing.

As his slave-force grew, Solomon had entire families of slaves. No numbers are placed on Solomon's slave force, but they must have numbered high in the thousands. I Chronicles 8:7-8 provides some information on some of the sources of Solomon's slave force.

"All of the people who were left of the Hittites, the Amorites, the Perizzites, the Hivites and the Jebusites, who were not of Israel, [8] namely, from their descendants who were left after them in the land whom the sons of Israel had not destroyed, them Solomon raised as forced laborers to this day."

2. He Possessed Flocks and Herds 2:7b

"Also I possessed flocks and herds larger than all who preceded me in Jerusalem."

The number of animals which Solomon offered in sacrifice at the time of the dedication of the temple gives us just a glimpse of how many animals Solomon could afford to give up. II Chronicles 7:5 tells of the sacrifice of 22,000 oxen and 120,000 sheep!

Even the record of the provisions required for his own household on a daily basis staggers the imagination! I Kings 4:23 reports a daily grocery list of ten fat oxen, twenty pasture-fed oxen, one hundred sheep, in addition to unnumbered deer, gazelles, roebucks and fowl.

3. He Accumulated Gold and Treasures 2:8a

28

"Also, I collected for myself silver and gold and the treasure of kings and provinces."

We get a glimpse of some of Solomon's treasures in I Kings 10:16-22.

"King Solomon made 200 large shields of beaten gold, using 600 shekels of gold on each large shield. [17] He made 300 shields of beaten gold, using three minas of gold on each shield, and the king put them in the house of the forest of Lebanon. [18] Moreover, the king made a great throne of ivory and overlaid it with refined gold. [19] There were six steps to the throne and a round top to the throne at its rear, and arms on each side of the seat, and two lions standing beside the arms. [20] Twelve lions were standing there on the six steps on the one side and on the other; nothing like it was made for any other kingdom. [21] All King Solomon's drinking vessels were of gold, and all the vessels of the house of the forest of Lebanon were of pure gold. None was of silver; it was not considered valuable in the days of Solomon. [22] For the king had at sea the ships of Tarshish with the ships of Hiram; once every three years the ships of Tarshish came bringing gold and silver, ivory and apes and peacocks."

4. He Enjoyed Music 2:8b

"I provided for myself male and female singers"

Solomon's exploration into the realm of music, like his other explorations, was done on a grand scale. He didn't just deal in soloists. He arranged for choirs to perform for his enjoyment.

5. He Enjoyed Women 2:8c

" . . . and the pleasures of men—many concubines."

As you may be aware, Solomon's report here is something of an understatement. I Kings 11:1-3 tells us that Solomon loved "many foreign women" of Moabite and Ammonite and Edomite and Sidonian and Hittite extraction, for a total of "seven hundred wives, princesses, and three hundred concubines"! If sex were life's ultimate good, as many modern messages from the worlds of media and entertainment would seem to suggest, Solomon should surely have known about it! But that isn't what Solomon is writing to tell us!

III. Solomon's Discovery 2:9-11

A. His Greatness 2:9

"Then I became great and increased more than all who preceded me in Jerusalem. My wisdom also stood by me."

A bumper sticker of recent years tells us that "He who dies with the most toys wins." By that

29

standard, Solomon was clearly a winner. If greatness is measured on the basis of material possessions and worldly achievement, Solomon rises right to the top of the heap - even by modern standards. All of the things which his world had to offer were available to him - and he obviously tasted freely of the things available to him.

It sometimes happens that people who "have it all" lose their minds in the pursuit of the things of this world. The case of Howard Hughes has often been cited. At the end of a life of unusual accomplishment and incredible wealth, Mr. Hughes became a recluse and a social misfit. But in all of Solomon's extravagant pursuit of satisfaction in life, he claims that his wisdom remained with him. And we have his writings to bear witness to the truth of his claim.

B. His Reward 2:10

"All that my eyes desired I did not refuse them. I did not withhold my heart from any pleasure, for my heart was pleased because of all my labor and this was my reward for all my labor."

If it felt good, Solomon did it! If it looked good, Solomon tried it! If it tasted good, Solomon ate it or drank it!

Solomon did his best to have a great time for the many years of his pursuit of satisfaction. He felt good about his accomplishments and his possessions for a period of time. But the day of reckoning came around when he stopped to add up all that he had accomplished and obtained and enjoyed. And he came to see things in a different light.

C. His Frustration 2:11

"Thus I considered all my activities which my hands had done and the labor which I had exerted, and behold all was vanity and striving after wind and there was no profit under the sun."

What Solomon discovered centuries ago, people are still discovering in our day. O.J. Simpson, the football superstar and millionaire, was quoted in People Magazine of June 12, 1978, as saying:

I sit in my house in Buffalo and sometimes I get so lonely it's unbelievable. Life has been so good to me. I've got a great wife, good kids, money, my own health - and I'm lonely and bored . . . I often wondered why so many rich people commit suicide. Money sure isn't a cure-all."[5]

---

[5] Josh McDowell, *The Resurrection Factor* (San Bernardino, CA: Here's Life Publishers, 1981), p. 11.

30

Worldly aims and accomplishments will never provide soul satisfaction. If you, as Solomon was, are in search of lasting satisfaction, you will never find it in pursuing the things of this world. It is not to be found "under the sun." But it is available to those who take the time, which Solomon didn't take until later in his life, to look "above the sun" where God is. Those who allow the Lord to direct their lives and His Son to save them from frustration will find meaning in their lives at a much lower price than Solomon paid! As Jesus said to His disciples in John 10:10: "The thief comes only to steal and kill and destroy; I came that they may have life, and have it abundantly." Though Solomon did not know Jesus, who had not come to live on earth by his day, he did come to soul satisfaction before his life was over (as we will see later in Ecclesiastes), but he didn't find it "under the sun" - and no one else will find it there either. So I hope "under the sun" is not where you are looking for meaning and satisfaction in your life!

31

Even Wisdom Has Its Limits
Ecclesiastes 2:12-17

Life as we know it is short, at best. So we ought to make every effort to make good use of the time we have. It sometimes happens that a man's best efforts are cut short by death, but whether we are making our best efforts or not, death (apart from God's intervention at Christ's return) is an appointment we all will have to keep.

In the study of Sir Walter Scott at Abbotsford visitors may see the last words written in his journal: "Tomorrow we shall . . ." The entry was never finished. Franz Schubert left his great "unfinished symphony," and Charles Dickens laid down his pen in the middle of writing a novel - so students have wondered ever since how the work would have ended.[6]

Both the brevity and uncertainty of life and the word of God challenge us to make the most of the time we have available to us, but just what is the best use of our time?

As Solomon reported in Ecclesiastes 2:1-11, it wasn't only time which he invested in his search into man's best use of time and energies and resources. His search took him in pursuit of pleasure and humor, intoxicating drinks, building and horticultural projects, the accumulation of wealth, the enjoyment of music, and relationships with women. In it all he was guided by the greatest store of earthly wisdom any mere man has ever possessed. Because God was left out of the picture, it wasn't spiritual wisdom - God's heavenly wisdom - which Solomon possessed. His investigation concerned only that which is "under the sun" - but apart from that single omission, Solomon's experiment was conducted with unparalleled skill and with incredible material wealth at his disposal.

So what did Solomon find for all of his time and effort? He found that those who seek ultimate satisfaction under the sun won't find it - even with the aid of the greatest of human wisdom. So if you are in search of satisfaction in life, be sure to take into full consideration that which is "above the sun," because not even wisdom will enable you to find it "under the sun."

---

[6] Paul Lee Tan, *Encyclopedia of 7,700 Illustrations* (Rockville, MD: Assurance Publishers, 1979), p. 1547, #7028.

I. Solomon's Considerations 2:12-14

A. The Subjects of His Considerations 2:12

Solomon makes it very clear in the book of Ecclesiastes that he did very extensive research in his pursuit of satisfaction in his life.

1. The Subjects Enumerated 2:12a

"So I turned to consider wisdom, madness, and folly . . ."

Solomon decided that if satisfaction was not to be found in pursuit of the pleasures and accomplishments and possessions which so many people invest their lives in, he would try another approach to satisfaction: he would try to find satisfaction in more "ethereal" areas of investigation.

Solomon turned his attention to "wisdom" (*chochmah*). "Wisdom," as Solomon referred to it, is "skill" - the ability to take knowledge and apply it so that it yields the best possible result. For example, an artist shows skill when he takes his knowledge of paints and colors and brushes and surfaces, along with his observation of scenery, and turns it all into a beautiful painting.

Solomon had used his great wisdom/skill in achieving all the things he says he achieved in the first part of Ecclesiastes two, but now he decided to pursue "wisdom" for wisdom's sake. He decided to gain all the knowledge he could gain and to understand all he could understand about the application of his knowledge in every conceivable field of endeavor. The perpetual student who adds course to course for the sake of the information and understanding he can gain in the process may be headed down a similar path to the one Solomon was on.

The pursuit of knowledge and wisdom for their own sake sometimes leads people to the border of insanity, and it may have done that for Solomon because, in addition to his pursuit of wisdom for wisdom's sake, he also turned to madness and folly - something like the brilliant graduate student who decides to look into spiritism or nudism or the life of a recluse or some other bizarre notion.

It would be interesting to know what kinds of madness and folly Solomon turned to in his search for satisfaction, but he doesn't tell us. It may have been his flirtation with the "gods" of his foreign wives - as recorded for us in I Kings 11:4-8:

> For when Solomon was old, his wives turned his heart away after other gods; and his heart was not wholly devoted to the Lord his God, as the heart of David his father had been. [5] For Solomon went after Ashtoreth the goddess of the Sidonians and after Milcom the detestable idol of the Ammonites. [6] Solomon did what was evil in the sight of the Lord, and did not follow the Lord fully, as David his father had done. [7] Then Solomon built a high

place for Chemosh the detestable idol of Moab, on the mountain which is east of Jerusalem, and for Molech the detestable idol of the sons of Ammon. [8] Thus also he did for all his foreign wives, who burned incense and sacrificed to their gods.

From the perspective of a follower of the Lord, the pursuit of other "gods" and of the "idols" which represent them is madness and folly of the highest order! Why would a man who had begun his reign with such an apparently genuine walk with the Lord even think of engaging in the worship of worthless idols and false "gods"? Perhaps Solomon was ashamed to tell us exactly what he did, but (for whatever reason) we are left to wonder what he gave his attention to that he considered "mad" or "foolish." What we do know is that he was satisfied that his investigations would not be improved upon in terms of their thoroughness.

2. The Subjects Evaluated 2:12b

" . . . for what will the man do who will come after the king except what has already been done?"

We don't have many details concerning the specific paths Solomon's investigations pursued, but it may well be that we read about some of the results in Scripture. I Kings 4:29-34 attributes Solomon's wisdom to God and is written in the context of his early life, but it certainly speaks of the accomplishments of a lifetime.

> Now God gave Solomon wisdom and very great discernment and breadth of mind, like the sand that is on the seashore. [30] Solomon's wisdom surpassed the wisdom of all the sons of the east and all the wisdom of Egypt. [31] For he was wiser than all men, than Ethan the Ezrahite, Heman, Calcol and Darda, the sons of Mahol; and his fame was known in all the surrounding nations. [32] He also spoke 3,000 proverbs, and his songs were 1,005. [33] He spoke of trees, from the cedar that is in Lebanon even to the hyssop that grows on the wall; he spoke also of animals and birds and creeping things and fish. [34] Men came from all peoples to hear the wisdom of Solomon, from all the kings of the earth who had heard of his wisdom.

Solomon had the time and the wealth and the resources and the mind and the inclination to do his investigation in search of satisfaction like no other man who has ever lived - or ever will!

There have been other men who pursued some of the same paths Solomon pursued, but they haven't been able to improve on his performance or discover kinds of knowledge which Solomon didn't find. As Solomon observed earlier in Ecclesiastes (1:9):

> That which has been is that which will be,
> And that which has been done is that which will be done.
> So there is nothing new under the sun.

Solomon's investigation was thorough, and his findings were thought-provoking, even if they weren't very uplifting in some respects.

34

B. The Substance of His Considerations 2:13-14

1. The Value of Wisdom 2:13-14a

For those who have been thinking that wisdom is worth having, Solomon had some good news.

"And I saw that wisdom excels folly as light excels darkness." 2:13

Wisdom is worth having and pursuing. Compared with folly - what we might call "stupidity" - wisdom is like light contrasted with darkness. We all know how difficult it can be to try to find your way around in the dark. Who of us haven't stubbed a toe trying to make our way through a house we are familiar with in the dark of night? And you may have had the more frightening experience of being lost in open country in the darkness of night.

It is so much easier to find your way around in the light. I have hiked hundreds of miles in territory I didn't even know and have never gotten lost when there was light to allow me to get my bearings. But I have gotten disoriented in even familiar territory a time or two in the dark. Compared with folly, wisdom is so much better that the difference is just as obvious as the difference between darkness and light. If you are pursuing wisdom, here is more good news.

"The wise man's eyes are in his head, but the fool walks in darkness." 2:14a

A wise person is comparable to someone who has eyes and can see where he is going. A wise man anticipates that there may be some times of inconvenience - even times of emergency - for himself and those he loves, so he tries to plan ahead for the unexpected.

A fool, on the other hand, is comparable to someone whose eyes do him no good because there is no light to guide them. A fool makes no plans for tomorrow because he can't see or think that far ahead.

It is much better to live by wisdom than by folly and madness. But Solomon also has some bad news, even for the man who lives by wisdom.

2. The Fate of the Wise 2:14b

" . . . and yet I know that one fate befalls them both."

The man who devotes himself to doing everything in his life in the best way possible is going to end up - if you are looking only at that which is "under the sun" - in exactly the same fix as the most foolish of the fools. They are both going to die. And, once death catches up with a person, there is no amount of wisdom available "under the sun" which can make things any better for the

35

wisest of the wise, humanly speaking, than for the worst of fools. When you are dead, you are dead. It makes no difference, from an "under the sun" perspective, whether you were wise or foolish!

Now, when you consider all the effort that some people put into doing everything just the way it ought to be done, is it fair that they are going to die just like a fool dies? It may not seem fair but, fair or not, that is just the way it is.

II. Solomon's Conclusions 2:15-17

A. The Vanity of Wise Effort 2:15

"Then I said to myself, 'As is the fate of the fool, it will also befall me. Why then have I been extremely wise?' So I said to myself, 'This too is vanity.'"

Solomon put a great deal of time and energy and wealth and wisdom into his accomplishments in this life, and his specialty (more than any other mere man) was wisdom. But when his life of extraordinary ability and accomplishment was over, the exact same thing happened to him that happened to the worst fool in his kingdom. He died. So why all of the effort? Why all of the accomplishment? Why all of the wisdom?

"Under the sun" it ended up amounting to nothing as far as Solomon was concerned. He could no more enjoy his accomplishments as a dead man than any other corpse in Israel. So he returned to his dreary assessment of life "under the sun." It is nothing more than vanity.

Alexander the Great, we are told, when he was on his death bed, commanded that, when he was carried to the grave, his hands should not be wrapped, as was usual, in the grave cloths, but should be left outside the casket, so that everyone could see them and see that there was nothing in them: they were empty. He was born to one empire, and he conquered another - so he was possessor, while he lived, of two worlds, of the east and of the west, and of the treasures of both. But when he died he couldn't retain a single treasure! The poorest beggar and Alexander the Great were on equal terms![7]

B. The Brevity of Wise Accomplishment 2:16

"For there is no lasting remembrance of the wise man as with the fool, inasmuch as in the coming days all will be forgotten. And how the wise man and the fool alike die!"

A man's wisdom won't do him personally any good when he is dead; nor will it cause him to

---

[7] Paul Lee Tan, *Encyclopedia of 7,700 Illustrations* (Rockville, MD: Assurance Publishers, 1979), p. 1547, #7033.

36

be remembered very long. True, Bible students remember Solomon many centuries after his death (because his life is recorded in Scripture), but Bible students also remember Balaam and his donkey and Lot and his wife (also recorded in Scripture), though they certainly weren't pinnacles of wisdom! And, even among students of God's word, Solomon is remembered for his excesses about as much as he is remembered for his wisdom.

Napoleon summarized his own fading fame in these interesting words: "I am doing now what will fill thousands of volumes in this generation; in the next, one volume will contain it all; in the third, a paragraph; in the fourth, a single line."[8]

So it was with Solomon and Napoleon, and so it will be with us - except that most of us probably won't rate even a single line a generation or two from now. So we could go, along with Solomon, into bitter despair.

C. The Bitterness of Life 2:17

"So I hated life, for the work which had been done under the sun was grievous to me; because everything is futility and striving after wind."

Evaluating a whole life of work and accomplishment, leaving God out of the picture completely, Solomon could see only pain and emptiness and fruitless effort. And we might do the same - looking at things from Solomon's chosen perspective. Those who seek satisfaction "under the sun" won't find it in the end - not even if they live their lives with all the wisdom they can muster.

So what are you doing in search of satisfaction in your life? Are you pursuing education? Pleasure? Material wealth? Artistic accomplishment? Deeper friendships? Fame? Athletic achievement? Political power? What are all your achievements going to amount to after your death?

You may become wealthy and well known and almost as wise as Solomon, but if your accomplishments don't reach above the sun they eventually won't amount to a single thing! Even wisdom has its limits if it is only man's wisdom!

So consider the apostle Paul's "above the sun" perspective in I Corinthians 1:20-25:

"Where is the wise man? Where is the scribe? Where is the debater of this age? Has not God made foolish the wisdom of the world? [21] For since in the wisdom of God the world through its wisdom did not come to know God, God was well-pleased through the foolishness of the message preached to save those who believe. [22] For indeed Jews ask for

---

[8] Paul Lee Tan, *Encyclopedia of 7,700 Illustrations* (Rockville, MD: Assurance Publishers, 1979), p. 1551, #7052.

37

signs and Greeks search for wisdom; [23] but we preach Christ crucified, to Jews a stumbling block and to Gentiles foolishness, [24] but to those who are the called, both Jews and Greeks, Christ the power of God and the wisdom of God. [25] Because the foolishness of God is wiser than men, and the weakness of God is stronger than men."

38

Only God Knows
Ecclesiastes 2:18-26

We are living in an age when many people are groping to find any meaning to their lives. God has been dismissed as an ancient and unnecessary myth; man has been elevated to the throne as supreme being; and truth, with a capital "T," is increasingly disappearing from human consideration.

For many people in our day the only absolute truth is the truth that there is no absolute truth. There are no blacks or whites; everything is grey. Modern man's assessment of life has been capsulized in phrases like the following:

> "Do your own thing."
> "If it feels good, do it."
> "Right and wrong are determined by the situation in which you find yourself."
> "What is right for you may not be right for anyone else."

If you throw out the absolutes in this life, and you throw out the God who speaks in absolutes, life will cease to make much sense! It is only when human life is seen through the eyes of our Creator, God, that it can be full of the meaning it was intended to contain. If God is not a part of life's picture, the picture will become meaningless. It won't really make any sense.

Solomon did, for a time, what many people in our day are doing. He tried to find satisfaction in his life in things and experiences and efforts - apart from God. So he experienced disillusionment, because God is the key to finding satisfaction in life on our sin-cursed earth.

It is true that life is complex, and it contains some experiences which nobody fully understands. But if God is placed at the center of our lives, where He belongs, even some of life's simplest experiences can be filled with meaning. On the other hand, if God is not at the center, nothing will make much sense.

I. Solomon's Complaints 2:18-23

A. The Working Man's Heir 2:18-21

With all the time and energy and resources he was investing in his search for meaning in life, Solomon had the sense we all have, that it should all have some lasting significance. But as he pondered the eventuality of his demise, Solomon found little reason to be encouraged.

1. Solomon's Frustrations 2:18-19

Solomon's frustrations regarding the future, for all of his hard work, arose both out of some things he was certain about and some things he was uncertain about.

a. The Frustrating Certainty 2:18

"Thus I hated all the fruit of my labor for which I had labored under the sun, for I must leave it to the man who will come after me."

Ecclesiastes 2:1-11 has described a time Solomon went through in his life when he worked hard and accomplished a great deal and experimented with many things in his search for meaning in life. He tried wine, work projects (houses, vineyards, gardens, parks, orchards, ponds), wealth (slaves, flocks and herds, silver, gold, and treasures), music, and women (1,000 or them!).

When Solomon had "tried it all," he came to some very discouraging conclusions because of his "under the sun" perspective. He concluded that "all was vanity and striving after wind and there was no profit under the sun" (2:11b). And he concluded "as the fate of the fool [the fate of death], it will also befall me" (2:15). And now, as if adding insult to injury, Solomon has come to another despairing conclusion. He has come to see that he can't take anything he has accomplished with him - "for I must leave it to the man who will come after me."

There is no doubt about it. Whatever you may accomplish and accumulate in this life - no matter how hard you worked for it; no matter how valuable it might be - **will** be left to someone else! For Solomon this was a frustrating certainty. But it was only one half of the reason for his frustration.

b. The Frustrating Uncertainty 2:19

"And who knows whether he will be a wise man or a fool? Yet he will have control over all the fruit of my labor for which I have labored by acting wisely under the sun. This too is vanity."

Not only was Solomon faced with the frustration that he was bound to die and leave all of his accomplishments to someone else. He was also faced with the frustration of not knowing who that person would be. Even those who prepare for their death by drawing up a will can't be sure it will all work out the way they want it to work out. Even if their assets end up in the hands of the person they chose to receive them, there is no certainty that the person chosen will handle the assets well. What if Solomon's fortune and accomplishments were inherited by a fool?

Some time ago a student died in New York City at age 63. He had been a student all his life and the degrees after his name looked like the alphabet. He never had a job, never taught anyone else from his store of knowledge.

When he was a youth, a rich relative had bequeathed him several thousand dollars a year as long as he remained in school, but his income was to cease as soon as he left school. The relative merely wanted him to get a good education. But the youth took advantage of the

40

technicality and stayed in school all his life.[9]

Solomon realized that everything he had worked to accomplish might be wasted away by some foolish heir. And, of course, Solomon's fears were justified! His son, Rehoboam, did very little to bring credit to his father's name - splitting the nation of Israel into two nations because of his foolish policies as a young king.

2. Solomon's Despair 2:20-21

When a man who is living "under the sun" comes to realize what a slippery slope he is living on, there is plenty of cause for a serious case of depression. And that is where Solomon's frustrations took him.

a. The Fact of Despair 2:20

"Therefore I completely despaired of all the fruit of my labor for which I had labored under the sun."

If a man's labor is all aimed at earthly pursuits and ambitions, there isn't any encouragement in the realization that earthly pursuits and ambitions are soon going to come to an end, and that he won't have any real control over what he has accomplished during his lifetime. So Solomon found himself in despair. He saw no reason to be encouraged about his life and his future. All that he had accomplished would soon do him no more good whatsoever. Furthermore, all that he had accomplished would soon be turned over to others who might not make good use of what he had done.

b. The Reason for Despair 2:21

"When there is a man who has labored with wisdom, knowledge and skill, then he gives his legacy to one who has not labored with them. This too is vanity and a great evil."

The citizen who has worked hard and faithfully paid his taxes and who has found that he can get by in life by cutting corners has reason to feel satisfied in what he has accomplished. But it will probably not make him happy to see a person who has done little or nothing receiving a welfare payment from the taxes he has worked so diligently to pay. Why should the man who works hard all his life pay the bill for someone who may not work at all?

It isn't right, but sometimes it may seem that there isn't much return for diligent effort in this

---

[9] Paul Lee Tan, *Encyclopedia of 7,700 Illustrations* (Rockville, MD: Assurance Publishers, 1979), p.723, #3024.

life. And if there is no God in the picture, and no future, and no hope, and no justice, it might cause the hard-working taxpayer to feel as Solomon felt. Here he saw another encounter with "vanity" (heel - breath, breeze, nothingness). Here he saw another example of "great evil" in his world - the working man robbed of his reward!

B. The Working Man's Reward 2:22-23

The apostle Paul asked those sensible questions in I Corinthians 9:7: "Who at any time serves as a soldier at his own expense? Who plants a vineyard and does not eat the fruit of it? Or who tends a flock and does not use the milk of the flock?" And he answered such questions in his letter to Timothy (I Timothy 5:18): "The laborer is worthy of his wages."

Solomon was clearly on solid ground in suggesting that there should be a reward for the working man. But, as we all know, it doesn't always turn out that way in real life!

1. Solomon's Question 2:22

"For what does a man get in all his labor and in his striving with which he labors under the sun?"

With God in the picture, Scripture assures us that we can expect life's inequities to be resolved in glory. But if God is not in the picture, it may well be that a man could work hard, but fail to be properly paid for his hard work. Solomon's question: "If there is no God in view, what do all of a man's efforts actually amount to?" His answer is not very encouraging!

2. Solomon's Answer 2:23

"Because all his days his task is painful and grievous; even at night his mind does not rest. This too is vanity."

If you put God out of the picture of life, Solomon says, you can boil all of a man's labors down to two words: pain (suffering) and grief (sorrow).

Because we live on a sin-cursed earth, everything a man does is going to have a negative side to it. It all started in the Garden of Eden, when the Lord said to Adam (Genesis 3:17b): "Cursed is the ground because of you; in toil you shall eat of it all the days of your life."

Just so he can eat, a man will have to bend his back or his brain (or both) in effort which will leave him tired and a little bit older - and if he wants to live "well," he will have to work harder (or at least smarter). And when his day's work is done and he goes home to rest up for more of the same the next day, his mind may not let him rest! Who of us haven't gone home from work to experience a restless night as some aspect of the job we have been doing has returned to give us troubling dreams?

42

Life will have its frustrations at best. And for those who leave God out of the picture, it can be so empty that it is hardly worth living. So Solomon repeats the dreary refrain: "This too is vanity."

But no one has to leave God out of the picture! In fact, no one should leave God out of the picture - as Solomon acknowledges.

II. Solomon's Conclusions 2:24-26

A. The Blessings of God 2:24

"There is nothing better for a man than to eat and drink and tell himself that his labor is good. This also I have seen that it is from the hand of God."

For the first time in his book, Solomon takes a look through the clouds of his despair about life's emptiness and lets in some light from "above the sun." When a man stops excluding God from his life, it doesn't take much to brighten up the picture.

Without regard for God, all of the major accomplishments a man might invest his life in (as Solomon did) amount to nothing. But even the seemingly inconsequential things in life can be full of meaning when they are done with God in full view. The person who eats a meal which he is fully aware has been provided by God can find it a deeply meaningful experience - even if it is only a peanut butter and jelly sandwich. The person who quenches his thirst, recognizing as he does it that the Lord has provided for the needs of his body by creating thirst-quenching drinks (even if it is only a glass of water), can enjoy himself and his good God to the fullest in the process. The person who goes to work sincerely thankful that God has given him the ability to work, as well as a job to do, will find a rich sense of fulfillment in doing it.

Now what is it that has so suddenly changed Solomon's attitude from despair to delight in the simplest things in life? It is a glimpse of the Lord God. "This also I have seen, that it is from the hand of God." God doesn't have to do amazing things in order to make life worth living and full of meaning. He only has to be there.

B. The Importance of God 2:25

"For who can eat and who can have enjoyment without Him?"

The same Solomon who discovered that meals, even meals "fit for a king," can be an empty experience "under the sun" - apart from God - now confesses that you only have to add God to the picture and you can eat your meals and enjoy them too. We are painfully aware that some of the world's best looking, wealthiest, and most famous people have ended their sad lives by committing suicide. But we also know that some of God's great saints have thrived on prison fare!

43

It was from a prison cell that the apostle Paul wrote his letter to the Philippine which has often been described as an "epistle of joy." Consider the positive outlook he displayed from prison when he penned the words of Philippine 4:12-13:

> I know how to get along with humble means, and I also know how to live in prosperity; in any and every circumstance I have learned the secret of being filled and going hungry, both of having abundance and suffering need. [13] I can do all things through Him who strengthens me.

The secret to a full and meaningful life is not any amount of food or clothing or wealth or intelligence or fame. The secret to a full and meaningful life is the Lord! So Solomon asks the question, "Who can eat and who can have enjoyment without Him?"

Many of this world's godless "well-to-do" seem, from outward appearances, to be having a great time in life. But we occasionally get a glimpse of their private lives where there is evidence that all is not well. And many of them, who have eventually come to salvation in Christ, have confessed that their former plastic smiles were hiding empty hearts. Appearance doesn't always equal reality.

C. The Assignments of God 2:26

Whether people choose to give to the Lord the recognition He deserves or not, He remains the sovereign God of the universe. So He is the one who ultimately determines how life will go for every person. And He makes a distinction between those who honor Him and those who do not.

1. God's Assignment to the Good 2:26a

"For to a person who is good in His sight He has given wisdom and knowledge and joy."

The person who gets God's good assignment is not the person who merely appears to be good, but the person "who is good in His sight." Goodness is not measured by human standards but divine standards.

To such people the Lord gives the three things Solomon has listed in this verse:

1. Wisdom (*chokmah*) - the skill to live well, whatever that might involve in a person's life. For the Jewish artisan Bezalel, as an example, it involved the "skill and understanding to know how to perform all the work in the construction of the sanctuary" (Exodus 36:1). For the apostle Paul it involved the proclamation of Christ (Colossians 1:28).

Wisdom is available to everyone, because its principles are spelled out in the pages of Scripture. But those who reject the Lord won't bother to investigate the pages of His word. Nor

44

will they come to know the wisdom personified in the person of Jesus Christ (Colossians 2:2-3).

2. Knowledge (*daath*) - the truth about life and people and God - irrespective of the level of a person's academic achievement.

Such knowledge is available to every person who correctly assesses the message of the creation which surrounds him, because it is revealed in the heavens (Psalm 19:2). But, like the wisdom just considered, it won't be found by people who reject the Lord, because "The fear of the LORD is the beginning of knowledge" (Proverbs 1:7). Again, of course, its primary source is the word of God (Psalm 119:66).

3. Joy - the kind of gladness which seems to accompany a banquet but which, in this case, is the "real thing."

God can reward a person with everything he needs and wants for a full and rich experience in this life if that person is seeking to live according to the Lord's direction. But the Lord has another assignment for those who choose to do otherwise.

2. God's Assignment to Sinners 2:26b

" . . . while to the sinner He has given the task of gathering and collecting so that he may give to one who is good in God's sight. This too is vanity and striving after wind."

We shouldn't be deceived by that fact that a godless person seems to be living well - in spite of his sinful lifestyle. Whatever that person is able to accumulate during his life will be reassigned by God - to the person and at the time which the Lord chooses. Consider, for example, the way He chose to turn the accomplishments of Nabal (husband of Abigail) over to David (I Samuel 25)!

God is the key to finding satisfaction in this life, even with its frustrations.

Are you finding satisfaction in this life because you are seeking it in the person and the blessing of the Lord? Or have you perhaps been getting along without satisfaction in your life because you haven't given the Lord the place He deserves in your life?

Section Three:
Solomon's Illustrations
of Life's Futility

3:1-11:10

46

God Is the Key
Ecclesiastes 3:1-13

Have you ever locked yourself out of your car (or maybe your house)? Life can suddenly become very complicated when you don't have the key you need to open the doors that give you access to the things you need.

There are many people in the world who are trying to make their way through this life and finding the experience very frustrating because they don't have the key that gives them access to an understanding of all that is happening in their lives.

The Lord is the key to an understanding of what life is all about, because He is the one who makes the appointments which all men keep in this life. Trying to go through life without taking Him into consideration at every bend in the road is something like trying to get into your car (or your house) without the proper key. It can be done - but it is much more complicated than it was ever intended to be.

The person who does take God into consideration at every bend in the road won't necessarily have answers for all of his questions. But he will enjoy the satisfaction of knowing that God is alive and at work in the affairs of men, and that everything is eventually going to work out for his good because God is in control of the events of his life - whether mere man understands them or not.

Israel's King Solomon got off to a very good start in his life. As the son of King David he not only enjoyed the many physical benefits of life in the palace, he also enjoyed the spiritual heritage of a man after God's own heart as his father.

So Solomon started his tenure as king of Israel with a heart which was sensitive to the Lord. When God gave him the privilege of asking for anything that he wanted from God he asked for a heart of wisdom so he could rule well over God's people - and God gave him such a heart (as reflected in the book of Proverbs which he wrote, apparently as a young king).

But as Solomon became older and wealthier he disobeyed God's word to His people, and to their kings, by marrying foreign wives in increasing numbers. God had said that Israelites were not to marry foreigners, and that kings were not to multiply wives. But, as a result of Solomon's disobedience on both counts, his wives drew his heart away from God (I Kings 11:4). It was apparently in his degenerate spiritual condition that Solomon gave himself to the search for satisfaction in life which is recorded in Ecclesiastes. He looked in every possible direction except up, toward the Lord (as Ecclesiastes 1:12-2:11 recorded for us). Solomon finally concluded that satisfaction in life is not to be found "under the sun" (apart from God). He came to see that life doesn't make much sense if you throw away its key - and God is the key.

God has assigned man's task in life in such a way that man can enjoy it - even though he doesn't fully comprehend it. Only God can fully comprehend the mysteries of our earthly lives. But God made mankind for bigger things than merely earthly life, so man isn't going to fully discover soul satisfaction until he finds it in God, his Maker. God is the key! Are you trusting Him to make the final appointments in your life - and asking Him to help you face them as they come your way?

I. God's Appointments for Mankind 3:1-8

A. Introduction to God's Appointments 3:1

"There is an appointed time for everything. And there is a time for every event under heaven -"

Though this verse doesn't come right out and say it, it is God who has appointed a time for everything. It is God who has established a time for every event under heaven. James 4:13-15 makes it clear who it is that is behind the scenes of our lives.

> Come now, you who say, "Today or tomorrow we will go to such and such a city, and spend a year there and engage in business and make a profit." [14] Yet you do not know what your life will be like tomorrow. You are just a vapor that appears for a little while and then vanishes away. [15] Instead, you ought to say, "If the Lord wills, we will live and also do this or that."

The point of our verse is that God knows exactly when everything that happens will happen, because He controls its happening! If God controls and therefore knows the exact time of "every event under heaven" (and He does), then it should be rather obvious that we would do well to keep in touch with Him concerning the unfolding events of our lives.

The Bible teaches us that man can influence the course of his own life. It is not as though we were robots. Though God is sovereign, He has granted mankind a measure of freedom regarding life's choices. In addition, man can communicate with his Maker and influence God's hand by his prayers. And man can influence the outcome of events by the way he responds to the events of life. But since God arranges all of man's appointments, it would be well worth a man's time to keep in touch with the Lord. Do you consult the Lord for each day's activities, asking Him to keep you out of temptation and to deliver you from evil, as Jesus taught His disciples to pray?

B. Illustrations of God's Appointments 3:2-8

1. Birth and Death 3:2a

"A time to give birth, and a time to die."

Doctors can guess when a baby will be born, and mothers and fathers can hope for one thing or another, but when all is said and done babies are born according to the time appointed by God.

48

Who of us have not awaited the day of a baby's birth with our plans on "tentative"?

God controls the time of birth. He also controls the time of death. Though He often allows what would appear to be the normal time of death to be postponed - by personally arresting or reversing the course of events, or by enabling doctors to intervene with medical procedures - when a person's time comes to go, he will go. When death's appointment arrives, all of the doctors and medical equipment and procedures in the world can't keep it from taking place.

The truth of this verse is popularly recognized in the comment we sometimes hear: "It was his time to die," or "His time was up." God appoints the moments of birth and death - but He also appoints many other moments we might not have considered.

2. Planting and Uprooting 3:2b

"A time to plant, and a time to uproot what is planted."

God controls the seasons - so that spring is generally the time to plant and fall is generally the time to uproot what is planted. But He also controls the hands and feet and machinery and momentum of the farmer or gardener.

And it isn't only the birth and death of people the Lord controls. He also controls the birth and death of plants and animals and insects and other living things.

3. Killing and Healing 3:3a

"A time to kill, and a time to heal."

The taking of human lives by murder or capital punishment or by war would seem to be in the hands of men, but God so controls the hands of men that no one really dies by accident. Though we don't think of God as the cause of death, He is certainly the controller of death. Consider, for example, the demise of ancient Israel's King Ahab.

Wishing to recapture Ramoth Gilead from his enemies, Ahab invited Judah's King Jehoshaphat (and his army) to join his nation in battle at Ramoth Gilead. Perhaps it was in part the prophet Micaiah's prediction that Ahab would die in the battle (I Kings 22:17) which caused him to dress as a commoner, while Jehoshaphat dressed as a king for the contest (I Kings 22:30). But, while Jehoshaphat came through the losing battle unscathed, King Ahab was killed when (I Kings 22:34) "a certain man drew his bow at random and struck the king of Israel in a joint of the armor."

What applies to killing also applies to healing. Doctors practice medicine, but it is God who controls the healing process and the timing of it. Who of us have not known someone who seemed to be getting all the proper treatments without a healing response?

49

4. Tearing Down and Building Up 3:3b

"A time to tear down, and a time to build up."

Anyone who has gone through the process of having a home built will probably tell you that the timing didn't go exactly as planned. It a rare event when construction plans move along as quickly and smoothly as a buyer would like them to progress. So it is wise to keep the Lord in the "loop" of the building process, because it is ultimately His to control.

And He will decide when it is time for the completed project to come down. This truth was dramatically illustrated in Jesus' prediction of the destruction of the Jerusalem temple (Matthew 24:2). But the Lord is ultimately the one who decides the fate of every building project constructed by mankind. So we should be taking Him into consideration not only in the building projects of our lives but in all of the maintenance issues as well.

5. Weeping and Laughing 3:4a

"A time to weep, and a time to laugh."

If we chose the times in which we weep there wouldn't be any. But there come into the life of every person times (e.g. distress in a friendship) when weeping is the most appropriate response to events. And if we chose the times in which we laugh we might choose more of them. But we certainly ought to be grateful for the many joyous occasions the Lord grants in virtually every human life.

God appoints, in each life, just enough weeping and just enough laughing so that everything stays pretty much in balance and in proper perspective. Our sadness makes us more fully appreciate our happiness, and our happiness makes us able to bear up under sorrow. And those who know the Lord, and who are sensitive to His control in the affairs of our lives, can respond to the challenge of the apostle Paul in I Thessalonians 5:16 to "Rejoice always" - even in times appropriate for weeping - out of the conviction that He has our best interests at heart.

6. Mourning and Dancing 3:4b

"A time to mourn, and a time to dance."

Mourning speaks of the very sad times of life (e.g., the death of a loved one) and dancing speaks of those times when we literally jump for joy (something the ancient Jews were more likely to do than many in western culture).

And God keeps these extremes of emotion in balance in our lives just as He keeps our lesser emotional swings in balance. Those who pause to ponder the affairs of human experience would have to acknowledge that balance is certain to be one of God's specialties!

50

7. Throwing and Gathering Stones 3:5a

"A time to throw stones, and a time to gather stones."

The land of Solomon's ancient kingdom makes this verse particularly appropriate, because it is a land of very rocky terrain. In an agrarian society (which much of ancient Israel was), the management of the soil for effective farming and ranching involved the removal of stones from fields destined for crops. But stones thrown out of the fields were often used to build homes and walls for the protection of the crops and the control of animals, so thrown stones often became gathered stones. And there was benefit in both activities, and in God's gracious provision of fertile fields and plenty of building materials.

8. Embracing and Shunning Embracing 3:5b

"A time to embrace, and a time to shun embracing."

It is great to have someone to be close to - and sometimes being close is the most appropriate order of the hour. The benefits of physical touch are well known to lovers, but physical touch has beneficial broader applications as well.

Of course, if people spent all of their time in close, even physical, contact with people they care about, they wouldn't get much accomplished. So, as inviting and encouraging as an appropriate embrace can be, life is full of occasions when embracing would be an obstacle to progress in matters of practical importance to our best interests. And, of course, time spent without an embrace becomes all the more reason for returning to the warmth of life's dearest friendships, because "absence makes the heart grow fonder."

9. Searching and Giving Up as Lost 3:6a

"A time to search, and a time to give up as lost."

Some years back my wife lost the diamond out of her wedding ring while she was walking the dog, with a leash wrapped around her hand. Because of the stone's value (more as an emotional symbol than a monetary investment) she spent more time than usual trying to find it. But it eventually became clear that there was no reason to continue the search. We have all had experiences of the kind, I am sure.

God Himself sent Jesus to this earth "to seek and to save that which was lost" (Luke 19:10). But even God Himself stops seeking people who refuse to be found when it becomes evident that there is no reason to continue the search.

10. Keeping and Throwing Away 3:6b

51

"A time to keep, and a time to throw away."

Young people, and couples, who are setting up housekeeping are normally on the keeping end of the continuum. But the passing of the years brings most people to the time in life when there isn't room or reason to keep any more. And they often discover that much of what they have kept down through the years has little enough value to anyone else that they have to throw it away (and Solomon's word - *shalak* - is as likely to have the trash can in mind as it is to refer to some charitable organization).

11. Tearing Apart and Sewing Together 3:7a

"A time to tear apart, and a time to sew together."

Though this line may have reference to such things as the alterations our clothing needs from time to time, it had special significance in Jewish culture where a person's response to a tragic situation might well be to tear ("rend") his clothing.

How grateful we should be that life's occasional tragedies are soon over and we can sew together the torn pieces of our garments and our lives.

12. Being Silent and Speaking 3:7b

"A time to be silent, and a time to speak."

Though there is much to be said for a word well-spoken, there are also times in our lives when the more appropriate and even more eloquent thing would be to say nothing at all. Job's three "friends" and "comforters" provided their greatest service to him, in his time of grief, during the seven days they spent sitting in silence (Job 2:11-13). People who recognize and who make use of times appointed for silence are likely to speak more profoundly when they speak up (though it didn't turn out that way for Job's friends, because they based their observations on conventional wisdom far more than on divine revelation).

There is great value, of course, in well-spoken words. As Solomon himself wrote in Proverbs 25:11: "Like apples of gold in settings of silver Is a word spoken in right circumstances." God has shown the way to verbal excellence in His own written revelation, so we do have a flawless source from which to draw well-spoken words of our own. The challenge of wisdom then, beyond knowing what to say, is knowing whether to say anything at all.

13. Loving and Hating 3:8a

"A time to love, and a time to hate."

Love is probably more often appropriate in our lives than hatred, so the New Testament commands Christians to love one another (John 13:34,35) and to walk in love (Ephesians 5:2) as a habit of life. But there are some things in life which God's people ought to hate as well. A short list could include abortion, alcohol abuse, crime of every sort, drug abuse, immorality, and pornography - and the list could go on and on.

Love is very important in its place - and its place is very large, to be sure. But hatred is also important in its place. Our lives don't have the keen edge they should have until we keep our God-appointed meeting with hatred of the things He Himself hates.

14. Warring and Experiencing Peace 3:8b

"A time for war, and a time for peace."

God sent His ancient people to war more than a few times, so that they could also enjoy the blessing of peace which was His greater appointment for them. And, of course, He sent His own Son to engage in serious spiritual warfare to make possible our peace with Him (Colossians 1:20). So it should come as no surprise that, while peace is His gift to us in Christ, He also calls us to war against the enemy of our souls, along with our enemy's demonic hordes (Ephesians 6:10-18). As much as we would enjoy unending peace, we need to be alert to the possibility of war which God has also appointed as part of mankind's experience in this life.

As the swinging pendulum of an old-fashioned clock keeps the hands in touch with time, man's life on earth moves along by God's design with a variety of emotions and experiences, flowing together to create balance and interest and beauty. If God is not appreciated in all of it, it will never make as much sense as it should. As those who love Him and who are called according to His purpose, the Lord assures us that He is taking all of the events of our lives and is causing them all to "work together for good" (Romans 8:28).

Do you see the hand of God in balancing the positives and negatives of your life so that it continues to move ahead in the meaningful balance which makes for progress? Like electricity, which works by the alternating forces of positive and negative charges, our lives work as they find balance in the middle of life's positive and negative charges.

II. Man's Response to God's Appointments 3:9-13

A. Observation of God's Appointments 3:9-10

As Solomon pondered the appointments of God in the lives of His creatures, he found it hard to take it all in and to comprehend what it all means. You can probably sympathize with him in his perspective as a puzzled "preacher."

1. Solomon's Question 3:9

53

"What profit is there to the worker from that in which he toils?"

Having spent a significant amount of time and energy and money seeking satisfaction in life without giving any thought to God's important part in it all, Solomon now wondered out loud what earth's workers might expect to get for all their efforts.

Most people invest a great amount of effort in a lifetime of labor! It certainly makes sense that they should hope it would get them something, or somewhere, of value.

2. Solomon's Observation 3:10

"I have seen the task which God has given the sons of men with which to occupy themselves."

Make no mistake about it, if you want to make some sense out of the ups and down and backs and forths of this life you must give God His proper place in it all. He is the one who has assigned man to his earthly task. So He is the key to making sense out of it all.

As Solomon has already reported in the opening chapters of his book, the alternative (leaving God out of the picture) is very bleak, because life "under the sun" is full of vanity and futility!

B. Evaluation of God's Appointments 3:11-13

Challenging assignment that it is, every person would like to be able to make some sense out of life as he knows it. We all want to have a sense of the meaning of life, so Solomon turns to an attempt at evaluating the divine appointments he has just enumerated.

1. They Are Unfathomable 3:11

"He has made everything appropriate in its time. He has also set eternity in their heart, yet so that man will not find out the work which God has done from the beginning even to the end."

In His plan for mankind, the Lord has characteristically done all things well. He has assigned our tasks in perfect balance so that human life, taken as a whole, turns out to be an experience of that which is "appropriate." For example, there are just enough fall and winter days to make us enjoy the spring and summer, and just enough spring and summer days to make us appreciate fall and winter.

In addition to the perfect balance the Lord has programmed into human lives, He has also given us a sense of something bigger and better. In Solomon's words, "He has set eternity in their heart." The sense all people share, that there should be more than we are experiencing in this life, is the force behind man's religious pursuits. God has given every man the feeling that this life isn't all there is - which is the thing which drove Solomon in search of satisfaction in the first place.

54

God has made human life a beautiful experience, and He has given man the distinct impression that there is more to life than just the surface reveals. But God, in His infinite wisdom, has done it all in such a way that only He fully understands it all. So, if a man leaves God out of his life, he leaves out the only person who has the "big picture" clearly in view. As a result, he may experience the sense of futility and confusion which belongs to people who are not grateful to the source of life's many blessings.

2. They Are Desirable 3:12-13

"I know that there is nothing better for them than to rejoice and to do good in one's lifetime; [13] moreover, that every man who eats and drinks sees good in all his labor—it is the gift of God."

Whether a person acknowledges the Lord in his life or not, he can enjoy the good things of life because the Lord, in His goodness, has made this His "gift" to every person. Such things as physical life, health, the joys of love and home and family, and the satisfaction of a job to do are all gracious gifts from the Lord. It is God's intention that mankind find joy in this life, and that he dedicate his life to doing good. That which is good, of course, is defined by the Lord, so "doing good" works best for those who are giving God the recognition He deserves as life's creator and director.

God has assigned man's task in life in such a way that man can enjoy it without fully comprehending it. Comprehending life with all of its variety and complexity is God's department. He is the key to an eventual understanding of our lives, so those who recognize and appreciate His importance in it all find life much more satisfying than those who do not.

Are you giving the Lord the recognition and trust He deserves as the one who, having planned our lives, fully understands them? Life's greatest satisfaction will be ours through a close and personal relationship with Him. He is the key!

55

The Big Picture
Ecclesiastes 3:14-22

The *Humanist Manifesto II* contains this confession and observation:

> We can discover no divine purpose or providence for the human species. While there is much that we do not know, humans are responsible for what we are or will become. No deity will save us; we must save ourselves.[10]

This is the viewpoint which was adopted by King Solomon during the time in his life which is covered by the book of Ecclesiastes. He put God out of the picture - "above the sun" - and set about to assume responsibility for what he was and would become. He decided to try to save himself - to find a sense of meaning and direction for his life by his own mind and effort and achievement.

When Solomon had "done it all," he still hadn't found what he was looking for. He hadn't managed to discover God's purpose and providence for his life. So he stepped back and took another look - this time taking in the "big picture," including the God of heaven who is "above the sun" - and he saw and confessed that there is a divine purpose and providence for the human species. He saw that, if you leave God out of the picture, this life will never make much sense, but if you take the Lord into consideration, things will begin to fall into proper perspective.

There are many things in life which don't come into focus for us - which don't make much sense at the time - because we get so caught up in the details of the present that we can't see "the big picture." Meanwhile, God is working behind the scenes to put together all the pieces of human life in such a way that, one day, seen from His perspective, it will all make sense.

There isn't anything in our lives which isn't touched by the providence of God (His guidance and care). God's providence encompasses everything in life - and also beyond. So you can't leave God out of the picture of your life and expect life to make much sense.

I. The Nature of God's Providence 3:14-15

A. The Permanence of His Providence 3:14

"I know that everything God does will remain forever; there is nothing to add to it and there is nothing to take from it, for God has so worked that men should fear Him."

Not only is God behind the scenes in every aspect of our lives, but He is also behind the

---

[10] *Humanist Manifestos I and II* (Buffalo, NY: Prometheus Books, 1973), p. 16.

56

scenes doing all things well in every aspect of our lives. When He does something, He does it perfectly and permanently (it "will remain forever"). He never makes a mistake.

There is nothing to add to it, because God never does too little. He does just enough to accomplish His purposes each time He acts. He may come back another time and add to what He previously did, because His full purpose isn't yet accomplished, but each step of the process is done to completion. For example, when God was preparing David for his contest with Goliath, the Philistine giant, He first sent into his life a lion and a bear; then he sent David up against Goliath, and David was ready.

There is nothing to take from God's preparation. He never does too much. He knows how much we can handle, so He does in our lives just enough to accomplish His purposes each time He acts. He has promised, for instance, that He will never give us more than we can handle in the area of testing/temptation (I Corinthians 10:13).

God's providential dealings in our lives are perfectly balanced, and they are intended to make us sensitive to Him. This is what Solomon means when he writes "for God has so worked that men should fear Him."

To fear God is to recognize our accountability to Him. It is to recognize that He is God and that we, His creatures, owe Him our attention and our allegiance and our obedience. It is to realize and respond to the fact that one day we must report to Him for the way in which we have conducted ourselves on this earth during this life. It is to give Him the reverence He deserves as our Maker and our judge.

Now, of course, not everyone does fear God, but it isn't because He hasn't created in their lives the perfect opportunity. His providence touches everything and everyone and He has done all things well. And He does all things well again and again.

B. The Scope of His Providence 3:15

"That which is has been already and that which will be has already been, for God seeks what has passed by."

The surface issues of this life keep changing with the passing of time. Manufacturers, for example, keep changing the designs of the things they manufacture. You may not be able to buy a new car like the one made last year, because the car makers have redesigned their cars for the current year.

But the big issues of life - the real issues - remain the same from year to year and generation to generation and age to age. In every age people are born; people need care; people grow up; and people establish relationships (normally including marriage and family relationships). And then the cycle starts over. People in every age need food and clothing and shelter and

57

transportation and someone to care about them. Though there may be stylistic changes in some of these things, the basic issues never change.

God has seen to it that all people experience essentially the same experiences in life, whatever the time and wherever the location, because He wants to face all people with the biggest issue of all - the issue of man's relationship with his Maker. In every age and in every life, God providentially faces men with the same basic issues - seeking (in Solomon's words) "what has passed by."

Now it bothers many people - when they hear that God guides and cares in all things - that there are evidences of evil and injustice all around us. How, they ask, could a good God allow evil in His universe?

That is a good question, but even evil falls within the sphere of God's providence.

II. The Problem of Evil in God's Providence 3:16-17

A. The Presence of Evil 3:16

"Furthermore, I have seen under the sun that in the place of justice there is wickedness and in the place of righteousness there is wickedness."

The "place of justice," in human terms, would be the court system. But, as we all come to realize, the place of justice isn't always characterized by justice. Good people are sometimes treated like bad people - as in the case of believers down through the ages who have been persecuted and even killed for their faith. And bad people are sometimes treated like good people - as when people who are criminally insane are set free from custody, often to take innocent lives and commit other criminal acts. Not even the highest courts of our land come up with just decisions every time around. How can a good God allow it that "in the place of justice there is wickedness"?

The "place of righteousness," in human terms, would be the place of worship (the tabernacle, the temple, the church building). But, as we all know only too well, the place of righteousness isn't always characterized by righteousness. The sons of Eli defiled the tabernacle by their wicked ways. The temple was not well-served by many of its priests and Levites, nor by all who were known as prophets - nor by many of the religious leaders of Jesus' day. And, in our own day, Jim Jones and Jim Bakker and Jimmy Swaggart, and others, have given the church a bad name in the thinking of many. How can a good God providentially allow wickedness in the "place of righteousness"?

B. The Solution to Evil 3:17

"I said to myself, 'God will judge both the righteous man and the wicked man,' for a time for

58

every matter and for every deed is there."

Make no mistake about it, God is going to call to account every person before His judgment bar - both those whose lives have been characterized by righteousness and those whose lives have been characterized by wickedness! II Corinthians 5:10 tells of the coming of the "judgment seat of Christ," when the Lord will judge His own on the basis of their performance (as described, many believe, in I Corinthians 3:10-15). And Revelation 20:11-15 tells of the coming day of the "great white throne" judgment of the unbelieving.

A time is coming when every wrong will be made right before the great judge of the universe. People won't get away with their wickedness. It only appears in this life that they do.

The reason that humanists "can discover no divine purpose or providence for the human species" is that they see only a small part of "the big picture." Unfortunately, when they finally see "the big picture," it will be forever too late!

Are you seeing "the big picture" while you still have time to do something about it? Are you giving the Lord the place of importance He deserves in your life? Life on this sin-cursed earth will never make very good sense if you leave God out of the picture.

III. The Presence of Death in God's Providence 3:18-21

The Bible refers to death as man's "enemy" (I Corinthians 15:26). But we need to keep in mind that death was not a part of the original plan. It has come into human experience because of sin. But there can be no doubt that its presence seems dehumanizing.

A. The Beast-Like Nature of Man 3:18

"I said to myself concerning the sons of men, 'God has surely tested them in order for them to see that they are but beasts.'"

A superficial look at mankind may bring a person to the conclusion which Solomon initially came to: "People are just animals, like any other animal." They have basically the same appetites and needs - food, shelter, some kind of companionship, and sex. Mankind sometimes behaves no better than a wild animal - as suggested by the bumper sticker: "Support wildlife - throw a party."

It is interesting (but not entirely surprising) that modern humanists have come to conclusions so similar to those which Solomon initially came to:

Humanist Manifesto I, section 2, states that "Humanism believes that man is a part of

59

nature and that he has emerged as the result of a continuous process."[11]

Humanist Manifesto II, section 2, states that "Science affirms that the human species is an emergence from natural evolutionary forces. As far as we know, the total personality is a function of the biological organism transacting in a social and cultural context."[12]

Not only does a man sometimes look and act like nothing more than a "beast," he appears (superficially) to die like a beast as well.

B. The Beast-Like End of Man 3:19-20

1. Man and Beast Have the Same End 3:19

"For the fate of the sons of men and the fate of beasts is the same. As one dies so dies the other; indeed, they all have the same breath and there is no advantage for man over beast, for all is vanity."

There comes a time in the life of both man and beast when there is no longer any breath, and death sets in. Man and beast breathe similarly, and when they stop breathing they each die - so what is the difference?

Life appears (superficially - with no God in the picture) to be an exercise in futility. It hardly seems to make any difference whether you are a man or a dog - both are going to stop breathing and die. Some people have even sought to tie man and beast together as to origin and destiny.

2. Man and Beast Have the Same Origin and Destiny 3:20

"All go to the same place. All came from the dust and all return to the dust."

By "the same place" Solomon refers to the grave. It is interesting that, even in his despairing mood when he thought these thoughts, Solomon hadn't abandoned the Biblical teaching that both man and beast were created out of dust by God. But it is evident to anyone who cares to check it out that both man and beast return to dust after death.

It is interesting, again, that modern-day humanists have come to essentially the same conclusion that Solomon came to in his despair.

Humanist Manifesto II, section 2, states "There is no credible evidence that life survives the

---

[11] *Humanist Manifestos I and II* (Buffalo, NY: Prometheus Books, 1973), p. 8.

[12] *Humanist Manifestos I and II*, (Buffalo, NY: Prometheus Books, 1973), p. 17.

60

death of the body."[13]

But Solomon came to realize that there is a difference between man and the beast. Though Solomon's statement in the next verse is phrased as a question, it isn't the question of man's destiny distinguished from the beast's destiny that is at stake. It is the question of man's knowledge of the difference that is at stake.

C. The Distinction Between Man and Beast 3:21

"Who knows that the breath of man ascends upward and the breath of the beast descends downward to the earth?"

Not all men know this, of course. The humanist doesn't know it, but (when he stopped to factor in God's word) Solomon knew it, and we can know it, if we take God at His word. There is a difference between man and beast. When a beast dies it is all over. His "breath" descends downward to the earth. The beast's breath is buried with the beast's body. But when a man dies, though his body is buried to return to dust, his "breath" (*ruach* - "soul") "ascends upward" - "to God who gave it" (as Solomon will put it in 12:7). Solomon isn't saying, of course, that all men go "up to heaven." He is saying that all men report back to God, the one who made them.

All appearances to the contrary notwithstanding, men are not just like animals. Even in death, the providence of God is clearly seen and firmly in control, because men stand before the Lord! We haven't yet gotten "the big picture" until we see men standing in fear (at last) before their Maker. Don't ever forget man's accountability. But also don't imagine that God planned it, as He did, in order to take all the happiness out of human life.

IV. The Prospect of Happiness in God's Providence 3:22

A. The Happiness of Man 3:22a

"I have seen that nothing is better than that man should be happy in his activities, for that is his lot."

God is not the heavenly killjoy that many people make Him out to be. It is His desire and intention that people should be happy in life's activities, and He has made every provision to that end. He has provided life and health and family and friends and food and shelter and something to do with our hands and our minds - and even His word to direct and increase our happiness.

---

[13] Ibid., 1973, p. 17.

61

God has done His work, and done it well, and He has given every one of us a chance to come to know Him as we respond to His world and His word. He is going to settle all injustices. He is going to provide relief from death. And He wants us all to enjoy His generous provision for our happiness in this life. But He also wants us to remember that, in His providence, we do have an appointment to keep with Him.

B. The Accountability of Man 3:22b

"For who will bring him to see what will occur after him?"

The answer to Solomon's question is this: If nobody else brings man to see what will occur after him, God will do it. God's providence encompasses everything in this life - and beyond this life as well. So you can't leave God out of the picture of your life and expect life to make much sense. But if you will recognize the Lord and the place which He rightfully deserves in your life on earth, things will fall into proper perspective. So be sure you get the big picture.

God wants you and me to give Him all the credit which He deserves while we are still in this life. If we don't, His providence will call us into account anyway. Here is how the apostle Paul explained things to the Philippians with regard to God's exaltation of Jesus Christ, His divine Son in Philippians 2:9-11.

For this reason also, God highly exalted Him, and bestowed on Him the name which is above every name, [10] so that at the name of Jesus every knee will bow, of those who are in heaven and on earth and under the earth, [11] and that every tongue will confess that Jesus Christ is Lord, to the glory of God the Father.

62

Oppression Under the Sun
Ecclesiastes 4:1-3

Oppression is a way of life for many, many people in our world today - as it has been for many people down through the centuries.

Imagine yourself living with the sounds of gunfire and exploding bombs, sounds familiar to people who are living today in many places on earth, under the stresses of various religious and political conflicts. What would it be like to live in the middle of a battleground, forced to flee or be killed. Where would you go? How would you get there? What would you take with you? And, once you arrived in a safe place, would anyone there help you? What would you eat? Would you find shelter?

There are many people for whom these kinds of questions are a part of daily life. Millions in today's world do not have the blessings of life which we easily take for granted - because we have always had such blessings. Our world is full of people whose circumstances make life hardly worth living - especially if they don't know the Lord, or don't have His truth to add God's perspective to their lives.

King Solomon is a man who experienced very little of the bitter side of life. But during that period of his life when he chose to live "under the sun" even Solomon got a view of life through the eyes of those less fortunate than he was. In the process he came to realize that, viewed apart from God's perspective, life for those who are oppressed can be hardly worth living.

I. The Problem of Oppression 4:1

A. The Frequency of Oppression 4:1a

"Then I looked again at all the acts of oppression which were being done under the sun."

Solomon writes as if there were, in his day, many acts of oppression being done "under the sun" - and we can be sure there were. Though we don't know exactly what they were or who was involved, what is known about the depraved condition of the human heart assures the existence of oppression in Solomon's day! The prophet Jeremiah pondered the issue of man's depravity in Jeremiah 17:9:

The heart is more deceitful than all else
And is desperately sick;
Who can understand it?

Little children have always been victims of oppression, because they are readily available and very easy to oppress. And in our day, of course, that oppression often reaches into the lives of children who haven't even been born! Women have often been the subject of oppression at the hand of mean-tempered fathers and husbands (and others) - and on occasion they have managed to turn the tables and oppress their oppressors. Employees often receive the brunt of oppression at the hands of inconsiderate bosses - even in America. And, as everyone knows, minority races have had more than their share of oppression. Europe and America's sorry experience with slave trade is a clear illustration of that.

Acts of oppression occur often enough in our world - and they almost always have - as to be commonplace. Just think for a moment of countries around the world you know about where oppression has been taking place because of corrupt political systems and conditions of violence, much of it a result of war. Your thoughts could easily take you around the globe. Oppression takes place all over the world, affecting the lives of countless people.

B. The Sorrow of Oppression 4:1b

"And behold I saw the tears of the oppressed and that they had no one to comfort them."

I have sat in a room with people grieving the death of loved ones who died in acts of meaningless violence. If tears ever seemed appropriate, they seemed appropriate then. And there isn't much that can be said at such a time to alleviate the sorrow and help dry up the tears.

If we don't see it in the lives of people around us, we can't help but see it on television and in newspapers and magazines almost every day. How many people have lost loved ones to senseless acts? How many families have been made homeless as a result of wars? How many tribal peoples have been caught up in the middle of seemingly endless intertribal violence? How many people have become victims of terrorist acts?

The tears of oppressed people are often bitter tears because oppression is generally so senseless. Oppression's tears often cannot be stopped, and in many cases there isn't even anyone to try to bring comfort in the face of oppression.

C. The Power of Oppressors 4:1c

" . . . and on the side of their oppressors was power, but they had no one to comfort them."

The child who is oppressed by a cruel parent can hardly do much to stop the oppression. And if it is a child's parent who oppresses him, who can he go to for help and comfort? The wife who is oppressed by a cruel husband probably doesn't have the physical strength to fight him off, if that were her choice, and if she can't turn to her husband for comfort, who can she turn to? The religious or political prisoner under a repressive government can't do much to fight off the governing authorities, and when you are in jail, who do you turn to for help and comfort?

The oppressed people of the earth are generally in a position of weakness in relation to their oppressors, and they are often cut off from almost any source of help - if, in fact, there is anyone who even cares enough to help.

Try to put yourself, for a moment, in the place of some oppressed person who comes to your mind or your imagination. How would it feel to be numbered among the oppressed people of the earth? How do you think you would feel toward your oppressor? How do you think you would feel about yourself? How do you think you would feel about life in general?

As Solomon thought about the awful burden of oppression which he saw in the world around him "under the sun," he could hardly think in terms other than terms of despair. As he looked at the oppression in his world and tried to find some kind of a solution to it, his view did not include the Lord. God, of course, is "above the sun," and Solomon wasn't thinking that direction.

Now, no matter how you look at it, oppression is a very ugly subject. But if you leave God entirely out of the picture, it is even uglier! It is very close to a hopeless thing! So Solomon's viewpoint is very pessimistic. He was hard-pressed to think of any way around the problem of oppression.

II. The Escape from Oppression 4:2-3

Because of his "under the sun" perspective, the best solution Solomon could find to the problem of oppression was anything but encouraging!

A. The Lot of the Dead 4:2

"So I congratulated the dead who are already dead more than the living who are still living."

Most of us, if we know we have a painful experience coming our way, would like to get it over as soon as possible. The best view of a bad thing is the backward look. If your parents made you eat beets or spinach at dinner time as a youngster, you may have eaten them first so you could move ahead to things you found more palatable.

As Solomon considered the lot of the oppressed, he congratulated those who had the experience of oppression behind them now - because they were dead. As much as we all value physical life, Solomon couldn't imagine death being any worse than life, if life had to include oppression.

If that seems pessimistic, it is nevertheless the view which oppressed people sometimes come to when the burden of oppression gets them down. It doesn't take something as serious as oppression to make a person wish that he were dead. I have heard people say "I wish I were dead," and mean it, for lesser causes than oppression. But, as Solomon continued to think of the problem of oppression, there was one more condition which occurred to him which would even

65

be better than death.

B. The Lot Of the Non-Existent 4:3

"But better off than both of them is the one who has never existed, who has never seen the evil activity that is done under the sun."

If you are only seeing life apart from God, and you have to figure oppression into the picture, the best thing possible would be to never come into existence in the first place. If oppression can no longer hurt those who are dead, it doesn't even touch those who never come into existence. It is worth noting, at this point, that Solomon is talking about the non-existent, not the unborn, because the abortion holocaust in America today is proof enough that simply being unborn isn't enough to keep a person from "seeing" the evil activity which takes place "under the sun."

If you leave God out of the picture of life, oppression is so ugly that it would be better never to exist than to come into existence and have to face the possibility of oppression. Viewed apart from God's perspective, life for those who are oppressed is hardly worth living.

Now, some may be wondering, since oppression is such an ugly thing, what difference could it possibly make to bring God into the picture in a situation where oppression is going to be a part of the scene anyway? Would oppression be any better just because of God's presence in the life of the person enduring it?

C. The Lot of the Believer

We are blessed that not many Americans need to testify, from personal experience, about the difference the presence of the Lord can make during times of oppression. American believers have been shielded from much of the world's oppression. But the Bible shows us that there have been saints who could answer such a question from personal experience - people who, in spite of oppression, found life well worth living because of the Lord's presence with them in it.

Consider the apostle Paul's viewpoint - the viewpoint of a man in prison because of his faith in the Lord - as he voiced it in Philippians 1:12-20:

> Now I want you to know, brethren, that my circumstances have turned out for the greater progress of the gospel, [13] so that my imprisonment in the cause of Christ has become well known throughout the whole praetorian guard and to everyone else, [14] and that most of the brethren, trusting in the Lord because of my imprisonment, have far more courage to speak the word of God without fear. [15] Some, to be sure, are preaching Christ even from envy and strife, but some also from good will; [16] the latter do it out of love, knowing that I am appointed for the defense of the gospel; [17] the former proclaim Christ out of selfish ambition rather than from pure motives, thinking to cause me distress in my imprisonment. [18] What then? Only that in every way, whether in pretense or in truth, Christ is proclaimed;

and in this I rejoice.

Yes, and I will rejoice, [19] for I know that this will turn out for my deliverance through your prayers and the provision of the Spirit of Jesus Christ, [20] according to my earnest expectation and hope, that I will not be put to shame in anything, but that with all boldness, Christ will even now, as always, be exalted in my body, whether by life or by death.

Consider too the viewpoint of Peter, who (like Paul) gave up his life as a martyr for the Lord Jesus, as he expressed it in I Peter 3:13-18:

Who is there to harm you if you prove zealous for what is good? [14] But even if you should suffer for the sake of righteousness, you are blessed. And do not fear their intimidation, and do not be troubled, [15] but sanctify Christ as Lord in your hearts, always being ready to make a defense to everyone who asks you to give an account for the hope that is in you, yet with gentleness and reverence; [16] and keep a good conscience so that in the thing in which you are slandered, those who revile your good behavior in Christ will be put to shame. [17] For it is better, if God should will it so, that you suffer for doing what is right rather than for doing what is wrong. [18] For Christ also died for sins once for all, the just for the unjust, so that He might bring us to God, having been put to death in the flesh, but made alive in the spirit.

Knowing the Lord adds a vast array of bright perspectives to a believer's life - whether his life is an easy life or a hard life. Believers who came to Christ as teens or adults out of difficult backgrounds are often keenly aware of the richness that knowing the Lord can add to life in spite of oppression. Life can be tough, but no matter how tough it may become, it will always go better and be richer for those who are viewing it from God's perspective - "above the sun."

Do we sufficiently appreciate the viewpoint which God has given us in His word and in His Son? Life **is** worth living, and it always will be - even if we (like many saints before us) should be subjected to oppression - because of the Lord, and because of the lofty perspectives which can be ours in Him.

67

The Working Man
Ecclesiastes 4:4-8

Much of the time which earthly life makes available to us is spent working. The person who spends the frequently-mentioned 40 hours on the job is spending almost one fourth of the hours in a week working for his paycheck - and many people spend well above 40 hours a week bringing in a paycheck. In either case, there are certain to be some chores to do after work and on the week-ends, so it would be safe to say that over one fourth of the time available to us during our working years is spent working, either on the job away from home or doing work of some sort around the home. Even the housewife who, according to some of her critics, "does not work," puts in a large part of a 40-hour work week just planning menus, shopping, preparing and serving meals, and cleaning up the kitchen. And that, of course, is apart from her other normal tasks of running errands and house-cleaning and the care of clothing and, often, caring for children!

Working is a very important part of our lives and, generally speaking, a very satisfying part of life - as Solomon has observed already in our study of the earlier chapters of Ecclesiastes. For example, recall the message of Ecclesiastes 3:12-13: "I know that there is nothing better for them than to rejoice and to do good in one's lifetime; [13] moreover, that every man who eats and drinks sees good in all his labor—it is the gift of God."

We sometimes hear people complain about having to work, but their complaining is easily drowned out by the complaining of those who can't work - either because they are disabled or because they have no job at which to work.

Working is a very important part of our lives, but like everything else in life, it needs to be kept in proper balance with other things in life, because it isn't sufficient as our reason for being.

As Solomon, with all of his wisdom, wandered away from the Lord and began to look "under the sun" for a satisfying explanation for man's existence, one of the avenues he explored was the avenue of work, and he came to the conclusion that a man's work is not a sufficient reason for his being. It does not and cannot provide ultimate meaning and satisfaction in this life - even when, as in Solomon's case, work is done up in a big way.

Ecclesiastes 2:4-6,11
I enlarged my works: I built houses for myself, I planted vineyards for myself; [5] I made gardens and parks for myself and I planted in them all kinds of fruit trees; [6] I made ponds of water for myself from which to irrigate a forest of growing trees.
[11] Thus I considered all my activities which my hands had done and the labor which I had exerted, and behold all was vanity and striving after wind and there was no profit under the sun.

If a person's labor is not well balanced with other activities (including some leisure) and well aimed (so that he is working for a worthwhile cause), it will become very frustrating - even if he is a "workaholic." The person who does nothing but work will eventually come to see his labors as "striving after wind."

I. The Futility of Ceaseless Labor 4:4-6

A. The Reason for Ceaseless Labor 4:4

"I have seen that every labor and every skill which is done is the result of rivalry between a man and his neighbor. This too is vanity and striving after wind."

The truth of Solomon's observation that "every labor and every skill which is done is the result of rivalry between a man and his neighbor" is captured in the American phrase we all have heard - "keeping up with the Joneses."

"Rivalry" is one of the key motivators in almost everything we do in this life. Why, for example, does General Motors work so hard to update and improve their cars every year? Is it pure concern for the welfare of consumers? Of course, it isn't. The people at General Motors know that if they don't work hard, Ford and Chrysler (and Honda and Nissan and Toyota, etc.) will put them out of business.

Why do we want our shoes polished and our clothes cleaned and pressed and our hair combed when we go out in public? Is it our deep appreciation for aesthetic values? Not likely. We know that most of the other people we meet in public will be somewhat conscious of their appearance, and we don't want to compare too badly.

Some companies and some individuals are more competitive than others, but, generally speaking, the force which keeps human society moving in a forward direction is the sense of rivalry which exists between one person and the next.

Through hard labor and skillful effort, many things are accomplished for good in this life, but if God is not in the picture, the day will come when the basic futility of many of life's activities will become evident. You can't get to heaven in a General Motors car, so when all is said and done, what will all of the General Motors Cars (and others) really have amounted to? All of the well-made cars in the world are heading ultimately for the same place - the junk-yard.

The fact that a person is well-dressed and well groomed won't earn him any favor with God. Nor will it earn him a way into God's heaven. So no matter how many people we might impress along the way with our clothing and our appearance, it will all amount to nothing in the end.

There are people, of course, who have already decided that there isn't much point in competing with other people in a race which doesn't matter much in the end anyhow, so they have checked out of the race.

69

B. The Opposite of Ceaseless Labor 4:5

"The fool folds his hands and consumes his own flesh."

The man who chooses not to do any work - unless there is some good reason why he can't do any work - is labeled "a fool." Solomon's word (*kesil*) identifies a simpleton; someone who is willfully ignorant.

While working is admittedly not what this life is all about, it is recognized as necessary and even desirable by almost everyone. For a person to refrain from working simply because he or she doesn't want to work is a self-destructive route to take. Solomon addressed the problem in Proverbs 24:30-34:

I passed by the field of the sluggard
And by the vineyard of the man lacking sense,
[31] And behold, it was completely overgrown with thistles;
Its surface was covered with nettles,
And its stone wall was broken down.
[32] When I saw, I reflected upon it;
I looked, and received instruction.
[33] "A little sleep, a little slumber,
A little folding of the hands to rest,"
[34] Then your poverty will come as a robber
And your want like an armed man.

The person who simply folds his hands and refuses to work "consumes his own flesh." He will eventually (or should, anyway) end up without the necessary balanced diet to keep body and soul together, and without sufficient clothing and shelter to adequately protect himself, and without medical and dental care which are costly but necessary facts of almost every person's life.

To work one's life away (as some "workaholics" do) is "vanity and striving after wind," because work is not sufficient to give meaning and purpose to life in a final sense. And to fold one's hands and watch the world go by, refusing to work, is also not a satisfying or satisfactory course of action (or inaction) to take. So what every person ought to strive toward is a balanced life which includes enough work to provide for life's necessities (and perhaps a few amenities or even luxuries) and also enough leisure (or, at least, time away from work) to allow a person to rest and enjoy the fruits of his labors.

C. The Alternative to Ceaseless Labor 4:6

"One hand full of rest is better than two fists full of labor and striving after wind."

70

It is almost always a matter of necessity to have at least one hand full of labor - to work at what might well be called a "full-time" job. But life will be most enjoyable and potentially more fruitful if the other hand can be full of "rest" - opportunities to be refreshed, and to spend time doing what may be more enjoyable and even more important, in some cases, than what one must do to earn a paycheck. There is much to be said for time invested in service to the Lord (for which many people receive no paycheck), and even some forms of self-development (e.g., art, music, travel, social service, etc.).

Work is good and important, but it needs to be kept in balance with other good and important things in life - and sometimes doing this can become quite a struggle, because work has a way of taking over and ruling like a dictator in many lives.

An example of this fact is the way in which work can sometimes dominate the life of a person who is single and alone and who, it would seem, ought to be free to work less because he or she has less to support by means of work.

II. The Futility of Solitary Labor 4:7-8

A. An Evaluation of Solitary Labor 4:7

"Then I looked again at vanity under the sun."

Solomon took another look at the world of working people, and his keen eye picked out another situation which puzzled and disturbed him. He will define the situation which he saw in the next verse - the situation of the person who is working hard to support only himself or herself. But he begins his consideration with an evaluation of what he is about to explain. By now it is a familiar evaluation: "vanity under the sun."

What Solomon will describe in the eighth verse he first evaluates as "vanity." His word (which we have considered before, *hebel*) could be translated "nothingness" or "transitoriness" or "breath." It speaks of something which is meaningless. It is a passing thing. It leaves behind it no lasting result. It is something intangible and invisible, like a puff of wind.

The reason that the thing Solomon will describe in verse eight is "vanity" is that it is "under the sun." God is not in view in the picture. Only passing and earthly issues are in view. If the person under consideration were pouring out all of the energy and effort involved for the Lord, it all would make some sense, because it would result in something of eternal value, but this is not to be the case. God is not in the picture.

B. An Example of Solitary Labor 4:8a

"There was a certain man without a dependent, having neither a son nor a brother, yet there was no end to all his labor. Indeed, his eyes were not satisfied with riches and he never asked, 'And for whom am I laboring and depriving myself of pleasure?'"

If this verse sounds like an argument against the single life, it just might be. Solomon, you will remember was not exactly the world's most eligible bachelor when he wrote this book. We are told, in I Kings 11:3, that he had 700 wives and 300 concubines in his life!

But consider his argument. If a man can work hard and support a wife and five children and two dogs and a cat on his paycheck, from forty hours a week (and some people can), then the man who has no one to support except himself should be able to provide for all of his needs by working less than ten hours a week, right? It doesn't turn out that way, of course.

As we know, the person who has only himself to support often works just as hard, if not harder, than the person who supports a whole family (perhaps including a few pets). Though such a person may live alone, he still has many of the same needs experienced by a whole family! He still needs a residence with utilities, insurance, and transportation. Though he won't eat as much as a family, or wear as many clothes, it is more economical to cook (per serving) for many than for one, and clothing which can be passed down through a family (or shared with family members) provides better economy for multiples than for singles. And many of the home-entertainment items an entire family can enjoy are just as costly for a single person to obtain. So, while it may seem that the single person who has a full-time job should be living in luxury, Solomon's observation was that "His eyes were not satisfied with riches."

Solomon raises another issue by his question: "For whom am I laboring and depriving myself of pleasure?" As most married people (especially those who have a family of children to enjoy) can testify, there is some measure of satisfaction to be derived even in long hours of work when you know that others are benefitting from the fruits of your labors.

So what do we have as a result of Solomon's investigation into the work world - including the work of the solitary person?

C. The Frustration of Solitary Labor 4:8b

"This too is vanity and it is a grievous task."

It hardly seems fair or right that a single person working to support only himself should have to work so hard (generally speaking) to support just one, but that is the way it is. Solomon calls it "vanity" and "a grievous task." So, whether you are married or single, if you are looking to your job to provide you with a full and meaningful life, without giving much consideration to the spiritual dimension which looking "above the sun" provides in the matter, you will look long and hard and not come up with much.

A person's work is not a sufficient reason for being. If labor is not well-balanced with leisure, if it is not well-aimed at a worthwhile cause, and (most importantly) if it does not include

72

spiritual pursuits from "above the sun," it will produce nothing more lasting than exhaustion and frustration. A person's work - even if it is the work of spiritual ministry - does not and cannot provide ultimate meaning and satisfaction in life. Life's greatest satisfaction will be found in a warm and genuine relationship with the God who made us to find ultimate fulfillment only in Himself.

Where are you looking for meaning and satisfaction in your life?

73

Companionship
Ecclesiastes 4:9-12

One of the finest gifts God has given is the gift of friendship and companionship. This poem, patterned by Rosalie Carter after the famous poem "Trees," says it well:

I think that God will never send
A gift so precious as a friend.
A friend who always understands,
And fills each need as it demands,
Whose loyalty will stand the test,
When skies are bright or overcast,
Who sees the fault that merits blame,
but keeps on loving just the same.
Who does far more than creeds could do,
To make us good, to make us true.
Earth's gifts a sweet contentment lend,
But only God can give a friend.[14]

Who of us have not experienced the help of a good friend at some crucial time in our lives?

A large newspaper once offered a sizeable cash prize for the best answer to the question: "What is the shortest way to London?" The entry which won the prize was this: "The shortest way to London is good company!"[15]

As Solomon went searching for the secret of meaning in life, leaving God out of the picture, he looked in every direction he could think of, and one of the areas of life which he gave his attention to was that of companionship. The subject which led Solomon into his consideration of companionship was the subject of labor and its rewards, with the question we have just considered in the previous chapter (from 4:8): "If a man works full time to support only himself, what is the point of all his hard work?"

Working full time only to provide for oneself is a big undertaking for a small reward, so Solomon turned his attention next to the benefits of companionship - one of which is increasing the return for a person's labors.

I. Solomon's Statement on the Desirability of Companionship 4:9a

---

[14] Paul Lee Tan, *Encyclopedia of 7,700 Illustrations* (Rockville, MD: Assurance Publishers, 1979), p. 464, #1797.

[15] Ibid., p.463, #1791.

74

"Two are better than one . . ."

There are many things in life which either cannot be done well by only one person, or cannot be done at all. There have been many jokes, for example, about the person who talks to himself, but the truth is that there isn't much satisfaction in talking to oneself. Sharing the thoughts on your mind works best when you have someone with whom to share them.

Solomon's argument in this passage is not necessarily an argument for marriage, though it applies to marriage. It is broader than a consideration of only relationships between the sexes. What he has to say applies to almost any friendship or companionship situation. It applies, for example, to people working together on a job, to people traveling together on a trip, to children playing together, and (clearly) to people living together in marriage.

There are many situations in life where two or more people can function better than one. People were not made to live in total isolation from other people. Though there are people who are "loners," there are many more who like to be with other people and who appreciate the benefits that come where two or more people are cooperating with each other and coordinating their energies and efforts. This is what makes families and communities and cities and nations what they are.

Even people who are "loners" can't live in total isolation. They often don't even wish to. Many "loners" choose to marry. And all "loners" need other people for some things in their lives.

II. Solomon's Defense of the Desirability of Companionship 4:9b

"Two are better than one because they have a good return for their labor."

The presence of two people speeds up almost any job, and makes possible many others which couldn't be done by one person alone. My college job of folding and taping large mattress boxes could probably have been done by one person, but it would have taken much longer to get the work done. I was glad that my dentist had an assistant to help with my most recent dental appointment. And performing major surgery requires a team of skilled people working together.

If a job doesn't move faster because of a second person, it seems faster when a second person becomes involved just because of the companionship of a second person. So labor becomes more efficient and more enjoyable when two or more people work side by side than when one works alone. And, thinking back to the argument of verse eight (where Solomon described a man working only to support himself), labor becomes more meaningful if someone other than the worker alone is going to benefit from its rewards.

God has made us social creatures, a fact which He Himself acknowledged on the first day of man's existence when He declared that it was not good for the man to be alone. Things go better

75

with companionship in almost any situation in life.

III. Solomon's Illustrations of the Desirability of Companionship 4:10-12

Solomon continues to press home his point with three illustrations, showing three of the benefits of companionship.

A. The Assistance of Companionship 4:10

"For if either of them falls, the one will lift up his companion. But woe to the one who falls when there is not another to lift him up."

My wife and her father were hiking in the San Juan Mountains of Southwestern Colorado one summer when he slipped and fell over the edge of a cliff around thirty feet high. With his leg badly broken, he was in no shape to continue his hike, or to call for help. So it was good that they were hiking together, and that she could go for help, or the incident could easily have been the end of my father-in-law's life.

Married couples experience the truth of this verse every time one of them experiences an illness - and the truth is really driven home on those rare occasions when both partners in a marriage, or all of the members of a family, become disabled because of illness or injury.

B. The Comfort of Companionship 4:11

"Furthermore, if two lie down together they keep warm, but how can one be warm alone?"

Franz Delitzsch offers this appropriate reminder in his commentary on Ecclesiastes:

> The marriage relation is not excluded, but it remains in the background; the author has two friends in his eye, who, lying in a cold night under one covering cherish one another and impart mutual warmth.[16]

All hints of immorality aside, there are ancient writings which inform us that sleeping together was a sign of a healthy friendship in ancient times. Remember, these were the days before indoor heating was perfected and before electric blankets were invented. In our day perhaps a mountain camping trip among friends would be the most likely setting for discovering what most married couples know to be true - even with indoor heating and electric blankets.

If we may broaden the lesson of this verse beyond the issue of physical warmth, there are

---

[16] C. F. Keil and F. Delitzsch, *Old Testament Commentaries* (Reprint, Grand Rapids, MI: Eerdmans, 1968), Vol. 6, page 277.

many, many ways in which a companion - either within marriage or outside of marriage - can provide some form of comfort to a friend, whether in a material context (perhaps a gift), an emotional context (a word of encouragement), a social context (perhaps a compliment), or a spiritual context (a witness or a ministry).

So companionship offers almost unlimited opportunities for comfort of one kind or another.

C. The Strength of Companionship 4:12

"And if one can overpower him who is alone, two can resist him. A cord of three strands is not quickly torn apart."

A third illustration of the potential benefit of companionship is seen in the matter of security.

As we all know, "there is strength in numbers" when it comes to security. In fact, sometimes just the impression of numbers is enough to lend security. Recall Gideon's noisy attack on the Midianites in the dark of night (Numbers 7:15-23) when they couldn't tell he had only 300 soldiers with him!

As a general rule, two are stronger than one; and three are stronger than two. All other things being equal, we expect the larger number of people to prevail over a smaller number in contests of most any kind.

Companionship is one of life's richest blessings, providing many benefits to those who enjoy it, whether in marriage or otherwise. Solomon has nothing negative to say about companionship in this passage, though he was well aware that not all companionships are created equal - as he reveals more than once in Proverbs (e.g., 21:19: "It is better to live in a desert land / Than with a contentious and vexing woman").

In the larger context of Ecclesiastes, it is important to remember that, though companionship is good and beneficial in many respects, it is still "under the sun" if the Lord is not in the picture. As an earthly issue it can't provide lasting satisfaction for the soul and the spirit of man who was made to enjoy the fellowship and companionship of the Lord.

Companionship is one of life's richest blessings - but don't look to companionship, any more than to any other earthly thing, for the satisfaction of your eternal soul. Companionship too is only "vanity" if God is not a central part of the picture, because (1:2) "all is vanity" if it is "under the sun."

Do you appreciate the blessings of companionship? Are you grateful to those who make your life more fulfilling by their presence and their partnership in your life? Have you discovered the companionship of that friend whom Solomon described in Proverbs 18:24 as "a friend who sticks closer than a brother"? - a friend personified most clearly in the person of the Lord Jesus Christ?

77

Approval Ratings
Ecclesiastes 4:13-16

Everyone likes to be well thought of. We all invest considerable amounts of time and energy attempting to be and to say and do the kinds of things which will make people accept us; maybe even admire us.

Take, for example, the noble attempts which young children can make to please their parents and impress their friends (on special occasions, at least). Or consider the careful attention which young people pay to dressing and grooming and speaking and acting in such a way that they will be accepted by the "in crowd." And then there are the efforts adults invest in "keeping up with the Joneses."

There is nothing wrong with being well-liked - accepted and even admired - as long as a person doesn't have to compromise important standards and deny important truths in order to gain the approval of men. Johnny Urso of Halifax, Nova Scotia, was only nine years old when his playmates dared him to touch a 23,000-volt transmission line near his home. Though he was young, he knew it was dangerous, but under pressure from his "friends" he climbed the pole and touched the wire - flying up and landing on top of a grid of high-powered lines where he suffered third degree burns which took his life.[17] Sometimes the price to be paid for acceptance by one's peers is too high, and a wise person must learn when he can't afford it.

People's approval can be a good thing - increasing a person's influence for good and even for God. But, like other good things or potentially good things in this life, approval has its limits, so it isn't worth pursuing (as some pursue it) as if it were a God or an ultimate goal in life.

As Israel's King Solomon searched his world - leaving God out of the picture - for a source of lasting satisfaction, he took a look at approval and fame and influence as possible sources of satisfaction. But, like other fleeting things in life, Solomon concluded that man's approval is not worth pursuing as a source of lasting satisfaction - because it doesn't **last**.

I. The Description of Two Kings 4:13

"Better is a poor and a wise child than an old and foolish king, who will no more be admonished."

A king would have to be considered one of the most important people in any kingdom. He is known to virtually everyone, and his influence can be felt from the throne room to the farthest

---

[17] Paul Lee Tan, *Encyclopedia of 7,700 Illustrations* (Rockville, MD: Assurance Publishers, 1979), p.388, #1429.

reaches of his domain - and especially so in the case of ancient kings, who ruled (or thought they did, anyway) with absolute authority. When King Solomon himself, for example, was displeased that his half-brother Adonijah requested to marry Abishag the Shunammite, he sent one of his servants to kill Adonijah on the spot (I Kings 2:19-25)! Crossing the king can be lethal!

A king normally enjoys, by virtue of his office, a certain measure of popular approval (or respect, at least), but Solomon reminds us by his illustration that even the throne is no guarantee of approval. The king in Solomon's illustration has gotten "old" - and though increased age doesn't always diminish popular approval, it often does. Further, the king in Solomon's illustration is "foolish." He may not always have been foolish, but he has at least become foolish (perhaps because senility is setting in). In addition, he is a king who "no longer knows how to receive instruction." Perhaps he once felt his limitations and turned to learned counselors for advice, but he doesn't do that anymore. He now acts as if he knows it all.

When the tide of popular approval begins to turn against a person, the things we often think of as advantages in life may turn out to be of little or no help.

In many respects, and in many situations in life, age gives a person an advantage. Those who are older have more experience and knowledge and resources. But the king in this verse is not in a place of advantage because of his age. It has become, it would appear, a liability.

It is usually the old who have wisdom and the young who act foolishly, but in this case the opposite is true.

Normally a king is better off than a poor man. Most kings are not poor, and most poor people lack leverage in many respects because of their poverty. But in this verse the king's liabilities have come to outweigh the advantages of position and possessions.

So Solomon's assessment of the situation is this: the poor, wise lad is a better person in a better position than the old, foolish king.

Here is an illustration of the problem with popular approval. Sometimes even the person who has the position and the possessions which usually go along with approval is not popular (or no longer popular). Popular approval doesn't last.

II. The Ascendance of the Young King 4:14

"For he has come out of prison to become king, even though he was born poor in his kingdom."

The poor, wise lad of verse thirteen has now become king in place of the old foolish king - and to top it off, he has come to the throne from prison! Why was he in prison? Was it his poverty that put him in prison? Was he unable to pay some indebtedness so that he had to go to prison? Was it some form of injustice which sent him to prison? Was he just the victim of an unfortunate set of circumstances, though he had done no wrong? Or was he placed in prison by the old and foolish king because he was considered a threat to the king's position?

79

We don't know why the young lad was in prison or how he happened to get free. But what we do know is that, somehow, he has now become the king. And we know, as well, that such things can happen, because there have been times when we know they did! We know that Joseph, Son of Jacob was taken from prison to become second in command in the land of Egypt (Genesis 41:14, 38-41). And perhaps you recall that Jeroboam, first king of the northern kingdom of divided Israel, came out of exile in Egypt to become king of the northern kingdom (I Kings 11:40; 12:20).

A change in leadership is almost always an exciting time. The higher the leadership role, the greater the excitement. Solomon takes us, in thought, to a scene where the wise young lad has ascended to the throne as the new king - with popular approval running high.

III. The Popularity of the Young King 4:15

"I have seen all the living under the sun throng to the side of the second lad who replaces him."

Solomon's use of the word "second" has made some Bible students conclude that there are two young kings in view in this verse. But most commentators are in agreement that there are only two kings under consideration: (1) the old and foolish king - the first; and (2) the poor and wise lad - the second.

The new king enjoys immediate popular approval, even though his background makes him an unlikely candidate for king. His youth and wisdom make him appealing, and his position as king makes him popular.

When "all the living under the sun" throng to his side, Solomon is probably picturing the coronation festivities to which representatives from foreign nations come to wish him well and pay their respects. We know that Solomon himself was visited by many foreign dignitaries who had heard of his wealth and wisdom and who came to see for themselves.

"Long live the king" is a popular sentiment when the administration is fresh and new - but how long does the enthusiasm last? Often not very long!

IV. The Problem for the Young King 4:16

"There is no end to all the people, to all who were before them, and even the ones who will come later will not be happy with him, for this too is vanity and striving after wind."

For a while the new king is thronged with well-wishers, just as his predecessor was for a time during the first years of his administration. But then the crowds of well-wishers begin to be replaced with the critics - and the familiar story goes down hill from there.

If you are looking to popular approval for satisfaction in this life, you may as well forget it,

80

because any satisfaction it brings will only last for a while. Even kings run into problems with the approval of the crowds before very long. It is interesting, but not very encouraging, to watch the approval ratings of United States presidents go up and down like a roller coaster. The polarization of American society virtually assures every president that, even if he is highly approved by many citizens, there will be many others who will strongly disapprove.

In the June 25, 1984 edition of U.S. News and World Report, several former presidential families were asked what it was like to leave the White House. Here is the interaction with Betty Ford, wife of President Gerald Ford:

Q - "Mrs. Ford, how difficult was it for your family to become private citizens after the White House years?

A - "The transition, particularly for me, was initially very traumatic. As my daughter, Susan, has put it, Jerry's defeat was like a slap in the face. Jerry had never lost an election, and Susan was caught up - as we all were - in his pain over a lost agenda of programs he wanted to complete for the country. We had worked very hard as a family during the campaign and for 2 and ½ years in office, so rejection at the polls hurt."

Anyone who is looking to continuing popular approval as a source of satisfaction in this life will almost certainly be disappointed - "for this too is vanity and striving after wind." Like other fleeting things in life, the approval of people is not worth pursuing as a source of satisfaction in this life. Popular approval doesn't provide deep and lasting satisfaction, because it can't last forever, and it often doesn't even last very long.

So where should we be looking for approval which can provide lasting satisfaction? "Above the sun"!

The apostle Paul adopted a realistic stance in his ministry before men, as I Thessalonians 2:4 expresses it: "but just as we have been approved by God to be entrusted with the gospel, so we speak, not as pleasing men, but God who examines our hearts."

Whose approval are you seeking in your life? If your approval in life does not come from above the sun, it doesn't come from high enough, and it won't last long enough.

81

Serious Business
Ecclesiastes 5:1-7

We have probably all heard of the problem among some in our day which has been termed "easy-believism." "Easy-believism" is the notion some people have that all a person needs to do in order to please God in this life is to believe on Him.

Now it is true, of course, that all a person has to do be become a child of God - to be "saved" - is to believe. Paul and Silas made this fact clear in their response to the Philippian jailer (Acts 16:30-31): "And after he brought them out, he said, 'Sirs, what must I do to be saved?' [31] They said, 'Believe in the Lord Jesus, and you will be saved, you and your household.'"

With the understanding that "belief" (faith) is an enlightened decision to trust in Christ who died for our sins, was buried, and rose again as God's provision for our eternal salvation, it is true that all we need to do to be saved is "believe."

To suggest, though, that a person's initial decision to believe in Jesus Christ is all that God wants or expects of people who want their lives to be pleasing to Him is not the whole truth. Having begun the Christian life by faith, God wants His people to continue the Christian life by faith. He wants His people to grow in their ability to trust Him by continually and increasingly trusting him, day by day and month by month and year after year and decade after decade!

And having learned to trust the Lord (to "believe" Him) there are some other things which the Lord tells us He wants us to add to our faith. The apostle Peter provided a list of such things in II Peter 1:5-8:

> Now for this very reason also, applying all diligence, in your faith supply moral excellence, and in your moral excellence, knowledge, [6] and in your knowledge, self-control, and in your self-control, perseverance, and in your perseverance, godliness, [7] and in your godliness, brotherly kindness, and in your brotherly kindness, love. [8] For if these qualities are yours and are increasing, they render you neither useless nor unfruitful in the true knowledge of our Lord Jesus Christ.

Because there is much more to living the Christian life the way God wants it lived than just "believing," "easy-believism" has often been a problem among professing Christians. Many people who have come to faith in Christ through ministries of mass evangelism, for example, have been invited to pray a prayer or fill out a response card in order to become a part of "God's forever family." Without proper follow-up, such individuals might be left with the impression that they have done all they need to do as far as salvation is concerned.

"Easy-believism" is a serious spiritual malady which has been around for many centuries. It was addressed by Solomon as a problem in his day (though not by the title "easy-believism," of course). In every age there have been people who would substitute religious "games" for spiritual realities, but it never has worked and it never will, because spiritual matters are serious business. God is not interested in religious games but in spiritual reality.

I. Solomon's Caution Concerning Man's Worship 5:1-3

A. The Challenge to Be Cautious 5:1

"Guard your steps as you go to the house of God and draw near to listen rather than to offer the sacrifice of fools; for they do not know they are doing evil."

There were people in Solomon's day (as there are in ours) who assumed that their regular participation in the religious life of Israel at the temple (in our day it would be the program of a local church) was all that God was asking of them. They made regular visits to the temple, and they offered sacrifices just as faithfully, but God was not impressed as they thought He should be (cf. Proverbs 21:3). As God viewed their sacrifices, He saw them as the sacrifices of "fools" - sacrifices (the right things) offered by simple-minded ritualists (the wrong reasons).

When God's people come into God's presence, they ought to be coming with a sensitive spirit. They should be open to hearing what God wants to say, and open to doing what God wants them to do. They ought to come carefully - with "guarded steps" - into the presence of God, eager to learn from Him.

What Solomon observed though (through the eyes of God's Spirit) was the regular appearance of some of His people at the temple with the proper sacrifices, but no sensitivity to the Lord in the process. His description of their activity as "the sacrifice of fools" should cause us to ponder the possibility of becoming so active in our "service" for the Lord that we have no time to listen to the Lord we claim to serve.

Solomon's concluding observation in this verse ("for they do not know they are doing evil") is a strong warning regarding meaningless ritual - even when it is religious ritual. Doing the right thing in the wrong way turns it into the wrong thing - "evil."

A person's walk with the Lord is serious business and is always deserving of cautious consideration. To do the right thing for the wrong reason can get us into trouble.

B. The Way to Be Cautious 5:2a

"Do not be hasty in word or impulsive in thought to bring up a matter in the presence of God."

The words we speak can be a very constructive part of our relationship to and our service for the Lord , just as they have potential for great good in our relationships with one another. But, in order to be constructive, words need to be carefully and skillfully chosen. It takes time to choose words carefully and skillfully. We often fail to say what we should say because we speak too soon, not having taken the time to think through what we ought to say. I am reminded of the words to a popular song from the latter half of the twentieth century - "I love you, I love you, won't you tell me your name." Who doesn't want to be loved, and to be told they are loved? But does real love take place between people who don't even know each other's names?

Ill-chosen words are the product of insufficient thought, so we need to be careful not to voice every thought that comes to mind - and especially so when we are thinking about God and talking to Him. Jephthah's infamous vow (Judges 11:30-31) appears to have been a case of words too hastily spoken in his relationship with the Lord - words which were spoken before they had been thought through carefully enough.

Hasty words and impulsive thoughts which arise in our relationship with the Lord are a result of our failure to sufficiently understand and appreciate the heights at which God exists and the depths to which man is capable of falling.

C. The Reasons to Be Cautious 5:2b-3

1. The Elevation of God Above Man 5:2b

"For God is in heaven and you are on the earth; therefore let your words be few."

By his statement "God is in heaven and you are on the earth," Solomon calls our attention to the significant differences between man and his Maker. God is supernatural and divine, while man is only natural and human. God is holy and good, while man is unholy and sinful - both by nature and by practice. God is the "uncaused cause" and eternal, while man is a creature bound by time. God is infinite and omnipresent, while man is finite and able to be in only one place at any given time (and sometimes seemingly not even "all there").

The mind of man cannot comprehend the incomprehensible God, but every glimpse of insight we receive informs us of our need to be very careful in all that we think and say and do before our all-seeing God. Consider, for example, the response of the prophet Isaiah when he saw the Lord in the year that King Uzziah died (Isaiah 6:1-5):

In the year of King Uzziah's death I saw the Lord sitting on a throne, lofty and exalted, with the train of His robe filling the temple. [2] Seraphim stood above Him, each having six wings: with two he covered his face, and with two he covered his feet, and with two he flew. [3] And one called out to another and said,
"Holy, Holy, Holy, is the Lord of hosts,
The whole earth is full of His glory."
[4] And the foundations of the thresholds trembled at the voice of him who called out, while the temple was filling with smoke. [5] Then I said,
"Woe is me, for I am ruined!
Because I am a man of unclean lips,

84

And I live among a people of unclean lips;
For my eyes have seen the King, the Lord of hosts."

Isaiah's view of God in His holiness filled the prophet with a strong sense of his own unholiness - specifically with reference to his "unclean lips" (i.e his inappropriate speech). The knowledge we have that we will one day stand before this holy Lord to account for our behavior calls for all of us to be very cautious any time we come before Him.

2. The Inclination of Man to Folly 5:3

"For the dream comes through much effort and the voice of a fool through many words."

Down through the ages people have tried to attach spiritual significance to the dreams they have had. We know, of course, that the Lord has often spoken to men through their dreams. But all it takes to produce a dream is a busy mind, not a voice from heaven. We have probably all experienced nights of dream-troubled sleep in response to busy days (or, perhaps, a spicy meal).

Other people have tried to attach religious or spiritual significance to their many words. Merit has often been attached, for example, to prayers said (or repeated) out of religious devotion - or ritualistic habit. But the more words we speak the more folly they are likely to contain. Because sinful humans frequently say sinful things, the more a person speaks the more he is likely to speak sinfully.

The proverbs of Solomon frequently warn of the dangers of the tongue and of the many words they speak. Consider, for example, Proverbs 10:19:

"When there are many words, transgression is unavoidable,
But he who restrains his lips is wise."

Because God is so far above us, and because we are so inclined to empty activity and sinful words, we need to be very careful when we come before the Lord in worship. What He has to say to us is far more important than any sacrifice or service we can offer to Him.

We all need to watch our step every time we approach the Lord, whether in private devotion or public worship. God's "loftiness" and our "lowliness" call for caution, even in our worship. Are you careful to seek God's cleansing from sin when you come before Him - either in private or in public? Because of who God is, our worship is serious business - as are our words.

II. Solomon's Caution Concerning Man's Words 5:4-6

A. The Challenge to Pay What You Vow 5:4

"When you make a vow to God, do not be late in paying it; for He takes no delight in fools. Pay what you vow!"

A "vow" is a solemn promise or pledge, and God knows well that human beings have made many solemn promises to Him. We can only begin to imagine how many promises have been made to God in "altar calls" down through the years - to say nothing of all the things men and women in difficult circumstances (like "foxholes" in battle) have promised to do, if only God would do one thing or another for them.

When God speaks, He says what He means and He means what He says. So He wants His people to do as He does in their speech. When a man makes a promise, God wants him to keep it, and He tells us clearly that He considers the person who doesn't keep his word a "fool." If we have made any solemn promises to the Lord, He expects us to fulfill our word!

B. The Advisability of Making Vows 5:5

"It is better that you should not vow than that you should vow and not pay."

Because God holds His people responsible to do what they say they will do, it is very important that we be careful about what we say we will do. God holds truthfulness in such high regard that He would prefer His people not make promises - even if their promises are good and noble promises - than that they make a promise and then fail to keep it.

C. The Seriousness of Making Vows 5:6

Solomon was well aware that the Hebrew Bible spoke clearly regarding the seriousness with which the Lord views the vows of His people. A vow, once made, was never to be retracted by the one who made it!

1. Man's Futile Attempt to Retract His Vow 5:6a

"Do not let your speech cause you to sin and do not say in the presence of the messenger of God that it was a mistake."

Solomon's teaching on vows in these verses is similar to the teaching on the subject which was contained in the law. Deuteronomy 23:21-23 summarizes the Lord's words through Moses on the subject.

"When you make a vow to the Lord your God, you shall not delay to pay it, for it would be sin in you, and the Lord your God will surely require it of you. [22] However, if you refrain from vowing, it would not be sin in you. [23] You shall be careful to perform what goes out from your lips, just as you have voluntarily vowed to the Lord your God, what you have promised."

86

The law made no provision for cancelling a vow, except in the case of a woman under the authority of a father or a husband. Only in this case could a vow be cancelled, and only under the circumstances given in Numbers 30:3-8:

> Also if a woman makes a vow to the Lord, and binds herself by an obligation in her father's house in her youth, [4] and her father hears her vow and her obligation by which she has bound herself, and her father says nothing to her, then all her vows shall stand and every obligation by which she has bound herself shall stand. [5] But if her father should forbid her on the day he hears of it, none of her vows or her obligations by which she has bound herself shall stand; and the Lord will forgive her because her father had forbidden her.
> [6] However, if she should marry while under her vows or the rash statement of her lips by which she has bound herself, [7] and her husband hears of it and says nothing to her on the day he hears it, then her vows shall stand and her obligations by which she has bound herself shall stand. [8] But if on the day her husband hears of it, he forbids her, then he shall annul her vow which she is under and the rash statement of her lips by which she has bound herself; and the Lord will forgive her.

As Solomon points out in this verse, God didn't want His people making promises to Him and then going to His "messengers" (the priests, who often were the ones who "collected" for the Lord on the promises of His people) and trying to get excused from their promises on the grounds that they had made a mistake.

That God was serious about His people's promises is made clear in the last part of verse 6.

2. God's Judgment Against Insincerity 5:6b

"Why should God be angry on account of your voice and destroy the work of your hands?"

If God's people didn't keep their promises to Him, He threatened to become angry and to complicate their lives. He might "destroy the work of [their] hands" in many ways - e.g., crop failure or family problems or health problems. II Samuel 21:1 records, for example, a three year famine which occurred during the days of King David. When David inquired of the Lord, he learned that the famine was God's judgment for Saul's dealings with some Gibeonites he had put to death. The nation of Israel had taken an oath during the days of Joshua not to take the lives of the people of Gibeon (Joshua 9:15). Because Israel, under Saul, did not keep that oath, the Lord brought judgment.

If you are getting the impression that God is serious about the words His people speak, you are getting the message. He is very serious. Living life before the all-seeing eye and the all-hearing ear of the Lord is serious business. We need to be careful to live up to promises we make to Him. Unkept promises to God could be the explanation for some of the problems which come into our lives and the lives of others.

III. Solomon's Conclusion Concerning Man and God 5:7

"For in many dreams and in many words there is emptiness. Rather, fear God."

As Solomon pursued his search for meaning in life, as it takes place "under the sun," he didn't find it. He didn't even find it in the realm of worship and many of the commitments people make to the Lord, because there he encountered the problem of insincerity and words not spoken in honesty.

In many of the dreams people report as a part of their spiritual experience, Solomon discovered "emptiness." Though people often attach spiritual significance to their dreams, Solomon could see that dreams often have nothing to do with communication from the Lord. A stressful day, or a spicy meal, can produce a memorable dream. So it is dangerous to put too much stock in someone's dream - particularly when the interpretations of dreams can be such a subjective experience. In a world where dreams come frequently, "in many dreams . . . there is emptiness."

Unfortunately, what is true of many dreams is equally true of many words. The fact that a person talks more or prays more than someone else doesn't necessarily make him a spiritual person. In fact, the more a person says, the more likely he will be to say something foolish. Like dreams, words are many, but God is not looking for words in His people's lives as much as He is looking for deeds. And right deeds start with the right attitude toward the Lord. So Solomon's advice is "Rather, fear God."

It isn't how often we show up at the "house of God," or how impressively we speak about Him, that makes or breaks our relationship with the Lord. Rather it is how fully we give Him the reverence He is due in every facet of our lives. The day is coming when every person will give an account before the Lord of all that he has thought and said and done. So the wise person lives in view of his accountability to the Lord. God is not interested in the religious games people often play, but in spiritual reality.

Because our relationship with the Lord is serious business, our lives and worship should be characterized by caution. It is important that our words be worthy of trust. It is important that our lives be lived in sincere reverence for who the Lord is in view of our accountability to Him.

88

Good News, Bad News
Ecclesiastes 5:8-9

Some years ago now someone came up with a "good news, bad news" situation or joke, and the idea took off across the land, until it seems that nearly everyone has gotten in on the act. A friend of mine was told by her doctor that he had some good news and some bad news for her. The good news was that her tumor hadn't gotten any bigger; the bad news was that it hadn't gotten any smaller.

Though the proliferation of "good news, bad news" evaluations has been something of a fad in recent years, "good news, bad news" situations have been with us from the beginning. In the Garden of Eden the first "bad news" was God's observation that "it is not good that the man should be alone;" the "good news" was that the Lord was going to make a helper suitable for him (Genesis 2:18). Even the first "gospel" announcement (Genesis 3:15) juxtaposed the "bad news" of the bruising of the heel of the woman's seed (ultimately, Christ's death on the cross) against the "good news" of the bruising of the head of the serpent's seed (ultimately, Satan's defeat).

Life is full of "good news, bad news" scenarios. And in many cases they are no joking matter, but dead-serious business. Life on a sin-cursed earth is a complex mixture of both the good and the bad. But that in itself is both bad news and good news. The bad news is that everyone is going to experience some problems in this life. The good news is that even in the middle of our problems there is almost always some benefit to be found.

The passage before us brings to our attention just one of those anomalies which can be observed in many places in the world in which we live. The "bad news" is this: the world is full of oppression, injustice, and unrighteousness. But the "good news" is that even an oppressive, unjust and unrighteous situation can have some beneficial side effects. For example, even an oppressive authority is better than no authority at all. And even an unjust decision can produce some good results. And even an unrighteous action can spin off some righteous reactions.

As realists, we need to be prepared for both the bad and the good. But as God-trusting optimists, we ought to be looking for something to be grateful about - even when bad news comes into our lives.

As Solomon spent his energies looking for meaning in life, he was looking (unfortunately) in the wrong place ("under the sun"). As a result, he comes across, in the book of Ecclesiastes, as something of a pessimist. But, looking at his pessimistic book optimistically, we get the benefit of a better understanding of how life really looks for people who don't give the Lord the place which He deserves. And if we don't give the Lord the place which He deserves, life is at best a mixture of bad news and good news.

I. Solomon's Exhortation 5:8a

89

A. The Potential Situation

[8a] "If you see oppression of the poor and denial of justice and righteousness in the province, do not be shocked at the sight."

1. Oppression Observed

If you look around and don't see any signs of oppression, you probably should have your eyes examined. Solomon has assured us already (4:1-3) that he saw "acts of oppression" in great numbers in his world. There he saw "the tears of the oppressed and that they had no one to comfort them."

Oppression is always taking place in varying degrees in many ways and many places on the face of our earth. In every age there are oppressive regimes in power, withholding from their citizens the "inalienable rights" with which the Lord Himself has endowed them. Even in our own land and our own communities ("in the province") there are examples of oppression taking place in our streets and in our schools and in our workplaces and even in many homes. What can be said, for example, in defense of the husband who beats his wife or abuses his children?

2. Injustice Observed

Just as the world is full of oppression, so the world is full of injustice. Look around carefully and you will find people in many places who are being treated unfairly. Even in the halls of our judicial system you are likely to have good reason to doubt that justice is always being well-served. The discovery of a "right to abortion" in the U.S. Constitution - where the word "abortion" never occurs and the concept had never been seen before by generations of the nation's top jurists - serves as a classic example in the thinking of many.

3. Unrighteousness Observed

Unrighteousness is a broader concept than either oppression or injustice - encompassing both. Unrighteousness is taking place wherever people are not conforming their lives to the will of God in what they think or say or do, so it should be rather obvious that unrighteousness is all around us. What, for example, is righteous in a terrorist event, where someone is injured or killed by a person they have never met or had any dealings with?

Without any reasonable doubt, the world is full of oppression, injustice, and unrighteousness. And you don't have to check out the whole world to find it. Just look around you "in the province" (on the local scene) and you will find sufficient examples. Human nature is so infused by sin that we have learned to expect some oppression and injustice and unrighteousness!

B. The Practical Exhortation

90

[8a] "Do not be shocked at the sight."

The Scriptures assure us in many places that there is no reason to be shocked when we find oppression and injustice and unrighteousness in our world. The natural condition of the human heart makes it inevitable.

Jeremiah 17:9 is a classic statement of the heart's condition: "The heart is more deceitful than all else / And is desperately sick; / Who can understand it?" More extensive descriptions of man's heart problems can be seen in Psalm 14:1-3 and Romans 1:18-21 and Romans 3:9-18 and Galatians 5:19-20

Given the truth of the depravity of man, we might be surprised not so much by how much wickedness we see around us as by how much goodness we see around us. This is because, by the grace and wisdom of God, man's wickedness has been put under some practical restraints - though, of course, even those restraints are flawed by the sinfulness of man.

II. Solomon's Observation 5:8b

" . . . for one official watches over another official, and there are higher officials over them."

A. The Presence of Lower Officials

Because man is by nature a sinful creature, God has ordained human government to help restrain man's sin. The Noahic Covenant (Genesis 9:5-6) records the earliest Biblical allowance for human government.

> [5] "Surely I will require your lifeblood; from every beast I will require it. And from every man, from every man's brother I will require the life of man.
> [6] Whoever sheds man's blood,
> By man his blood shall be shed,
> For in the image of God
> He made man."

To help maintain order, mankind appoints (under God's authority) "officials" to exercise authority. But even "officials" don't have their acts entirely together, so men live under a hierarchy of officials. Officials need to be regulated by other officials - so the officials who most immediately supervise the public are themselves supervised by higher officials.

B. The Presence of Higher Officials

To keep order on our sin-cursed earth we have a whole network of government officials. But government officials too are cursed by sin, so we have more officials to govern our officials, and even more officials over them! And at the top of the heap of human authorities we have still another sinner in authority over lesser authorities. Because humans are all characterized by sin, all of the human officials who govern sinful humans are also marred by sin. So "If you see oppression of the poor and denial of justice and righteousness in the province, do not be shocked at the sight"!

The "bad news" is that oppression and injustice and unrighteousness are here to stay in our world in its present condition, because all people are sinners. Not even a proliferation of officials will eliminate oppression and injustice and unrighteousness, because even officials are oppressive and unjust and unrighteous.

Does this mean, then, that the human scene is bad news and only bad news? No, it doesn't. There is also some good news, and the good news is this. Even an oppressive, unjust, and unrighteous situation can have some beneficial side effects. Even an oppressive, unjust, and unrighteous authority can be better than no authority at all.

III. Solomon's Conclusion 5:9

"After all, a king who cultivates the field is an advantage to the land."

A. A King's Activity 5:9a

While the person who is in power - the "king" in Solomon's words - may not be the best of authorities, he still brings some benefits to the land which he serves by some of the things he does. In order to keep his kingdom in operation, the king of Solomon's example cultivated the land. He had to arrange for the growth of crops in order to feed his household. In our own day, the cultivation of the land might be expanded to include the paving of roads, the provision of educational opportunities, and the maintenance of a police force and fire-fighting force and military force. And the benefits could be greatly expanded - depending on the functionality of the official in question.

B. The Land's Advantage 5:9b

Though the people may not appreciate all that the person in authority does and stands for, because he is (as they are also) sinful, he still brings some benefits to those over whom he exercises authority by the activity of his administration.

Anyone who thinks the "system" under which he lives is worthless needs only to be reminded of what happens when a social crisis or a natural disaster shuts down the "system" for a period of time, and people think they can do as they please! Natural disasters like floods and earthquakes and hurricanes and tornadoes, for example, are often followed by times of social chaos with looting and rioting - until the authorities in power can reassert their control. Such occasions illustrate the truth that even an oppressive, unjust, and unrighteous government can have some beneficial side-effects.

92

Looking at life from a pessimistic point of view (which is Solomon's point of view in Ecclesiastes - "under the sun") there is still some good news along with all the bad news in the social structures of our world.

As Christians who know that "above the sun" there is a God who sovereignly works in the affairs of men, we can see things from a much brighter perspective than Solomon did in Ecclesiastes. The apostle Paul put these things in good perspective for us in Romans 13:1-7.

Every person is to be in subjection to the governing authorities. For there is no authority except from God, and those which exist are established by God. [2] Therefore whoever resists authority has opposed the ordinance of God; and they who have opposed will receive condemnation upon themselves. [3] For rulers are not a cause of fear for good behavior, but for evil. Do you want to have no fear of authority? Do what is good and you will have praise from the same; [4] for it is a minister of God to you for good. But if you do what is evil, be afraid; for it does not bear the sword for nothing; for it is a minister of God, an avenger who brings wrath on the one who practices evil. [5] Therefore it is necessary to be in subjection, not only because of wrath, but also for conscience' sake. [6] For because of this you also pay taxes, for rulers are servants of God, devoting themselves to this very thing. [7] Render to all what is due them: tax to whom tax is due; custom to whom custom; fear to whom fear; honor to whom honor.

When all is said and done, the bad news is that those who are in authority over us in this life are all sinners, but the good news is that God can use them for our good in spite of their sinfulness, and that He is the ultimate authority - working all things out for His good pleasure and the good of His people.

93

Don't Love Your Money
Ecclesiastes 5:10-17

If money could buy happiness Israel's King Solomon could have bought a lot of it, and the book of Ecclesiastes would probably never have been written. I Kings 10:14 tells us that "the weight of gold which came to Solomon in one year was 666 talents of gold." Calculating 666 talents at around 800,000 ounces, at $500 an ounce Solomon would have received $400,000,000 each year in gold alone! No surprise, then, that "Solomon became greater than all the kings of the earth in riches" (I Kings 10:23).

As the richest king of his time and one of the richest men of all times, Solomon became a disillusioned man when he allowed the Lord to slip out of the place of central importance in his life. And so we have the book of Ecclesiastes, a record of his search for meaning in life "under the sun."

There are many people in days gone by, and in our own day, who have sought or are seeking happiness through the pursuit of wealth, but it isn't to be found in wealth. The apostle Paul could have been writing a commentary on the life of Solomon when, speaking for God, he advised Timothy as he did in I Timothy 6:9-10:

> But those who want to get rich fall into temptation and a snare and many foolish and harmful desires which plunge men into ruin and destruction. [10] For the love of money is a root of all sorts of evil, and some by longing for it have wandered away from the faith and pierced themselves with many griefs.

The person who loves money will live an empty life because money does not have the capacity to bring soul satisfaction. If anyone was ever in a position to speak with authority on the subject, it was Solomon. So let's consider what he had to say.

I. The Vanity of Riches 5:10-12

A. Riches Don't Satisfy 5:10

"He who loves money will not be satisfied with money, nor he who loves abundance with its income. This too is vanity."

Life's most satisfying relationships are not relationships between people and things. Life's most satisfying relationships are relationships between persons - between people and people, and between people and God.

The philosopher has often been quoted in his saying: "The soul of man is a God-shaped vacuum." Man will discover ultimate satisfaction only when he finds it in a personal relationship

94

with God.

Next to the satisfaction which God gives is the satisfaction we find in family and other significant human relationships. But least satisfying of all relationships are the relationships which exist through ownership and control - between people and things.

How often have you had a strong desire for some material possession which now sits unused in some corner of your house or yard? I watched with some amazement when a former neighbor purchased a very nice fifth-wheel trailer (for, I would estimate, around $80,000) and parked it in his yard adjacent to mine. He regularly drove the new pick-up truck which he purchased to pull it. But only once in the next six years did I see him take the fifth-wheel trailer out of his yard - for a short fishing trip to a lake about forty miles away! The fifth-wheel trailer he apparently loved enough to invest significant funds in purchasing didn't seem to give him much satisfaction for his investment.

Whether it is money itself or the things which money can buy, those who love wealth and place it ahead of life's more important pursuits are headed for disappointment because, when all is said and done, it is "vanity." Though many Americans (arguably the world's leading materialists) have learned the hard way of the vanity of material possessions, there are many, many more who are going to discover it in the years ahead. As a nation, the people of the United States in the early twenty first century are probably wealthier than any people have ever been before them. Today's necessities were yesterday's luxuries, while yesterday's necessities have come to be considered our birthright. I recall seeing a bumper sticker which read "housing is a right, not a privilege" - as if even those who do nothing to provide for their own shelter deserve to have it given to them on the proverbial "silver platter."

Be aware that money and material things will never bring lasting satisfaction to your soul. Only as money and material things are invested in eternal matters will they achieve anything of really lasting value.

Not only do riches not bring lasting satisfaction to the soul, they tend to attract "leaches" to those who possess them.

B. Riches Multiply Spenders 5:11

"When good things increase, those who consume them increase. So what is the advantage to their owners except to look on?"

The more money you have, the more "friends" you will have to help you spend it. Some will be true friends and loving family members - simply responding to your generosity. Others will be "fair weather friends" and not-so-loving family members (including relatives you didn't even know you had) who will be out to see what they can get. Still others will be businesses (good and bad) seeking you as a customer. And then there is the ever-hungry government seeking its share of the goods.

If you are rich, or planning to be rich, plan to take a lot of people with you for whatever ride you can provide. But in many cases your greatest satisfaction will be to watch while others enjoy the benefits of your wealth. You do enjoy sending politicians on "fact finding" tours to places you may never see, don't you?

And be aware that riches don't always improve your quality of life.

C. Riches Diminish Sleep 5:12

"The sleep of the working man is pleasant, whether he eats little or much; but the full stomach of the rich man does not allow him to sleep."

The "working man" puts in many a day of hard labor, after which his tired body and mind sleep soundly - even if he is too poor to eat a large and nutritious meal. But the "rich man" (by which Solomon obviously refers here to the man who is so wealthy he doesn't have to do any physical labor - if he does any work at all) goes to bed on a stomach full of rich food which won't allow him to sleep. And then his mind is full of plans and worries which would keep him awake even if his rich meal didn't. Where to invest next - and worries about what is already invested (whether it will pay off as expected). What to buy next - and worries about depreciation and disaster (e.g., theft, accident, etc.) with respect to what has already been bought.

For all of the time and energy which mankind invests in accumulating wealth, there is a very disappointing pay-off of "vanity" (emptiness; breath; nothingness). And what a person works so hard to acquire (or perhaps acquires without working) not only doesn't bring lasting satisfaction; it also doesn't even last!

II. The Transiency of Riches 5:13-17

Because our values are often overbalanced toward the physical and material things of life, we sometimes spend too much time and effort accumulating things we ultimately can't keep anyway.

A. Hoarded Riches Can Hurt 5:13

"There is a grievous evil which I have seen under the sun: riches being hoarded by their owner to his hurt."

The French millionaire miser, M. Foscue, in order to hide his treasure securely, dug a cave in his wine cellar, so large and deep that he could go down only with a ladder. At the entrance was a door with a spring lock, which would automatically shut itself. After some time, he disappeared and, though a search was made, he couldn't be found. At last his house was sold.

96

The purchaser of the house was making some improvements when he discovered the door in its cellar. Opening the door he found the house's former owner lying dead on the floor - his vast wealth stored away around him. He had apparently gone into the cave and been trapped when the door automatically closed behind him. Lacking food, he had eaten some candles and even gnawed the flesh off of both of his arms. His hoarded wealth had become his undoing.[18]

But hoarded wealth can hurt a man much more easily than this. Who of us have not invested some money in things which threatened to become our master? The more you own, the more you have to take care of. It is easy to become possessed by our possessions. You buy a second car, thinking that it will free up your family's transportation situation. And it does. But you soon discover that your insurance rates nearly doubled; your maintenance expenses nearly doubled; the car you want to use always seems to be blocked in by the other one; and the time you spend washing and caring for the second car makes you wonder whether it is an asset or a liability.

So our possessions can be very possessive. And even those possessions which become so possessive of us are not a secure investment.

B. Riches Are Easily Lost 5:14-15

"When those riches were lost through a bad investment and he had fathered a son, then there was nothing to support him. [15] As he had come naked from his mother's womb, so will he return as he came. He will take nothing from the fruit of his labor that he can carry in his hand."

The fact that a person possesses wealth is no guarantee that he knows how to live well. And it is no guarantee that he will retain his wealth even during this life on earth. Here is Solomon's warning on the subject from Proverbs 23:4-5:

Do not weary yourself to gain wealth,
Cease from your consideration of it.
[5] When you set your eyes on it, it is gone.
For wealth certainly makes itself wings
Like an eagle that flies toward the heavens.

In 1923 a group of the world's most successful financiers met at the Edgewater Beach Hotel in Chicago. Collectively, these tycoons controlled more wealth than there was in the United States treasury, and for years newspapers and magazines printed their success stories and urged the youth of the nation to follow them as examples. Here is what happened to some of them:

---

[18] Paul Lee Tan, *Encyclopedia of 7,700 Illustrations* (Rockville, MD: Assurance Publishers, 1979), p.803, #3430.

97

1. Charles Schwab - the president of the largest independent steel company - lived on borrowed money the last five years of his life, and died penniless.
2. Arthur Cutten - the great wheat speculator of his time died abroad insolvent.
3. Richard Whitney - the president of the New York Stock Exchange - spent time in the Sing Sing Mental Hospital.
4. Albert Fall - a member of the president's cabinet - was pardoned from prison so he could die at home.[19]

Riches in this world are so unpredictable that a person often departs this life with nothing more to claim as his own than he brought with him into life - even though he may have handled hundreds of thousands and even millions of dollars during his life time.

C. Riches Can't Go with You 5:16

"This also is a grievous evil—exactly as a man is born, thus will he die. So what is the advantage to him who toils for the wind?"

Many people who came into this world with nothing also depart this world with nothing they can claim as their own. But even those who die with earthly wealth are materially disinherited by death. No matter how much wealth you possess at the time of your decease, you can't take any of it with you. As the Spanish proverb has it: "Shrouds have no pockets." Or, as I have heard pastor Chuck Swindoll observe in a radio message, "You never saw a hearse pulling a U-Haul!"

No matter how much wealth you manage to store up during your life, you will leave it behind for someone else to enjoy (or fight over, or be burdened about). So don't lay up your treasures only, or even primarily, in things you will never be able to keep in the years to come anyhow.

D. Riches Can Be Frustrating 5:17

"Throughout his life he also eats in darkness with great vexation, sickness and anger."

The person who sets his affection on the material things of this life and then sees them slip through his fingers loses his reason for living. So his life becomes even more frustrating than it was when he was hotly pursuing the worthless things he now has lost. Many a formerly wealthy person has chosen to end his life through suicide rather than face the consequences of loss. His "light" goes out when his possessions slip away. His frustration (vexation) increases as he finds himself powerless to do anything about his situation. His body is consumed by the fever in his brain. He becomes an angry man.

---

[19] Paul Lee Tan, *Encyclopedia of 7,700 Illustrations* (Rockville, MD: Assurance Publishers, 1979), p.824, #3528.

98

Even when we have them, material things cannot provide satisfaction. So the person who lives for them and then loses them will probably go to a bitter grave. The person who loves money will live an empty life because money does not have the capacity to bring soul satisfaction.

What is your attitude toward material things? Is it the attitude Jesus taught His followers to adopt?

Matthew 6:19-21
"Do not store up for yourselves treasures on earth, where moth and rust destroy, and where thieves break in and steal. [20] But store up for yourselves treasures in heaven, where neither moth nor rust destroys, and where thieves do not break in or steal; [21] for where your treasure is, there your heart will be also."

99

Whistle While You Work
Ecclesiastes 5:18-20

While everyone needs a job and some resources in order to provide for the needs of his life and his family, there are many people who show very little appreciation for the work they are involved in. Consider, for example, all the complaints you have heard over the years about Monday morning - when work begins anew for most people for another week.

We only need to talk to someone who is trying to get along without a job which they need, or the resources which they need, in order to get a better perspective on the blessing we have when we have a job to do - a job which provides for the needs of our lives and our loved ones.

But there is more to be aware of than the fact that a job and some resources are an important part of our lives. Because even a job and some resources become a spiritual issue when we factor the Lord into the picture. Like every other "good thing bestowed and every perfect gift [which] is from above, coming down from the Father of lights, with whom there is no variation, or shifting shadow" (James 1:17), a job and some resources are among the many blessings which the Lord has given to mankind in order to make his life fulfilling and fruitful.

The Lord has enabled all people to find satisfaction in their labors as one of His good gifts to mankind. Do you see the hand of the Lord in the opportunity to be involved in work and to enjoy the fruit of your labors?

Though some people feel work is a curse of some kind, the truth is that it was a part of God's gracious provision for Adam even before the curse of sin came into the world to spoil God's good creation. And Solomon knew it very well - because he calls it to our attention not just once but several times in his search for meaning in life. He has already commended labor twice before in Ecclesiastes.

Eccles. 2:24 "There is nothing better for a man than to eat and drink and tell himself that his labor is good. This also I have seen that it is from the hand of God."

Eccles. 3:12-13 "I know that there is nothing better for them than to rejoice and to do good in one's lifetime; [13] moreover, that every man who eats and drinks sees good in all his labor—it is the gift of God."

Now Solomon is going to speak to the issue of work as a blessing once again.

I. God's Blessing on the Working Man 5:18

A. Solomon's Observation 5:18a

100

"Here is what I have seen to be good and fitting . . ."

Far from being something to shirk and reject, the ability to work and to enjoy the fruits of our labors in this life is something "good and fitting." Alternate translations for "good" (*tob*) include "pleasant" and "agreeable." And alternate translations for "fitting" (*yapheh*) include "fair" and "beautiful."

When you stop to think of the fact that the Lord has created people with such an amazing variety of abilities and interests, and that He has so designed our lives that almost everyone can find something he really likes to do - if he works hard enough at the pursuit, it really is a good and even a beautiful thing. I think of my brother's abilities with technical things - making his living as an electrician, and my own interests in ministry pursuits - making my living as a pastor. Our abilities and interests are very dissimilar in many respects, but we both find fulfillment in our work.

It is "good and fitting," says Solomon, that we are able to do what we do and enjoy what we enjoy.

B. Solomon's Enumeration of the Working Man's Blessings 5:18b

" . . . to eat, to drink and enjoy oneself in all one's labor in which he toils under the sun during the few years of his life which God has given him . . ."

God has beautifully designed our lives and our activities so that work is not only something good and beautiful in itself, but good and beautiful in what it enables us to do besides the job itself.

1. To Eat

Eating is a rather necessary part of our lives. So it is nothing less than a stroke of genius that the Lord has designed our lives so that the work we enjoy doing, in and of itself, can also make it possible to put a meal on the table to sustain our lives and significantly increase life's pleasure. How often in our lives do we find not only nourishment but a significant measure of pleasure in sitting down to a good meal - particularly when it is enjoyed in the company of others we love. And equally important to the well-being of the body as the food we eat are the beverages we drink.

2. To Drink

A great meal would not be as enjoyable or beneficial if it couldn't be accompanied by something to drink. If you have ever played the game where you eat some soda crackers and then try, as quickly as you can, to whistle a tune, you have experienced an exaggerated sense of the importance of the drinks which go along with our food.

And drinks are more than an accompaniment to our meals. We drink a variety of beverages throughout a normal day simply for the benefit they provide for our bodies. I keep a glass of water on my desk and empty it several times in a day, because the body needs liquids to function properly.

There is a great deal of potential enjoyment in the process of simply drinking something for the pleasure to be found in a tasty, invigorating drink. I enjoy the flavor of coffee and tea and various soft drinks and milk products and so forth - with their wide variety of forms and flavors. And some of them have significant health and medicinal potential as well. My eyes are sensitive to light, for example, so I find that a soft drink or a cup of coffee or tea helps control headaches, because my body responds quickly to the medicinal value of caffeine.

So the ability to eat and drink are two of the significant side-benefits of our work - and there are many others.

3. To Enjoy Oneself

My work as a pastor includes the stimulation of learning through study and the satisfaction of interacting with the Lord Himself and with a variety of people for a variety of purposes. It also includes the opportunity to take part in a wide variety of activities - each of which bring some measure of enjoyment in and of themselves. And, because I work, I am enabled occasionally to take a break for a number of recreational activities which are also very enjoyable and beneficial in many ways. Income earned from my employment has allowed me to take time to hike and ride my bicycle and travel to many interesting places and take part in such enjoyable experiences as viewing the Grand Canyon and hiking in the Canadian Rockies and riding to the top of the Arch in St. Louis, Missouri and taking in the rides at Disneyland and swimming in the Pacific Ocean and visiting the Kilauaeia Iki volcano on the island of Hawaii - and much more.

There are many things to enjoy for the person who takes his labors seriously and then takes advantage of the many experiences and opportunities which the fruit of his labors make possible. And this, Solomon assures us, is as it should be.

C. Solomon's Recognition of Work's Reward 5:18c

" . . . for this is his reward."

The word translated "reward" (*cheleq*) is more often translated "share" or "portion" or "lot" or "inheritance." But, however it is translated, the point is that work normally includes some benefits to be enjoyed as a result. And those benefits rightfully belong to the person who has invested the labor to achieve them.

Though other portions of Scripture warn us against the folly of using our employment only as an opportunity to indulge the flesh, there are legitimate benefits for the laborer - things to be enjoyed by those who pour themselves effectively into their work.

Do you see work as a God-given opportunity to find fulfillment and to acquire life's necessities - and to earn some enjoyment as well? That is how Solomon saw it. Even though the book of Ecclesiastes is written from the perspective of one who saw primarily what is "under the sun" (apart from the Lord), Solomon couldn't overlook the fact that the Lord has developed a very sensible plan for man's employment - a plan which contributes significantly to man's enjoyment.

And what is true for the "common man" is true as well - in an even fuller measure - for the man who has been blessed by the Lord with wealth.

II. God's Blessing on the Wealthy 5:19-20

A. Solomon's Recognition of God's Blessings 5:19a

"Furthermore, as for every man to whom God has given riches and wealth . . ."

There are the occasions in which riches and wealth belong to those who earn them by their fruitful labors. But riches and wealth are often the lot of those who have done little or nothing to earn them through their own labors. The legendary child born with "a silver spoon in his mouth" enjoys wealth because he is born into it. Others come into it as a result of inheritance.

Whether riches are earned by hard labor or handed down through the labors or fortunes of others, Solomon realized and recognized that their actual source is the Lord. He observed that "God has given riches and wealth" and that "this is the gift of God." And with God-given riches come God-given blessings.

B. Solomon's Enumeration of the Wealthy Man's Blessings 5:19b

However a person comes to be blessed with riches and wealth, Solomon recognized the truth that it is the Lord who has empowered him - in several respects:

" . . . He has also empowered him to eat from them and to receive his reward and rejoice in his labor . . ."

1. To Eat

If there is both the necessity and the opportunity for those who are hard workers to enjoy the blessings of good food, the wealthy also need to eat, and they also enjoy eating. And, of course, they are in a position to be even more selective about whether the food they eat is exactly to their liking! My pastoral ministry has sometimes involved me in weddings for wealthy families which included meals of much richer fare than my normal diet, and I will admit to enjoying such treats.

103

Wealthy people, like industrious people who are not quite so wealthy, have been blessed by the Lord with the blessing of good food to enjoy.

2. To Receive His Reward

Using the same word he used in verse 18 (*cheleq*), Solomon reminds us again that wealth comes with its "reward" (or "share" or "portion" or "lot" or "inheritance"). But that "reward" is available to the wealthy only because the Lord has empowered him to receive it. Anyone who doubts the importance of the Lord's hand in it all needs only to be reminded of some who have immense wealth and other benefits in life but who, for all they possess, are not empowered to receive it. They sometimes even take their own lives, in spite of their wealth, out of their sense of despair and desperation.

If the wealthy have been empowered to receive the "reward" which comes with their wealth, it is because they have been empowered by the Lord. And the Lord also has to empower them to rejoice in their labor.

3. To Rejoice in His Labor

While it may look otherwise to those who don't have it, possessing wealth is not all that easy. Wealth creates its own work, because it has to be managed. And if it isn't managed well, it will self-destruct. So even those who are wealthy, because the Lord has blessed them with wealth, need to be empowered to rejoice in the labor required to manage and maintain what they are blessed to have. Solomon himself possessed an amazing amount of wealth, but he obviously wasn't always empowered (while focused "under the sun") to rejoice in his labor - or he wouldn't have written the book of Ecclesiastes. And Solomon's son Rehoboam was born with a "silver spoon in his mouth" if any son ever was - but his failure to put the Lord first in his life also kept him from enjoying the empowerment God must give to allow a man to rejoice in his labors.

So Solomon acknowledged that the Lord must add His blessing to the mix, or even those who possess the blessing of wealth can't enjoy it as they might.

C. Solomon's Recognition of God's Gift 5:19c

" . . . this is the gift of God."

Riches and wealth, in and of themselves, will never make for healthy, happy meals and the reception of riches' reward and the enjoyment of wealth's labors. Howard Hughes, for example, was reputed to be one of the wealthiest men on the face of the earth in his day, but the Lord had no observable part in his life - and he ended his life a wretched, fearful, lonely man. There is far more to the Lord's gifting in a person's life than wealth.

D. Solomon's Recognition of Life's Gladness 5:20

104

"For he will not often consider the years of his life, because God keeps him occupied with the gladness of his heart."

The person who is gifted by the Lord with satisfying employment and the benefits it brings will not be found counting the years of his life out of concern or boredom. He will be blessed by the Lord with a sense of purpose and a happy heart as he goes productively about the business the Lord has given him to enjoy. The Lord enables people to find satisfaction in their labors as one of His good gifts to mankind.

Are you alert to and grateful for the things the Lord has enabled you to enjoy? Do you appreciate the ability to eat a good meal and to drink a refreshing drink and to find joy in your work as blessings which come from the hand of the Lord?

105

Not Enough Fun
Ecclesiastes 6:1-6

Perhaps you have puzzled, as I have, over the bumper sticker which reads "Pro-child / Pro-family / Pro-choice."

How can anyone even begin to imagine that they are supportive of children when they are in favor of the choice for women to have their children killed in the womb? How can anyone even begin to imagine that they are supporting the well-being of the family when they are supporting a woman's choice to abort her unborn child as a matter of public policy? We have clearly come to a day of contorted reasoning when it is considered pro-child and pro-family to promote the option of killing the unborn children who would contribute so much to the life of the family.

People who hold such views are apparently assuming that children who are an inconvenience to their mothers and families (as all children are, to some extent) will be unwanted. And they are apparently assuming that children who are not wanted will go through their lives unhappy. And they are apparently assuming that it would be better not to be born than to be unhappy.

The perspective that it is better not to have lived than to have lived and not to have enjoyed living is the perspective Solomon came to. He arrived at such thinking during that period of his life when he wandered from the Lord and from His word. Anyone who leaves the Lord out of his life is likely to become pessimistic and cynical, as Solomon became when he focused only on life "under the sun" for a period of time.

I. The Evil of Unclaimed Blessings 6:1-3

Advertisers who challenge us to "go for the gusto" are implying that life will be inferior for those who don't live at "full-throttle." If we can be convinced that we are missing out on something, we may feel motivated to buy what is being marketed as important to our well-being. And what could be more important to our well-being than wealth - or so goes the reasoning of the person who is focused only on this earthly life.

A. Unclaimed Blessings of Wealth 6:1-2

Though it may seem to many people in our world that the possession of wealth is the surest way to satisfaction, Solomon came to realize that there are some people - many by his assessment - who possess wealth, but who do not possess the satisfaction it should create because of their inability to use the wealth they possess. Solomon begins with the premise that this is an "evil" situation.

1. Solomon's Introduction 6:1

106

"There is an evil which I have seen under the sun and it is prevalent among men—"

The "evil" which Solomon observed came into focus because of his "under the sun" perspective. Though he grew up under the influence of the godly King David - a "man after God's own heart" - Solomon didn't always walk in the godly ways of his father.

Because he was extremely wealthy and influential as a young king, Solomon was sought out by foreign kings who wanted to enter into alliances with him. And some of those alliances were sealed, as foreign alliances sometimes were, by offering Solomon a king's daughter as a wife (as in the case of the Egyptian Pharaoh's daughter, who we are told in I Kings 3:1 became one of Solomon's wives in his early days).

With the passing of time, as I Kings 11:1 tells us, "King Solomon loved many foreign women along with the daughter of Pharaoh: Moabite, Ammonite, Edomite, Sidonian, and Hittite women." And I Kings 11:4 reports that "when Solomon was old, his wives turned his heart away after other gods; and his heart was not wholly devoted to the Lord his God, as the heart of David his father had been." So Solomon became a disillusioned man and spent years of his life and much of his fortune searching for the sense of meaning which had gone out of his life.

Instead of the rich blessings God had promised him, if he would walk faithfully in the way of the Lord, Solomon began to see the "evil" which is so prevalent in life for those who leave the Lord out of the picture. Solomon became focused, because of ungodly associations, on the prevalence of evil. So Solomon's observations in verse two are the observations of a man who wasn't factoring God into the picture of his life.

2. Solomon's Observations 6:2a

" . . . a man to whom God has given riches and wealth and honor so that his soul lacks nothing of all that he desires; yet God has not empowered him to eat from them, for a foreigner enjoys them."

Solomon may well have been thinking of some specific examples among his foreign kingly colleagues as he wrote the words of this verse - perhaps even one or more of his fathers-in-law. There were certainly many among the kings he knew and associated with who were given an abundance of riches and wealth and honor - whose souls (like his own) lacked nothing they desired. But Solomon was struck by the fact that even people who seem to have everything are sometimes not empowered by God to enjoy what they possess.

It would not be hard to imagine that Solomon knew of kings who had lost the ability to enjoy riches and wealth and honor they once possessed because they lost their kingdoms to foreign invaders.

3. Solomon's Assessment 6:2b

"This is vanity and a severe affliction."

There is certainly an emptiness to all the wealth and fame some people have if their wealth and fame aren't able to make them happy. The fall from power of the once wealthy and famous Sadam Hussein could be a modern example of the scenario Solomon has set before us. Solomon's assessment of such a fate was that of "vanity and a severe affliction."

Have you observed people who seem to have everything and yet don't seem to be able to enjoy anything they have? It really is a sad state of affairs - especially from the perspective of someone who, knowing the Lord, can get so much satisfaction out of so little in terms of wealth and fame!

Solomon's cynical mind puzzled over the man who is wealthy but not happy. And his cynical mind also puzzled over the man who has a large family and who lives a long life and doesn't enjoy any of it.

B. Unclaimed Blessings of Family 6:3

1. Solomon's Observations 6:3a-b

"If a man fathers a hundred children and lives many years, however many they be, but his soul is not satisfied with good things and he does not even have a proper burial . . ."

There are probably none of us who know any man who has ever fathered a hundred children. But Solomon knew men who had - because he was in circulation with numerous foreign kings who, like himself, had many wives. With his own seven hundred wives and three hundred concubines, he may easily have fathered a hundred children himself. We know that the wicked King Ahab, who later ruled over the northern kingdom of Israel, had seventy sons.

In addition to the blessings which family can bring into our lives, the blessing of longevity is something many people prize very highly. As Solomon looked around him, he witnessed people who had large families and lived many years, but still didn't experience all the joys of life it would seem a large family and a long life should bring. And even worse, Solomon was aware that some who had the luxury of large families and long lives ended their lives so ingloriously that they didn't even have a decent burial! Jeremiah 22:19 speaks prophetically of the burial of Israel's King Jehoiakim, the son of Josiah, king of Judah: "He will be buried with a donkey's burial / Dragged off and thrown out beyond the gates of Jerusalem."

Even for the "rich and famous," and for those who have large families and who live long lives, life sometimes comes to a very inglorious end! So Solomon summed up his observations with a very cynical assessment.

108

2. Solomon's Assessment 6:3c

" . . . then I say, 'Better the miscarriage than he.'"

There are few things in life which are sadder than the loss of a child even before he gets started in this life - especially if it happens late in a pregnancy, when anticipation is running high. But, as sad as the loss is for the parents who lose a child who didn't even make it out of the womb alive, you have to admit that things could have gone worse for the child. So we find Solomon actually expressing a sense of envy toward the child who exits this life before life can deal him any cruel blows - as life often does in the experience of those who come to birth and maturity.

II. The Alternative to Unclaimed Blessings 6:4-6

In his pessimistic frame of mind, Solomon pondered as preferable the fates of those who do not have to deal with the disappointment of unrealized blessing because they never make it to birth.

A. The Alternative of Futility and Obscurity 6:4

" . . .for it [the miscarriage] comes in futility and goes into obscurity; and its name is covered in obscurity."

Though the child who miscarries may have gotten off to a good start in the womb, if it doesn't come to birth there is little satisfaction for either the child or for his parents in his even having been conceived. It comes in futility. Children are conceived to be born and to grow to maturity - not to stop their short existence on the way to birth. So the child who miscarries becomes an unfulfilled promise. It "goes into obscurity."

Children who don't come successfully to birth don't make much of an impact on the lives of anyone on earth - except, perhaps (very briefly), the parents who were looking forward to the child's arrival. Even the time spent pondering the choice of a name for a child who miscarries amounts to very little when the child doesn't live to bear the name.

B. The Alternative of Darkness and Ignorance 6:5

"It never sees the sun and it never knows anything; it is better off than he."

Though the unborn child has eyes to see, those eyes never open to see the light of day if it doesn't come successfully to birth. And though the unborn child has a brain to think, we become aware of no conscious thought which ever goes through that brain if the child doesn't make a successful appearance on earth. So the unborn child's existence isn't all it promises to be.

But the unborn child, says Solomon, is actually better off than the man who comes to birth and who manages to succeed in life by accumulating wealth and honor and a family and long life - if he doesn't manage to enjoy all that comes into his life. Why even be born if all of life becomes only drudgery?

It is a pessimistic point of view - but it is a view which makes sense to the person who doesn't realize that there is more to life than simply experiencing good times.

C. The Alternative of Death 6:6

"Even if the other man lives a thousand years twice and does not enjoy good things—do not all go to one place?"

Solomon couldn't imagine wanting to live a longer life than any person has ever lived - two thousand years - without thoroughly enjoying every one of those two thousand years. He was so pessimistic, looking only "under the sun" (without any place for the Lord in the picture), that he could only see as far as the grave. After all, as in the case of the miscarried child, doesn't everyone arrive at death?

It is, of course, true that, if you leave the Lord out of the equation, there is little reason to get excited about life on a sin-cursed earth when it isn't filled with fun and fulfilling experiences. But, when you put the Lord back into the place of central significance, where He should be, what a different outlook you can have! Life wasn't exactly going well for Job when, looking beyond his troubled life, he spoke the words recorded for us in Job 19:25,26:

"As for me, I know that my Redeemer lives,
And at the last He will take His stand on the earth.
Even after my skin is destroyed,
Yet from my flesh I shall see God."

Or consider the perspective of the prophet Habakkuk, spoken out of his trust in the Lord at a time when things weren't going well for his nation - and were about to become much worse - as we have them recorded in Habakkuk 3:17-19:

"Though the fig tree should not blossom
And there be no fruit on the vines,
Though the yield of the olive should fail
And the fields produce no food,
Though the flock should be cut off from the fold
And there be no cattle in the stalls,
[18] Yet I will exult in the Lord,
I will rejoice in the God of my salvation.
[19] The Lord God is my strength,

110

And He has made my feet like hinds' feet,
And makes me walk on my high places."

And who of God's people have not found encouragement in the familiar words of the apostle Paul as we find them in Romans 8:28: "And we know that God causes all things to work together for good to those who love God, to those who are called according to His purpose."

From merely an earthly perspective, it is better not to have lived than to have lived and not to have enjoyed living. But from heaven's perspective it is good to have lived - even if life is not all that we had hoped it might be during this brief day on a sin-cursed earth - because this life is not all there is.

Even those who have no fun as far as the world sees it, but who come to know the Lord and to experience the satisfaction He gives to those who know Him (a satisfaction the world doesn't understand), have much to live for. Even if the present life doesn't result in great wealth and fame and a large family and many years, it can be full of satisfaction for those who know and love the Lord. Whatever may be lacking in this life will fade into obscurity with the revelation of the life to come - for those who enjoy a personal relationship with the God who lives "above the sun."

111

Emptiness Under the Sun
Ecclesiastes 6:7-12

The pages of history are full of the stories of people who have come to a despairing end in life because they didn't give the Lord the place of honor He deserves in every human life.

We are told that when Severus, Emperor of Rome, found his end approaching, he cried out: "I have been everything; and everything is nothing." Then, ordering the urn to be brought to him in which his ashes were to be enclosed on his body being burned, he said, "Little urn, thou shalt contain one for who the world was too little."[20] And it is reported that Philip III of Spain cried out his last words: "O would to God I had never reigned! Oh that those years I have spent in my kingdom I had lived a solitary life in the wilderness! Oh that I had lived alone with God! How much more secure should I now have died! What doth all my glory profit, but that I have so much the more torment in my death?"[21]

These and many other people - including people who have been famous and influential in their times - have found that life can be a very un-fulfilling experience if it is lived apart from a close and personal relationship with the God who made us. As Solomon might have said it from the perspective of Ecclesiastes, life "under the sun" is un-fulfilling and unpredictable. Leaving God out of human life is a sure path to emptiness. Human beings live with the sense that there should be more to life than this world is able to deliver.

I. Man's Insatiable Appetite 6:7-9

It doesn't take many years before most people begin to realize that, no matter what we do, there is always the desire for more. The things we crave never seem to deliver all we had hoped they would.

A. The Appetites of Men 6:7

"All a man's labor is for his mouth and yet the appetite is not satisfied."

The mouth of man is a symbol in this passage for man's insatiable appetites for things he hopes will bring satisfaction in life. Everything we do in life is done because of some satisfaction we believe will result. We get up each day hoping that the activities of another day will bring satisfaction in some form of accomplishment.   We sit down to every meal because we

---

[20] Paul Lee Tan, *Encyclopedia of 7,700 Illustrations* (Rockville, MD: Assurance Publishers, 1979), p.306, #1004.

[21] Ibid., p.307, #1006.

believe that food will satisfy our palates and temporarily end the pangs of hunger in our stomach. We go about the day's labors thinking that we will accomplish something of worth - if nothing more than earning a paycheck, so that we can keep food on the table and clothes on our backs. We go to bed at night thinking that some rest will strengthen us for the activities of another day.

But whatever we may do in a day to achieve satisfaction of one kind or another soon has to be done again, because life's satisfactions never satisfy for very long. We find that, having gotten up the day before, we need to do it again with each new day that comes along. The food we eat, however much we may have enjoyed it when we ate it, never satisfies for more than a few hours before we find ourselves in need of another meal. No matter how hard we worked yesterday and how much we accomplished as a result, there is always more work to be done today, and the ongoing need for a paycheck to buy more food and clothing and other necessities of life. And, having gone to bed last night to get some rest, we will need to go to bed again tonight to get the strength for another day tomorrow.

Everything we do, however satisfying it may be in the doing, soon has to be done over in order to bring satisfaction again. Nothing we do "under the sun" brings satisfaction that lasts on and on. And this is true without regard to intelligence or experience or social standing.

B. The Equality of Men 6:8

Though there are social distinctions of various kinds in life as we know it, the basic issues of life cut across all social barriers.

1. The Wise and the Foolish 6:8a

"For what advantage does the wise man have over the fool?"

The wise man has to keep feeding his mouth and pursuing the satisfaction of other appetites in his life just as the fool does. His wisdom doesn't make his satisfactions in life any more lasting than the fools' lack of wisdom does. It costs as much to run a good kitchen at a Christian university as it does to run a good kitchen at the county jail or the insane asylum. The wise man's blue jeans probably won't last much longer than the crazy man's blue jeans do, if they are both involved in physical activity. The wise man may sleep no more soundly than the fool does. In fact, with more on his mind, the wise man may sleep less soundly!

Life's satisfactions work about the same for both the wise and the simple. And life's satisfactions work about the same for both the rich and the poor.

2. The Poor and the Living 6:8b

"What advantage does the poor man have, knowing how to walk before the living?"

113

As long as the poor man manages to stay alive (because poverty can become so serious that it takes a man's life away), he deals with the same basic issues in his life as a rich man does. The poor man has to face his days one at a time - just as others do. Every time the poor man manages to satisfy his hunger with another meal, he has to begin to think toward the next meal, because the satisfaction which comes as a result of a meal will last only a few hours before the body begins to crave another meal - whether one is rich or poor. The poor man's clothing may not be as nice or as expensive as the rich man's clothing, but neither the poor nor the rich wear their clothing for long before they need to be replaced by garments less soiled or less worn.

Though wisdom is to be preferred over folly, and though almost everyone would rather be rich than poor, neither wisdom nor wealth can keep any man from dealing with the circuitous nature of life on earth, so you might well be wondering (as Solomon was) what is the real advantage of wisdom and wealth? Why bother?

C. The Possessions and Dreams of Men 6:9

"What the eyes see is better than what the soul desires. This too is futility and a striving after wind."

Everyone has things in his life which are tangible and visible (whether they are few or many), but no one has everything he wishes he had. It doesn't matter how much one possesses or how rich one becomes, there are always more things to possess and more riches to be had - so the wealthy have the same basic cravings as the poor. The rich man who is asked how much he will need to be satisfied says "a little more." No one ever feels that he has enough. So who is to say that the rich man is better off than the poor man if neither of them are satisfied.

Some years ago I heard some doctors discussing their incomes, and the level of satisfaction their incomes brought into their lives. One of them very candidly acknowledged that he had found it incredibly easy to get accustomed to his large annual income. But he also acknowledged that he didn't yet feel "rich" with the increase in his income because he found that his appetites increased right along with it.

Life is never satisfying for the person whose goals are worldly goals. Those who fail to believe the Lord and the teaching of His word, that this world is only a temporary stop-over on the way to that which is real and eternal and truly fulfilling, are bound to live their lives with a certain sense of frustration. They are going to say with Solomon "this too is futility and striving after wind."

Life "under the sun" is never as fulfilling as a person would like it to be. Nor is life "under the sun" as predictable as a person would like it to be.

II. Man's Unpredictable Direction 6:10-12

114

A. Man's Unavoidable Limits 6:10

"Whatever exists has already been named, and it is known what man is; for he cannot dispute with him who is stronger than he is."

Verse ten reads like a puzzle, unless it is seen as a description of the Lord and His works throughout the universe.

The ability to assign a name to something denotes the ability to exercise a measure of authority and control over it. So the Lord's ability to assign names to things which already exist (as He has done for every star in the universe!) is evidence of His authority and control over all things. What man can't even count, God created and has individually named - as the prophet Isaiah acknowledged in Isaiah 40:26:

Lift up your eyes on high
And see who has created these stars,
The One who leads forth their host by number,
He calls them all by name;
Because of the greatness of His might and the strength of His power,
Not one of them is missing.

And God not only controls the bodies in the universe around us, He controls the affairs of the people in His universe as well. Though we are often puzzled by human behavior, sometimes even our own behavior, to the Lord "it is known what man is." A classic revelation of the Lord's knowledge of mankind is seen in Psalm 139:1-4:

O Lord, You have searched me and known me.
[2] You know when I sit down and when I rise up;
You understand my thought from afar.
[3] You scrutinize my path and my lying down,
And are intimately acquainted with all my ways.
[4] Even before there is a word on my tongue,
Behold, O Lord, You know it all.

The Lord knows all there is to know about man, and the Lord controls the affairs of mankind - whether man likes to acknowledge it or not. Human experience has been full of what are often described as "acts of God" (earthquakes, floods, hurricanes, tornadoes, tsunamis, etc.) - vivid reminders that there are many things in our lives which are simply beyond our control!

Whether we like it or not, human life is subject to someone far greater than we are. So, in Solomon's words, "he [man] cannot dispute with him who is stronger than he is." Not only do we need to answer in life to every person who is placed in authority over us, we ultimately have to answer to the Lord - who has demonstrated His authority and control by naming every star in the universe, and by His inexhaustible knowledge of mankind.

Life "under the sun" can be a perplexing puzzle. But it isn't puzzling to the Lord, and it begins to make much better sense to everyone who is willing to share His perspective from "above the sun."

B. Man's Inability to Define 6:11

"For there are many words which increase futility. What then is the advantage to a man?"

Though much has been spoken and written over many centuries about life and about the nature of mankind, man still doesn't understand either life or himself very well. Check out the many different ideas of philosophers and psychologists concerning the meaning of life and the makeup and behavior of man and you will be bewildered by the wide diversity of opinions and theories proposed by various people about life and the nature of mankind.

If there were "many words" (as Solomon puts it) "which increase futility" already in his day, how much more futility do we have today - in view of the many more words which have been spoken and written? And many of them have been spoken and written without adding anything of significance to our understanding of man and the universe around him. The rejection in our day of the concept of "absolute truth" is evidence of modern man's commitment to the "under the sun" perspective which Solomon struggled with. What are the chances that we will get closer to the truth by denying its existence?

With all of his theorizing and philosophizing about himself and his universe, man is still a long way from really understanding what it is that makes him tick, so there is little advantage which results from all that man has done in this study of himself over the centuries. And nothing man has learned about himself in all of his study can tell him what he will find around the next bend in the road.

C. Man's Uncertain Future 6:12

"For who knows what is good for a man during his lifetime, during the few years of his futile life? He will spend them like a shadow. For who can tell a man what will be after him under the sun?"

If you ask people what is best to do with your life, you will get a wide variety of answers, because (as Solomon states it in this verse) there are few people who really understand "what is good for man during his lifetime." Even the best diagnostic tools available in our day cannot adequately take into account all of the complexities of the human mind and body and the many choices open to us. My wife still chuckles at the aptitude test she took as a high school student which indicated she would probably do well as a lumberjack!

116

So life can be an exercise in futility for many people - unable to find out what their lives are all about. And the few years of our earthly existence quickly speed by, leaving us not much farther along when we are finished with them than we were when we began - if we have only human wisdom to guide us.

And if human wisdom is sadly lacking in directing our lives in the present, it is even more sadly lacking in directing our lives into the future - a future which no one on earth can predict with any certainty (apart from the certainties of God's revealed word).

Life "under the sun" - leaving God out of the picture - is bound to be largely un-fulfilling and unpredictable. Leaving God out of human life is a sure path to emptiness.

Is your life as fulfilling as you would like it to be? Is it all adding up to something of lasting value because you have chosen to adopt God's perspective from "above the sun" as your guide through life's inevitable uncertainties?

If you are looking for a statement which can give definitive direction to your life, consider the apostle Paul's brilliant assessment of his own life - a life which mattered about as much for both time and eternity as any man's life has ever mattered. He wrote it down in Philippians 1:21: "For to me, to live is Christ, and to die is gain." Above the sun, in the "heavenlies" with Christ, we find direction for the present and security for the future which nothing "under the sun" can even begin to rival!

117

Surprise Values
Ecclesiastes 7:1-7

Give most people a choice between a trip to a famous theme park (e.g., Disneyland) and a trip to the dentist and they would choose the trip to the theme park without a moment's hesitation. But the reality of life is that the trip to the dentist may bring much greater benefit in the long run. Theme parks are flashy and fun, but when a day at a theme park is over there is little left - apart from the memories of a good time. The dentist's office isn't very flashy, and it often doesn't result in a very fun experience, but an hour or two in a good dentist's office can produce benefits which bring years - perhaps even decades - of significant benefit.

One of life's greatest challenges is the challenge of making the very significant distinction between that which is enjoyable and that which is important. We are living in a very hedonistic age - an age when many people are out to experience all the pleasure life can offer. But the reality is that there is more to human existence than the pleasures of the present. So there are going to be many, many people - who have spent much or even all of their lives pursuing pleasure - who are going to spend the rest of their eternal existence in some form of pain!

We wouldn't understand the issues involved without the aid of divine truth - so the Lord has given us His word to shed some light on the path of life and show us some surprise values. Experiences which bring life's real issues into clear perspective are of greater importance than those which merely bring enjoyment.

Are you caught up in the pursuit of pleasure? Or are you allowing God's word to give you divine perspective on life's greater values? If life isn't as pleasant as you had hoped it would be, are you making it as important as you can make it - in spite of any discomforts you may have to endure along the way?

I. The Value of a Good Name 7:1

"A good name is better than a good ointment,
And the day of one's death is better than the day of one's birth."

Good ointment can be a rather important part of a comfortable experience in this life - especially when you live in a dry climate (as Solomon did). A move I made from America's damp Pacific Northwest climate to the warm and dry climate of the Southwest soon left my skin feeling very itchy - until I discovered the value of some good skin lotion.

Physical comfort is something we all value in life, but it can't begin to compare with the importance of good character, and the good reputation which comes as a result of it - a "good name." We are all aware of spiritual leaders who have forfeited good reputations as servants of the Lord for the pleasure of a brief sexual encounter.

A good time isn't nearly as important or valuable as a good life. So "the day of one's death is better than the day of one's birth" because the day of one's death looks back on a life time of accomplishment, where the day of one's birth looks ahead only to the possibility that something might be accomplished. Accomplishment is better than the possibility of accomplishment.

II. The Value of a Good Funeral 7:2

"It is better to go to a house of mourning
Than to go to a house of feasting,
Because that is the end of every man,
And the living takes it to heart."

Given the choice between a funeral or a party with feasting, there is hardly anyone who wouldn't choose to attend the party! Parties are fun. A feast is physically satisfying and enjoyable. But funerals, frankly, are a little on the heavy side, and often even the stressful side. There are things, though, taking place at a funeral which are much more significant than the things taking place at a party.

At a funeral we are faced with the reality that life on earth won't go on as it is forever. At a funeral we are faced with the reality that what has happened to the deceased is one day going to happen to us. At the funeral we are reminded that we are accountable to the One who gave us life to begin with.

When it comes to thinking seriously about life's most important issues, we are much more likely to think those thoughts while we are staring death in the face than we are to think those thoughts in the midst of games and music and good food to eat and friends and family to visit with.

Because every person (barring the rapture) is going to end up his days on earth attending a funeral - his **own** funeral - what happens at a funeral is much more relevant and significant to our situation than the party we might enjoy so much more. Many more people have given serious thought to their relationship with the Lord and made decisions of eternal significance at funerals than at parties - so, even though parties are more fun, funerals are more significant to the important issues of life.

III. The Value of Sorrow 7:3-4

"Sorrow is better than laughter,
For when a face is sad a heart may be happy.
[4] The mind of the wise is in the house of mourning,
While the mind of fools is in the house of pleasure."

Sorrow is something most people actively seek to avoid, while laughter is something people

119

often pay to experience. So most people would say that laughter is better than sorrow. But the reality is that sorrow is much more likely to cause us to think seriously about things that are important - even eternally important.

As much as many people enjoy the comedy fare on evening television, it is not likely that many people have had their lives significantly changed for the good because of their devotion to television comedy. It is far more likely that lives have been changed for good as a result of the painful experiences of life which bring sorrow - illness and injury and broken relationships and other personal tragedies.

Though we enjoy laughter more than we do sorrow, we are challenged and changed far more often by sorrow than we are by laughter. And laughter is often only a very superficial indicator of what is going on inside a person anyhow. "For when a face is sad a heart may be happy."

Church audiences are often chastened by song leaders for failing to look happy - while almost any bar in town is filled with the sounds of laughter. But for all the sober expressions on the faces of worshipers and all the happy looks on the faces of the bar crowd, there is normally quite a different experience taking place in the hearts of the people in question.

The person who is skilled in handling the issues of life will far more often be thinking serious thoughts than drinking his problems away in the superficial gaiety of the party scene. Many of a country's most respected people seldom attend wild parties and are never found in bars or other haunts of the party crowd.

People who spend their lives in pursuit of pleasure are seldom the people who are most admired for their wisdom and their accomplishments. More often, those who spend their lives in pursuit of pleasure are people whose lives amount to the least - in terms of productivity. Any local rescue mission can put you in touch with people who have made the pursuit of pleasure one of life's goals - and who have bombed out as a result of worthless pursuits.

Wise people are often at least a little on the sober side, because they discover in their pursuit of life that life is serious business. But a sober expression often conceals a happy heart, because what wisdom lacks on the side of giddiness it makes up for on the side of accomplishment and satisfaction.

IV. The Value of Wise Rebuke 7:5-6

"It is better to listen to the rebuke of a wise man
Than for one to listen to the song of fools.
[6] For as the crackling of thorn bushes under a pot,
So is the laughter of the fool;
And this too is futility."

Because wise people come to see the seriousness of life, they are the ones most likely to rebuke whatever folly they see in the lives of those around them. The writings of Solomon (including the present passage) contain many serious thoughts and even rebukes, because he was granted enough wisdom to understand the seriousness of folly. Even Jesus, gracious as He was, spoke some rather stern words of rebuke from time to time, because He understood very well that people are accountable to the Lord for their lives!

If you are looking for comforting and positive words, you may not always find them on the lips of someone who is wise in handling the affairs of life, while you can almost always find them on the lips of those who are foolish. Solomon probably speaks of the "song of fools" in part, at least, because foolish advice often finds its way into the popular music of the day.

Fools often laugh at things which aren't really funny. We are hearing, in our day, more and more mocking laughter - laughter aimed at things the Lord and His people recognize as serious things. Only fools think such important matters as family values and moral standards and salvation truth are laughing matters. But the laughter of fools is nothing more than noise - the kind of noise you hear only briefly when a fire is kindled under a cooking pot using only thorn bushes for your fuel.

Solomon concludes the verse with the note that "this too is futility" because he has just reminded us that the songs and the laughter of fools are more noise than content.

V. The Value of Fairness 7:7

"For oppression makes a wise man mad,
And a bribe corrupts the heart."

Another example of futility is the example of oppression which, regrettably, has always been in more than abundant supply among earth's people. It began in Adam's family with the killing of Able by Cain. There are more than enough horror stories coming out of earth's repressive regimes in our own day to illustrate the ongoing nature of the problem. We are told, for example, with regard to the persecution of Christians, that more people died for their faith in Christ during the twentieth century than during the previous nineteen centuries combined! There are few things more frustrating ("maddening," to use Solomon's word) than to see people being treated oppressively and to be unable to do anything significant to change the situation.

People who aren't able to get what they want, or feel they have coming to them, often try to influence others to decide in their favor by offering money or favors as bribes. But bribes are a poor substitute for the just decisions which should be occurring in the first place. They have a way of short-circuiting just decisions, because people who receive bribes are no longer as interested in justice as they are in personal gain. Bribes result in corruption - as history has often demonstrated.

121

When oppressed people turn to those who are supposed to be wise, in hope of finding relief, but receive oppression instead of justice, they can't help but be frustrated. Life's greatest values are often found where you would least expect to find them - and people looking for life's values often fail to find them where they ought to be. No wonder, then, that Solomon - looking at life "under the sun" (without the Lord in view) - repeats his pessimistic refrain: "this too is futility."

But, like a visit to the funeral home, with all of the negative possibilities it entails, even oppression and corruption can serve a useful purpose if they help us to see the real issues of life with greater clarity. Experiences which bring life's real issues into clear perspective are of greater importance than those which merely bring enjoyment.

Looking "above the sun," we see that the Lord can use absolutely anything that He allows to come into our lives to perfect His purposes for His people - even things which make little sense in and of themselves. The life of Jacob's son Joseph is a classic Biblical example. Who would have thought the Lord could use his brothers' oppressive actions, in mistreating and selling him into slavery, to place Joseph in a position to save his family (along with the nation of Egypt) from disaster in a time of famine?

How are you at seeing life's issues from divine perspective? Are you so intent (as many are in our day) on finding enjoyment in life that enjoyment is all that matters? Or are you more intent on seeing things as they really are, and living life as it really is - even if the experience isn't always as pleasant as you might like it to be?

122

Secure in Sovereignty
Ecclesiastes 7:8-14

There are many people in our world today who would like to think that they are in control of their lives and their destinies. They feel self-sufficient in and of themselves, refusing to give any thought to the possibility of trusting in God - someone they see as a crutch for people who are weak to lean on.

The Humanist Manifestos make such an outlook a matter of humanistic faith in *Humanist Manifesto II* where the article on "religion" reads:

> We find insufficient evidence for belief in the existence of a supernatural; it is either meaningless or irrelevant to the question of the survival and fulfillment of the human race. As non-theists, we begin with humans not God, nature not deity.[22]

Needless to say, the humanist position is worlds apart from the Biblical outlook on life. The truth is that, whether people acknowledge the Lord's existence and importance or not, the Lord is both real and in control. The day is coming when every human being who has ever lived will answer to the Lord. So the sooner we realize it, the better things will be for us. The person who is wise learns to take life as it comes and when it comes, acknowledging and accepting the sovereignty of the Lord.

Do you recognize the Lord's sovereign control in the affairs of mankind? Are you growing in your ability to accept what comes from His hand, and to respond to it in the best way you can?

I. The Value of Patience 7:8-10

The Scriptures challenge God's people to place, and keep, their trust in the Lord. Because He is sovereign, He deserves to be trusted, but trusting the Lord requires a willingness to wait patiently on His leading and His timing.

A. Patience Versus Pride 7:8

"The end of a matter is better than its beginning;
Patience of spirit is better than haughtiness of spirit."

Because people are never able to see the end from the beginning (as God can), we never know how things are going to turn out in our lives - until they turn out. No matter how promising things look at the beginning, it is only at the end of any experience that we really know what we were able to accomplish. Ancient Israel's King Ahab stated this truth in the form of a

---

[22] *Humanist Manifestos I and II* (Buffalo, NY: Prometheus Books, 1973), p. 16.

proverb when he came up against the Syrian King Ben-Hadad, who was boasting about the victory he expected to have in battle against Israel: "Let not him who girds on his armor boast like him who takes it off" (I Kings 20:11).

People often try to improve their prospects for success by boasting about what they intend to accomplish, but a haughty spirit often ends up badly embarrassed. One of Charles Spurgeon's students went into a pulpit very confident about the message he had prepared, but it didn't go as well as he thought it would. So he came away distressed, almost brokenhearted, and he went to Spurgeon about it. The words of Spurgeon to him were these, "If you had gone up as you came down, you would have come down as you went up."[23]

How much better to approach our tasks with what Solomon calls "patience of spirit" (lit. "the long of spirit") than the haughtiness which grates on the nerves of men and invites the opposition of the Lord - the God who (according to James 5:6 and I Peter 5:5) "opposes the proud, but gives grace to the humble"!

As the American proverb has it, "Don't count your chickens before they hatch." Once they have hatched, you know exactly what you have to work with - which is why "the end of a matter is better than its beginning." But getting to the end of things will require some patience.

B. Patience with People 7:9

"Do not be eager in your heart to be angry,
For anger resides in the bosom of fools."

Our inclination to impatience in general leads us to get angry with people. The person who is "eager in [his] heart to be angry" is the short-tempered person. But a short temper is a telling sign! What is it that makes us angry? Unless we are dealing with that rare occasion of righteous anger, isn't it the feeling we have that someone has not recognized our "rights"? Isn't it the idea that we deserve better treatment than we are receiving which makes us feel anger?

So, once again, we are confronted with the problem of pride - the notion that our rights should come ahead of the rights of someone else. James 4:1-2 provides an exposé of unrighteous anger and its "fruits."

What is the source of quarrels and conflicts among you? Is not the source your pleasures that wage war in your members? [2] You lust and do not have; so you commit murder. You are envious and cannot obtain; so you fight and quarrel. You do not have because you do not ask.

---

[23] Paul Lee Tan, *Encyclopedia of 7,700 Illustrations* (Rockville, MD: Assurance Publishers, 1979), p.1100, #4826.

124

If we could content ourselves to take our desires to the Lord and leave them with Him - satisfied to receive what we think we need when He agrees that we need it and provides it in His own way - we wouldn't suffer nearly the heartburn we suffer otherwise. But trusting the Lord isn't what comes naturally. We want what we want when we want it, and we go after what we want to get it for ourselves, and our eager hearts lead to anger.

Nothing wrong with a little anger, you say? Solomon, speaking for the Lord, disagrees! "For anger resides in the bosom of fools." His word for "fools" (*kesilim*) is a word whose derivation speaks of one who is dull and obstinate. But it doesn't refer to a person who is inherently dull and obstinate; it refers to a person who has chosen (by foolish behavior) to be dull and obstinate.

We see children flare up in anger against each other at the slightest offense, and we attribute their behavior to "childishness" and "foolishness." But Solomon warns that we are childish and we are foolish when we allow anger to reside within us. How much better to be patient than to be haughty and, as a result, to be foolish. But our circumstances often don't lend themselves to patience.

C. Patience with the Present 7:10

"Do not say, 'Why is it that the former days were better than these?'
For it is not from wisdom that you ask about this."

Here is another way in which impatience manifests itself - the insistence that earlier days were better than the present days.

We can all remember some of the days of our lives which, looking back, were the "good old days." But the human memory is very selective, with an amazing capacity to forget the unpleasant parts of our past experience and to focus on the pleasant. So, for starters, the "good old days" probably weren't as good as we remember them! The person who remembers a more relaxed time in life, when the family used to spend more time together, may be forgetting that the family had no money for anything but necessities, or that the family had no car to allow them to get very far apart!

Then there are the advantages of progress which we enjoy in the present and have already come to take for granted, because that is another feature of the human mind - the tendency not to appreciate the good things we enjoy in the present. How often do you stop to think of the benefits you enjoy because of the power of the computer (even if you don't own one yourself, but only benefit from modern business practices which depend on them) - rather than complain because it is temporarily out of commission?

The person who has "wisdom" (*chokmah* - skill in handling the issues of life) is sensitive to the benefits and the bother of each succeeding period of life. He weighs them honestly against one another, without forgetting either the bad or the good of each stage in life. So you won't find the person who has wisdom longing for "good old days" which, in many ways, probably weren't all that good. And you won't find the person who has wisdom overlooking the good things he enjoys in the present.

Are you patient with the present, and as grateful for its benefits as you should be - as an indication that wisdom is at work in your life?

II. The Value of Wisdom 7:11-12

There isn't any aspect of human life which can't be improved by the application of wisdom. So Solomon turns to an evaluation of some of its benefits.

A. Wisdom with Wealth 7:11

"Wisdom along with an inheritance is good
And an advantage to those who see the sun."

We can all appreciate the blessings of an inheritance. Whether we have ever enjoyed one or not, we have certainly thought that it would be nice if some rich relative left us a million dollars to help us get our finances in order.

For the normal Israeli of ancient times an inheritance was even a more certain and more significant part of life, because the land of Israel (which was largely an agrarian society - tied to the land) was passed along from generation to generation as an inheritance.

But even a generous inheritance wouldn't be of much value to the person who doesn't have the wisdom to manage it well. In Proverbs 24:30-34 Solomon pictures the sluggard, pursuing "a little sleep, a little slumber, a little folding of the hands to rest" while "poverty [comes] as a robber, and . . . want like an armed man." It takes skill to run a farm well, so having a farm is only part of the path to advantage.

An inheritance managed with wisdom, writes Solomon, is an "advantage to those who see the sun." Since Solomon has been writing, throughout the book Ecclesiastes, about conditions "under the sun," his reference here to those who "see the sun" is apparently a reference to someone who is beginning to understand the truth about life - beginning to "see the light."

The truth is that, no matter how much a person possesses in this life, it won't be as valuable as it could be if it isn't used skillfully. And it can't be used as skillfully as it should be if the Lord isn't given the significant place He deserves in our lives. As Jesus stated it (Matthew 16:26): "For what will it profit a man if he gains the whole world and forfeits his soul? Or what will a man give in exchange for his soul?"

Do you possess the wisdom which enables you to view all of life with eternity's values in

126

view?

B. Wisdom's Protection 7:12

"For wisdom is protection just as money is protection,
But the advantage of knowledge is that wisdom preserves the lives of its possessors."

The word which is translated "protection" in this verse is an interesting one. The Hebrew phrase literally reads "wisdom is a shadow [just as] money is a shadow" or "wisdom is a shade, money is a shade." In warm, sunny climates a shadow, or shade, offers an important measure of protection from the ravages of the sun. During my pastoral service in the Sonora Desert (Tucson, Arizona), the shady parts of the parking lot filled up first during the hot, sunny days of summer.

Just as we find protection from the ravages of the sun in the shade, so there is protection from the ravages of life for the person who has enough money - if (as we were just told) that money is handled with wisdom.

Money alone will offer very little protection to the person who doesn't have the wisdom to use it well. Lottery prize winners, we are told, seldom retain their wealth over the long haul. So Solomon is quick to combine the protection which money can provide with the protection which wisdom can provide, because it is wisdom which maximizes the value of money.

It is worth noting that it is wisdom which we need, not just knowledge. In a day when the value of an education is so loudly proclaimed, it is important to understand that Solomon is talking about more than education (or "knowledge") when he writes of the importance of "wisdom."

Solomon ties together wisdom and knowledge in verse twelve. "The advantage of knowledge is that wisdom preserves the lives of its possessors." Wisdom is the proper use of knowledge. It doesn't matter what we know until we know how to put what we know to practical use. The person who knows how to put his knowledge to practical use can apply his knowledge to "preserve his life." For example, if he knows what it is that makes the body function well, and he skillfully puts that knowledge to work in managing his own body, he can save his physical life by enhancing his health. Or, to use Solomon's example from the first half of the verse, if he knows how to handle finances, and he handles his own finances skillfully, he can preserve his material well-being. And, most importantly, if he knows how to develop a healthy relationship with the Lord, and he skillfully uses his knowledge in developing a strong relationship between himself and God, he can save his spiritual and eternal life by the spiritual progress he achieves.

In every area of our lives, what is needed to live most successfully is wisdom. Since you can't get wisdom, at its best, without a healthy relationship with the Lord, the perspective of Proverbs 9:10 (one of several statements of the theme of the Bible's wisdom literature) is critical:

127

"The fear of the Lord is the beginning of wisdom, / And the knowledge of the Holy One is understanding."

III. The Value of Divine Perspective 7:13-14

Wisdom requires that we factor the Lord into every aspect of our lives, and when we do we will experience the benefits of divine perspective.

A. The Lord's Sovereignty 7:13

"Consider the work of God,
For who is able to straighten what He has bent?"

You can't be wise, in the final sense in this life, without giving the Lord a central place of significance, because He is sovereign in all the affairs of our lives. Solomon captured the thought in Proverbs 19:21: "Many plans are in a man's heart, / But the counsel of the Lord will stand."

So take time to "consider the work of God." Stop to learn as much as you can about Him and about His ways and about His will! Because, in the process, you will discover that the Lord has the final say in everything we do and say and are. If you don't think He does, just take something He has done and try to change it. For example, if you don't like the weather today, go ahead and change it - if you can.

There are many things - like the weather - which the Lord has designed with His own sovereign imprint and which we are powerless to change. So our best course of action is to simply accept what He has made and to submit ourselves to His workmanship and His lordship. It is a part of His divine genius that not only is He sovereign, He also owes an explanation to absolutely no one.

B. The Lord's Secrecy 7:14

"In the day of prosperity be happy,
But in the day of adversity consider—
God has made the one as well as the other
So that man will not discover anything that will be after him."

If the Lord blesses you with good days, you are wise to make the most of them. Rejoice and enjoy your prosperity as fully as you can, to be sure. But, even as you rejoice in prosperity, remain sensitive to the fact that prosperity may not last - and there may be little or nothing you can do that will make a significant difference. If the Lord, in His wisdom, knows that adversity is what you need to perfect His sovereign purposes in your life, you will have to learn to live with adversity.

128

The story of the ancient saint, Job, who went from prosperity to adversity, without even a clue as to why his fortunes changed, illustrates the point Solomon is making. And you have probably known someone whose life, like Job's, turned from blessing to adversity, or adversity to blessing, with no visible explanation for the change.

If the Lord sends blessings into our lives, as He often does, we ought to make the most of them. But if He chooses to send adversity, we can't do anything better than to accept what He sends and seek to respond to it with the wisdom we find in His word. The person who is wise learns to take life as it comes, and when it comes, accepting the sovereignty of the Lord in the process. As Moses expressed it in Deuteronomy 29:29: "The secret things belong to the Lord our God, but the things revealed belong to us and to our sons forever, that we may observe all the words of this law."

We are all very restricted in our ability to control the events of our lives - or even to fully understand the events of our lives. So the best we can do is grow in our ability to wisely accept the events of our lives, and put our trust in the Lord. How are you doing at trusting the Lord's sovereign control in your life?

129

Living in Balance
Ecclesiastes 7:15-18

Have you spent much time wondering how richly it pays to do what is right?

Though most Christians probably don't spend a great deal of time pondering such thoughts, we probably all have had our moments. I think, for example, of a missionary prayer letter which told of a time of trial in the life of a family who were deeply committed to the Lord and actively involved in His service. In one week their car's water pump quit working, the gas stove in their home blew up, the refrigerator quit operating, the landlord informed them that he wanted the use of his house, and their computer broke down! Such weeks could cause a person to wonder why being committed to the Lord and His cause doesn't come with better results in some of the practical matters of life!

Though we all have occasions when we may wonder why the Lord allows all the things He does to come into our lives, there are many people who have far more reason to wonder about the temporal reward of doing right and serving the Lord on a sin-cursed earth than we have. I think, for example, of someone like Joni Erickson Tada - a quadriplegic who has devoted her life to the Lord's service in addressing the needs of the handicapped. The international compassion ministry she has founded (Joni and Friends) speaks volumes of the effectiveness of her work, so would it be too much to ask the Lord she serves, who has performed miracles down through the ages for so many people, to lighten her load by improving her physical condition?

Any thinking person is bound to have occasion from time to time to ponder the complexities of life, and to wonder how to make the most of life with all of the challenges it can bring our way. But the Bible becomes an indispensable guide for those who will avail themselves of its wealth of knowledge and wisdom - including knowledge and wisdom about the most difficult challenges which life can bring into our lives and/or the lives of those we love. In spite of its ironies, life goes best for those who fear the Lord - committing themselves to His righteousness and wisdom.

Have you spent much time pondering things in life which don't easily add up - as Solomon did, in the passage before us? Have you figured out what is most important to concentrate your efforts on in a world which sometimes doesn't go the way it should go (even as God Himself says it should go)?

I. Solomon's Observations 7:15

A. The Breadth of Solomon's Observations 7:15a

"I have seen everything during my lifetime of futility; there is a righteous man who perishes in his righteousness and there is a wicked man who prolongs his life in his wickedness."

Though no one has seen everything, Solomon clearly felt as if he had seen everything as he wrote these verses. And he probably came about as close as anyone because of his keen mind, his amazing wealth, and his decision and determination to search out life "under the sun" in order to find out what it is that brings the greatest satisfaction.

Recall the many avenues Solomon told us, in the opening chapters of Ecclesiastes, that he explored in his attempt to find meaning and satisfaction in life "under the sun."

> He explored pleasure (2:1)
> He explored wine and folly (2:3)
> He explored various work projects (2:4-6)
> > The construction of houses (4)
> > The planting of vineyards (4)
> > The growing of gardens (5)
> > The building of parks (5)
> > The growing of fruit orchards (5)
> > The creation of ponds for irrigation (6)
> He explored possessions (2:7-8a)
> > The acquisition of male and female slaves (7)
> > The possession of large flocks and herds (7)
> > The acquisition silver, gold and other "treasures" (8a)
> He explored music with male and female singers (8b)
> He explored the company of many concubines (8)

Looking back on all he had explored as a possible source of meaning and satisfaction in life, Solomon described it all as "vanity and striving after wind" (2:11)!

As privileged as Solomon was in many respects, he was still a frustrated man because of the futility he observed in his own life and in the lives of other people. He was as keenly aware as anyone that we live on a sin-cursed earth - an earth which (as Paul explained it in Romans 8:20) has been "subjected to futility" as a result of the entrance of sin into human experience back in the Garden of Eden.

After all of his exploration, Solomon at least felt as if he had seen "everything during [his] lifetime of futility" - and some of the things he saw obviously left him very disillusioned.

B. The Ironies in Solomon's Observations 7:15b

1. The Righteous Man Who Perishes

" . . . there is a righteous man who perishes in his righteousness . . ."

Solomon's own mother (Bathsheba) may well have been married, in her first marriage, to a "righteous man who perish[ed] in his righteousness." Uriah the Hittite was a soldier in King David's army, listed among David's "great men," who was so loyal to his nation's army that he refused to sleep with his own beautiful wife when David called him home from the battlefield, where his fellow-soldiers were risking their lives for the cause of their nation and David, its king!

Whether Uriah the Hittite was, as a rule of life, a "righteous" man or not we cannot say for sure. But there have certainly been many righteous men who perished in their righteousness; sometimes even **because** of their righteousness. Able - son of Adam and Eve - died when his jealous brother became angry over his acceptance by the Lord because of his righteous sacrifice. Isaiah - prophet of God - was forced into a hollow log and sawed in two when his faithful service for the Lord angered his enemies. And, of course, Jesus Himself - the only perfectly righteous man who ever lived - was brutally killed in young adulthood through no fault of His own.

Though the general rule of life (as seen in Scriptures) is that righteousness prolongs life, there have been many occasions when righteous men perished before their time - not only in but because of their righteousness. And it is ironic as well that wickedness doesn't always produce exactly what we would think it should produce.

2. The Wicked Man Who Prolongs Life

" . . . and there is a wicked man who prolongs his life in his wickedness."

The Israeli general, Joab, who cooperated with King David in his scheme to put Solomon's mother's first husband, Uriah the Hittite, to death, was a man who brutally murdered at least two good men (Abner, son of Ner, and Amasa, son of Jether). But, in spite of his brutality, he lived to old age - until (as advised by David in I Kings 2:5-6) he was finally put to death himself by order of none other than Solomon.

The pages of history list many people who have lived wicked lives, but who have lived lengthy lives - in spite of the fact that the Bible itself tells us that wickedness generally reduces life's quality and even brings it to a premature end. Consider, for example, the message of Psalm 55:23:

> "But You, O God, will bring them down to the pit of destruction;
> Men of bloodshed and deceit will not live out half their days.
> But I will trust in You."

Like the psalmist, we need to trust in the Lord when we see wicked people living in apparent ease and security, because that sometimes appears to be the case on a sin-cursed earth (as Solomon will acknowledge again in Ecclesiastes 8:14). If righteousness doesn't always pay rich dividends and wickedness doesn't always receive immediate retribution, what should the thinking believer's response to righteousness and wickedness be? Solomon has some interesting thoughts on the subject.

II. Solomon's Advice 7:16-17

A. Regarding Righteousness and Wisdom 7:16

"Do not be excessively righteous and do not be overly wise. Why should you ruin yourself?"

The reality is, of course, that it isn't possible to be "excessively righteous." Only one person who has ever lived has been perfectly righteous - the Lord Jesus Christ - and He wasn't one bit too righteous! He is the only person who ever fully pleased His Father (who, on more than one occasion, audibly declared His pleasure in His righteous Son from the heavens).

So, by his terminology "excessively righteous," Solomon must be thinking about the extreme of righteousness as man views the subject - the kind of righteousness which was evident in the lives of the Pharisees and others of their kind: the kind of righteousness described by the term legalism. Jesus spoke to this kind of righteousness in one of His responses to the Pharisees and their scribes, as recorded in Luke 5:31-32: "It is not those who are well who need a physician, but those who are sick. [32] I have not come to call the righteous but sinners to repentance."

People who get caught up in legalistic self-righteousness are "excessively righteous," but their brand of righteousness does them no good in the sight of the Lord. So they waste their time and energies in pressing the law of God beyond its reasonable limits. In Solomon's words, they "ruin" themselves. Legalism can drive a person to distraction over a lengthy list of "rules" which don't drive him an inch closer to the heart of God!

Along similar lines, just as it is not possible to be "excessively righteous," it is also not possible to be "overly wise"!

Once again, Jesus Himself was the personification of perfect wisdom. No one could be wiser than He. Paul tells us, in Colossians 2:3, that "in [Him] are hidden all the treasures of wisdom and knowledge." But He was not too wise, just perfectly wise.

So what Solomon describes as "overly wise" must refer to the person who is overly impressed with his wisdom - though, in fact, there may be little or no wisdom involved. It is the condition warned against in Proverbs 3:7: "Do not be wise in your own eyes; Fear the Lord and turn away from evil." It is the condition which Jesus observed in the lives of the Pharisees of His day which caused Him to say of them what is recorded in Matthew 23:5-7:

> "But they do all their deeds to be noticed by men; for they broaden their phylacteries and lengthen the tassels of their garments. [6] They love the place of honor at banquets and the chief seats in the synagogues, [7] and respectful greetings in the market places, and being called Rabbi by men."

Like "excessive righteousness" (legalism), the condition of those who are "overly wise" can lead people to "ruin" themselves. Being "wise in your own eyes," while actually living in a foolish way, can take its practitioners right down the path to eternal separation from God just as fast as profligacy can. So "excessive righteousness" and being "overly wise" are to be avoided, as are their opposites as well.

B. Regarding Wickedness and Foolishness 7:17

"Do not be excessively wicked and do not be a fool. Why should you die before your time?"

Though it is not possible to be "excessively righteous," it is possible to be "excessively wicked"! Biblical history and contemporary society provide more examples than we need of those who have been "excessively wicked." Take, for example, ancient Israel's King Ahab, of whom the Scriptures say (I Kings 16:33): "Ahab also made the Asherah. Thus Ahab did more to provoke the Lord God of Israel than all the kings of Israel who were before him." Or take, as a more recent example, the infamous Adolf Hitler, who led millions of people to their deaths in a foolish flirtation with despotism. Or, even closer to home, consider today's drug dealers who will stoop to virtually any low in pursuit of their degraded business.

Being "excessively wicked" and foolish can lead to your premature death (as it often does, for example, in the lives of those who are engaged in the drug trade). And being "excessively righteous" (i.e. legalistic) and "overly wise" (i.e. wise in your own eyes) can lead to ruin. So the "middle road" of righteousness and wisdom is the way to go! But, as Solomon has argued, in a sin-cursed world there is no hard and fast guarantee that even righteousness and wisdom will get you through life without any scars, or even get you through alive. But, for all of life's uncertainties, there is still no better path than the path of righteousness and wisdom.

III. Solomon's Conclusion 7:18

A. The Importance of Balance 7:18a

"It is good that you grasp one thing and also not let go of the other."

Whatever righteousness and wisdom cannot guarantee in our lives on a sin-cursed earth, there is still nothing better for us to get a firm grip on than these twin virtues which figure so large in the wisdom literature of the Bible.

Righteousness and wisdom are still among the best pursuits we can commit ourselves to - and they come to those who set their sights on the most important pursuit in all of life.

B. The Secret to Balance 7:18b

" . . . for the one who fears God comes forth with both of them."

134

God deserves to be feared because He is the one to whom we will all ultimately answer for everything we have ever thought or said or done. Those who fear the Lord - living their lives in view of their accountability at His throne - will be careful to do what is right. So they will "come forth" with righteousness as fully as any human being can "come forth" with righteousness (because just two verses later we are going to be reminded that there is not a man on earth who is perfectly righteous all the time).

And those who fear the Lord will "come forth" with wisdom, because (as Solomon tells us in Proverbs 9:10): "The fear of the Lord is the beginning of wisdom, And the knowledge of the Holy One is understanding." In spite of its ironies, life goes best for those who fear the Lord - committing themselves to His righteousness and wisdom.

Are you committing yourself to the pursuit of righteousness and wisdom? Are you living your life in the "fear of the Lord" - the sober recognition that we are all going to stand before the Lord one day to account for the way in which we have lived our lives (the truth to which Solomon will ultimately lead us as the book of Ecclesiastes concludes)?

135

The Pursuit of Wisdom
Ecclesiastes 7:19-22

The Bible sets forth some very high goals for human behavior which the world knows or cares very little about. An example from the Old Testament was cited by Jesus when He was asked about the greatest of all the commandments of the law, and He quoted Deuteronomy 6:5: "You shall love the LORD your God with all your heart and with all your soul and with all your might." Another example would be the challenge of Jesus in His "Sermon on the Mount" from Matthew 6:33 to "seek first the kingdom of God and His righteousness," in the knowledge that He will provide the earthly things those who don't know the Lord spend their lives clamoring to possess. Or an example from the writings of the apostle Paul is found in Colossians 3:2-4 where he challenged "Set your mind on the things above, not on the things that are on earth. [3] For you have died and your life is hidden with Christ in God. [4] When Christ, who is our life, is revealed, then you also will be revealed with Him in glory."

The book of Ecclesiastes ends with a similar challenge in its final two verses, but for the most part it approaches life from a much different level of thought. Solomon wrote Ecclesiastes at a time in his life when he was so far from the Lord in his thinking and living (largely as a result of the influence of idol-worshiping wives) that he came to despair of the possibility of finding meaning in his life. As we have seen numerous times in earlier chapters of our study, the book is written from the perspective of the person who sees only that which is "under the sun" - i.e. apart from the Lord and the much higher considerations He and His truth bring into human life.

If you leave the Lord out of the picture, what is the highest goal worth pursuing with all the energy you can invest? If you seek political influence you may soon become disillusioned with how little it has to offer. If you seek perfection you will spend your life in frustration over your inability to achieve it. If you try to find satisfaction by making everyone happy with your performance in life you will find (as we are told Abraham Lincoln once put it) that "you can please some of the people some of the time, and you can please all of the people some of the time, but you can't please all of the people all of the time."

In all of his deliberations about life's highest goal, leaving the Lord out of the picture, Solomon came to the conclusion that the thing most worthy of one's persistent pursuit is the goal of wisdom. His word for "wisdom" (*chokmah*) refers to skill - in whatever you might happen to be pursuing. It is the ability to do whatever you do in the best possible way. Wisdom is a more realistic goal (for those who think only "under the sun") than the political influence or perfect behavior or people-pleasing with which Solomon is about to compare it.

What place does wisdom play in your life? We who know Christ, of course, don't need to live our lives in view of only what is "under the sun," but there is plenty of benefit for anyone who will seek to do everything they do as skillfully as they possibly can! Wisdom is something which can bring benefit even to those who live only "under the sun"(though, in fact, wisdom at its best comes from "above the sun" - I Corinthians 2:6,7). But the wisdom Solomon writes

136

about offers benefit also to those who have heaven in view, and who desire to please the Lord along their earthly path on the way to heaven.

I. The Advantage of Wisdom 7:19

A. The Preferability of Wisdom 7:19a

"Wisdom strengthens a wise man . . ."

Wisdom brings benefit to any area of our lives in which it is ever applied! The book of Proverbs, for example, makes it very clear that the Lord Himself made use of wisdom in all He did in the creation of our earth and universe (in Proverbs 8:27-30 where wisdom, personified, is doing the speaking):

"When He established the heavens, I was there,
When He inscribed a circle on the face of the deep,
[28] When He made firm the skies above,
When the springs of the deep became fixed,
[29] When He set for the sea its boundary
So that the water would not transgress His command,
When He marked out the foundations of the earth;
[30] Then I was beside Him, as a master workman;
And I was daily His delight,
Rejoicing always before Him."

When Moses was leading the people of Israel in building the tabernacle, which would be used in the worship of the Lord in the wilderness, and later in Canaan, he was instructed to seek out artisans to make its furnishings who had "wisdom" in their art.

Exodus 31:1-6
Now the Lord spoke to Moses, saying, [2] "See, I have called by name Bezalel, the son of Uri, the son of Hur, of the tribe of Judah. [3] I have filled him with the Spirit of God in wisdom [chokmah], in understanding, in knowledge, and in all kinds of craftsmanship, [4] to make artistic designs for work in gold, in silver, and in bronze, [5] and in the cutting of stones for settings, and in the carving of wood, that he may work in all kinds of craftsmanship. [6] And behold, I Myself have appointed with him Oholiab, the son of Ahisamach, of the tribe of Dan; and in the hearts of all who are skillful [chakam] I have put skill [chokmah], that they may make all that I have commanded you."

In any area of life, wisdom gives strength to the person who possesses it, so wisdom is always something well worth pursuing - even if the person pursuing it is seeing things from only an "under the sun" perspective.

As Solomon observes in this verse, the pursuit of wisdom will certainly put those who are involved in it well ahead of many others.

B. The Poverty of Political Influence 7:19b

"Wisdom strengthens a wise man more than ten rulers who are in a city."

We would like to think that the people who are in charge of public affairs would be the best in the land - people who are able to provide skillful leadership and solve all of the problems which come along with running our cities and states and our nation.

A city large enough to require "ten rulers" would be a fair sized city; and the larger the city, the more people there are to choose from, and the greater likelihood (it would seem) that people of superior intelligence and understanding and ability should be at the helm of leadership.

But if you have spent much time at city hall - any city hall in the land - you have probably discovered that it isn't necessarily the wisest people in town who are in charge of the affairs of the city! Political processes being what they are, the people who provide the leadership of our cities and our states and our nation are often where they are more as a result of political connections and influence than pure wisdom and intelligence and understanding.

One citizen armed with great wisdom can easily outperform all the "rulers" who are over the city! II Samuel 20 records an example in the account of the rebellion of Sheba, son of Bichri, when King David and his administrators were getting re-established in Jerusalem following the rebellion of Absalom. Fearing that Sheba might do his administration more harm than Absalom had done, David commissioned one of his military officers to pursue Sheba and deal with the threat he was creating. When Sheba took refuge in the small city of Abel, David's army, under Joab's command, was threatening to destroy the city in their attempt to put down the rebellion. But an unnamed "wise woman" spoke to Joab from the city wall, asking why he was threatening to destroy the city. When Joab explained that Sheba had taken refuge in the city, and that it was Sheba he was after, the wise woman convinced the leaders of the city to throw his head over the city wall - saving the city from destruction.

If you are looking for something to enrich every dimension of your life, look to wisdom. Seek to do everything you do just as skillfully as you can do it, and your life will be improved as a result. And your chances of living wisely are better than your chances of living perfectly.

II. The Scarcity of Righteousness 7:20

A. The Dearth of Righteous Men 7:20a

"Indeed, there is not a righteous man on earth . . .

138

This truth is taught in many places throughout the Scriptures - regardless of the fact that there are many people who seem to think that they might be an exception! Ask the average person why they think they might get to heaven and they will most likely tell you about how good they have been - or tried to be.

It isn't only New Testament revelation which informs us that people are universally sinful. This truth has been with us down through the ages. Compare the message of this verse with other passages which say the same thing throughout the Old Testament (e.g., Job 15:14-16; I Kings 8:46; Isaiah 53:6). New Testament students are very familiar with the disconcerting revelation of Romans 3:23, that "all have sinned and fall short of the glory of God." So Solomon's point (that there is not a righteous man on earth) is well substantiated in Scripture.

Biblical righteousness is complete conformity to the will of God - in thought and word and deed, and there is no person except Jesus who conforms completely to the will of God - or ever has!

B. The Dearth of Perfect People 7:20b

Solomon assures us that there is not anyone on earth " . . . who continually does good and who never sins."

Even those who try the hardest to do good run up against the problem of human depravity, and fail to be all that they would like to be. Though we are all capable of occasional acts of goodness and kindness, there isn't anyone who has ever lived - with the exception of the God/man Jesus - who has been able to keep up works of only goodness and kindness throughout an entire lifetime.

The apostle Paul put together a catalog of Old Testament Scripture references confirming the sinful human condition in the lengthy list found in Romans 3:10-18 - beginning with the condemnatory observation that "There is none righteous, not even one."

Anyone who would like to find satisfaction in life by being completely righteous and good and sinless won't last long before his attempt fails. So it makes better sense to try to be wise than it does to try to be perfect, because we have already failed any attempt to be perfect. The goal of perfection is too high a goal. Perfection is simply not within our grasp. Not even if we think in terms of perfection only in the use of our tongues!

III. The Insignificance of Critical Words 7:21-22

We probably all heard, as children, the little ditty which says "sticks and stones can break my bones, but words can never harm me." How nice it would have been if our experience had borne out such a statement. We have all had to learn to deal with unpleasant words as we have made our way through life.

139

A. How to Respond to Critical Words 7:21

"Also, do not take seriously all words which are spoken, so that you will not hear your servant cursing you."

Our standards for the speech of other people are normally much higher than our standards for our own speech. We want people to say what they mean and mean what they say, though it may be alright for us to "stretch the truth" a little from time to time. So people who speak evil about us are quickly on our "black list" because we assume that their words are carefully chosen and seriously spoken.

But Solomon challenges all of us to take with the proverbial "grain of salt" the things that people say, because not all words can be taken seriously. Speech is challenging enough to keep under control that everyone says things they shouldn't say, and things they didn't intend to say.

The New Testament author James amplifies the challenge of flawless speech in the colorful third chapter of his book (James 3:1-8).

> Let not many of you become teachers, my brethren, knowing that as such we will incur a stricter judgment. [2] For we all stumble in many ways. If anyone does not stumble in what he says, he is a perfect man, able to bridle the whole body as well. [3] Now if we put the bits into the horses' mouths so that they will obey us, we direct their entire body as well. [4] Look at the ships also, though they are so great and are driven by strong winds, are still directed by a very small rudder wherever the inclination of the pilot desires. [5] So also the tongue is a small part of the body, and yet it boasts of great things.
> See how great a forest is set aflame by such a small fire! [6] And the tongue is a fire, the very world of iniquity; the tongue is set among our members as that which defiles the entire body, and sets on fire the course of our life, and is set on fire by hell. [7] For every species of beasts and birds, of reptiles and creatures of the sea, is tamed and has been tamed by the human race. [8] But no one can tame the tongue; it is a restless evil and full of deadly poison.

As unruly as the tongue is, it is inevitable that we will say things we shouldn't say. So Solomon envisions the possibility that someone might even hear his "servant" - someone who works for him and is responsible to him - uttering a curse against his master!

If you happen to be the "master" you are likely to object. But, before you make a federal case out of someone's impious language toward you, stop and think about everything you have ever said about others.

B. How to Evaluate Critical Words 7:22

"For you also have realized that you likewise have many times cursed others."

140

Because there are no exceptions to the rule (i.e. that everyone has trouble taming the tongue), it is certain that you have said some rather unwise things yourself! Perhaps, as in Solomon's illustration, you have experienced the embarrassment of talking with someone on the job about the boss, and having him walk around the corner just as you called him an "air-head" (or some comparable uncomplimentary designation).

The apostle James warned of the same possibility in James 3:9-10:

> With it [the tongue] we bless our Lord and Father, and with it we curse men, who have been made in the likeness of God; [10] from the same mouth come both blessing and cursing. My brethren, these things ought not to be this way.

People who hope to find satisfaction in their lives by the flawless use of their tongues are biting off more than they can chew! Wisdom is a more realistic goal than perfect behavior or speech. While it is true that perfect wisdom would result in perfect behavior and perfect speech, imperfect wisdom (the only kind of wisdom we are capable of achieving) can make our behavior and our speech more skillful than they would be without it.

Righteous behavior is an un-achievable goal in the absolute sense; and flawless speech is an un-achievable goal in the absolute sense; but wisdom begins with the acknowledgment that we are all going to stand before the Lord and give an account of our failings (Proverbs 9:10), so it should motivate us to live and speak more carefully and constructively than we would apart from its application to our lives.

Wisdom doesn't deny human failings. Rather, it seeks to make the most of human potential in spite of its failings. And, at its best, wisdom takes a look "above the sun," improving its performance with help from the Lord, who is the source of wisdom!

How important is the acquisition of wisdom in your life?

141

Solomon's Enigma
Ecclesiastes 7:23-29

The United States Marines tell us that "the Marines are looking for a few good men." And the Marines have found a few good men - judging by their own set of standards. They have often excelled at what they do in their defense of their country!

But things would turn out quite differently if the Marines were looking for a few good men as God judges "good men" - by His standard of perfection - because the sad truth is that our world has only known one man who could be described as "good" by God's standards! That is the point Jesus was making the day He asked the "rich young ruler," who had just addressed Him as "good master," "Why do you call Me good? No one is good but God." Jesus wasn't denying His goodness; He was seeking, as evidenced by His goodness, to affirm His deity in the thinking of the "rich young ruler."

As the ancient King Solomon pursued his search for meaning in life, he arrived at the observation that there isn't any such thing as a perfectly good man on the face of the earth. As revealed in the last chapter, Solomon observed that "there is not a righteous man on earth who continually does good and who never sins." Because he wasn't privileged to meet Jesus in the flesh, he didn't know experientially about the one exception to his observation who has now lived on our earth.

Since he came to the realization that there wasn't one perfectly righteous person on the face of the earth, Solomon decided that the thing a person ought to seek, since he or she can't be perfect, is to be wise. As he observed in 7:19: "Wisdom strengthens a wise man more than ten rulers who are in a city."

But the more Solomon pursued the idea of finding wisdom, the more disillusioned he became about that pursuit as well because, just as there are no perfectly good people on the face of the earth, so there are no perfectly wise people on the face of the earth either. Wisdom is very rare among human beings, who have perverted God's design.

How many people would you say you have ever met who were consistently "wise" in the sense that, in every dimension of their lives, they operated with unadulterated skill? As much wisdom as Solomon himself had, he couldn't even say that he himself was the personification of wisdom.

I. Solomon's Pursuit of Wisdom 7:23-26

A. His Desire to Be Wise 7:23

"I tested all this with wisdom, and I said, "I will be wise," but it was far from me."

142

The gift of wisdom the Lord gave to Solomon was the gift to skillfully weigh life's issues. Though the book of Ecclesiastes seems to record a "detour" in Solomon's ability to always skillfully weigh life's issues, each of the books Solomon wrote, which we have as a part of our Scriptures, are additional evidence that Solomon really was blessed with the gift of wisdom - at least academically.

It would be hard to improve on the revelation of wisdom we find in the book of Proverbs. And the book of Ecclesiastes, for all of its wandering around the path of wisdom, finally ends up right in the middle of the path. And the Song of Solomon contains some serious wisdom concerning relationships between the sexes.

Solomon put a great number of things in his experience of life to the test of wisdom (as his books reveal). And he was seriously interested in being wise. But, in spite of his statement "I said, 'I will be wise,'" Solomon had to confess that even he didn't do too well in the discovery of wisdom. As he had to candidly acknowledge, regarding wisdom, "It was far from me."

Look, for example, how far the Biblical record reveals he wandered from the path of wisdom in his pursuit of meaning in life. Consider the domestic mess he created by the numerous marriages he entered into - producing a son as his successor (Rehoboam) who promptly split the kingdom of Israel by foolishly following taxation policies his father had initiated. And look at the spiritual mess he got himself into by pursuing the pagan religions and deities of his many wives, and straying quite a distance from the path revealed in God's law!

Solomon wanted to be wise, but he had to admit that wisdom isn't easy to come by.

B. His Difficulty Assessing the Past 7:24

"What has been is remote and exceedingly mysterious. Who can discover it?"

As Solomon studied the events of history and attempted to analyze them by means of the gift of wisdom the Lord gave to him, he had to admit that "what has been is remote and exceedingly mysterious." As wise as he was academically, Solomon wasn't able to analyze human history and explain why people have done what they have done down through the ages.

Not only does man's past history soon become "remote" - in the sense that the details get away from us, for our lack of care in recording and preserving an account of the things people do - but man's past history is full of "mystery."

For example, why did Adam and Eve do what they did in the Garden of Eden to spoil such a perfect setting when there was nothing they lacked as things were? Why did the people of Noah's day persist in their violent ways instead of joining Noah on the ark and saving their lives? Why did Abraham, "friend of God" that he was, tell a lie to the Pharaoh of Egypt about his

143

relationship with his wife? Why did Samson, with all he had going for him in terms of God's blessings, waste his potential on godless women? Why did David, Solomon's own father - a "man after God's own heart" - compromise an otherwise godly life by pursuing an illicit affair, when he already had a harem of, undoubtedly, beautiful wives?

You could do damage to your brain if you spent enough time trying to unravel the twisted course of human history - providing a sensible explanation for everything that has taken place in the lives of men. But Solomon gave it his best effort.

C. His Determination to Distinguish Wisdom and Folly 7:25

"I directed my mind to know, to investigate and to seek wisdom and an explanation, and to know the evil of folly and the foolishness of madness."

Solomon had a passion for knowledge. I Kings 10 tells us that the Queen of Sheba heard of his fame and came to Jerusalem to test him with difficult questions. And I Kings 10:3 tells us that "Solomon answered all her questions; nothing was hidden from the king which he did not explain to her."

Solomon committed himself to the task of learning all he could learn and researching things he didn't know or understand. He made a concerted effort to do what he did with skill and understanding. In addition to the many things we have seen about the breadth of his accomplishments in the opening chapters of Ecclesiastes, I Kings 4:33-34 tells us that:

He spoke of trees, from the cedar that is in Lebanon even to the hyssop that grows on the wall; he spoke also of animals and birds and creeping things and fish. [34] Men came from all peoples to hear the wisdom of Solomon, from all the kings of the earth who had heard of his wisdom.

Solomon tells us that he sought to understand how folly leads to evil. As we saw in Ecclesiastes 2:3, he testified that: "I explored with my mind how to stimulate my body with wine while my mind was guiding me wisely, and how to take hold of folly, until I could see what good there is for the sons of men to do under heaven the few years of their lives." So Solomon apparently intentionally experimented with mind controlling substances (like alcohol), and even engaged in some things he knew were foolish, to see if there was any enjoyment or profit in the things he was experimenting with.

And Solomon tells us as well that he sought to understand how madness results in foolishness. As he explained earlier, in Ecclesiastes 2:1-2: "I said to myself, 'Come now, I will test you with pleasure. So enjoy yourself.' And behold, it too was futility. [2] I said of laughter, 'It is madness,' and of pleasure, 'What does it accomplish?'" So Solomon experimented with pleasures and pursued entertainment and even comedy to such an extent that he decided laughter is "madness" and pleasure affords little pay-off.

144

Of course, Solomon's pursuit of pleasure got him involved with a large number of women, and he discovered that there was plenty of room for trouble in that realm.

D. His Discovery of Trouble 7:26

"And I discovered more bitter than death the woman whose heart is snares and nets, whose hands are chains. One who is pleasing to God will escape from her, but the sinner will be captured by her."

Among the pursuits of his life Solomon became involved with many women. Many of them came into his life, no doubt, through political alliances (e.g., the daughter of the Pharaoh of Egypt, one of his earliest wives). But it is obvious, by his confession in this verse, that some of the women he pursued turned out to be his pursuers - to the extent that he knew what it meant to feel trapped, apparently both emotionally (by hearts which were "snares" and "nets") and physically (by hands which were "chains").

Solomon came to realize that not all is good that looks good when it comes to women, and that the seductive and/or dominating woman is a "trap" the Lord allows in the lives of those who reject His ways. He began to wish that he had been more careful to please the Lord so that he could have escaped some of the women who caught him.

Along with his affluence and influence, some of Solomon's pain is undoubtedly captured in the record of I Kings 1:1,3-4:

Now King Solomon loved many foreign women along with the daughter of Pharaoh: Moabite, Ammonite, Edomite, Sidonian, and Hittite women . . . [3] He had seven hundred wives, princesses, and three hundred concubines, and his wives turned his heart away. [4] For when Solomon was old, his wives turned his heart away after other gods; and his heart was not wholly devoted to the Lord his God, as the heart of David his father had been.

Though he sincerely tried to devote his life to wisdom, Solomon discovered well before the end that wisdom is harder to come by than it might appear. He sometimes found himself caught up in the problems and pains and pangs of guilt which belong to sinners who are commoners - but also to those who are kings and who turn their hearts away from the Lord in sin.

There isn't any way you can successfully mix the pursuit of wisdom with the pursuit of sin. They are to be found on entirely different paths. So Solomon came to realize, apparently late in life, that he wasn't as wise as he may have thought he was (or that he had squandered much of the gift he was given by God). He certainly didn't apply all the wisdom he had access to. He should have read - and put into practice - some of his own writings! But he came to realize that he shared the failings of people in general.

145

II. Solomon's Problem with Mankind 7:27-29

A. His Search of Men and Women 7:27-28

"Behold, I have discovered this," says the Preacher, "adding one thing to another to find an explanation, [28] which I am still seeking but have not found. I have found one man among a thousand, but I have not found a woman among all these."

What Solomon "discovered" was an enigma - something which is hard to understand or explain. Though he "added one thing to another to find an explanation" - i.e. he really tried hard to analyze all the angles and come to a satisfying explanation - he never was successful.

Solomon's book of Proverbs makes it very clear that wisdom is readily available to any who are interested in pursuing her. Proverbs 1:20-21 expresses it this way:

Wisdom shouts in the street,
She lifts her voice in the square;
[21] At the head of the noisy streets she cries out;
At the entrance of the gates in the city she utters her sayings.

But, for all of wisdom's availability, there are amazingly few who ever find her. In Solomon's experience, there might be one man in a thousand who discovered wisdom. And in Solomon's experience there were fewer than one woman in a thousand who discovered wisdom!

Keep in mind, of course, that (along with Solomon's male perspective) the women in Solomon's life were not a very fair sample of the women of Israel! It appears that many of the thousand women in his life were foreign women - probably women of nobility and wealth from surrounding nations, whose leaders were seeking political alliances with Solomon. The Song of Solomon seems to indicate that the woman Solomon enjoyed as much as any woman in his life was probably a farmer's daughter from northern Israel. His chances of finding some wise women would probably have been increased if he had spent more of his time on the farms of his own country rather than in the stuffy circles of royalty and the political correctness of his day.

Solomon obviously came near the end of his days with a very pessimistic view of women - and of mankind in general.

B. His Summation of Man's Condition 7:29

"Behold, I have found only this, that God made men upright, but they have sought out many devices."

Solomon came to realize that man's lack of wisdom is not to be blamed on the Lord. The Lord created man in a state of goodness and innocence. Adam was created "upright." And every individual since creation has come into this life in a state of practical innocence - though headed for trouble because of an inherent sin nature.

The unfortunate truth of the matter is that man has always excelled at finding ways to spoil God's good creation. Adam and Eve did it in the midst of a perfect environment. And their descendants have been doing it ever since. As the apostle Paul summed up the problem in Romans 1:18-20:

> For the wrath of God is revealed from heaven against all ungodliness and unrighteousness of men **who suppress the truth in unrighteousness**, [19] because that which is known about God is evident within them; for God made it evident to them. [20] For since the creation of the world His invisible attributes, His eternal power and divine nature, have been clearly seen, being understood through what has been made, so that they are without excuse.

Solomon's search for wisdom lead him to the conclusion that there are very few upright people - either among men or among women. Wisdom is very rare among human beings, who have perverted God's design.

Have you observed the same? If you haven't, you might want to look again - more closely.

Solomon really pursued wisdom only as long as he pursued the Lord. And what was true of Solomon will be equally true of us. As the New Testament affirms, wisdom is not so much a subject or a process to be mastered as it is a person to be known. So the apostle Paul prayed for the Colossian saints the prayer recorded in Colossians 2:2-3:

> That their hearts may be encouraged, having been knit together in love, and attaining to all the wealth that comes from the full assurance of understanding, resulting in a true knowledge of God's mystery, that is, Christ Himself, [3] in whom are hidden all the treasures of wisdom and knowledge.

It isn't possible to be wise, in the fullest sense, without aggressively pursuing an intimate relationship with the Lord who, as revealed in Jesus Christ, is the personification of wisdom.

147

Responding Rightly to Authority
Ecclesiastes 8:1-4

A bumper sticker which has defaced many cars in recent years reads simply "Question authority."

In a modern democracy, and especially in the sorry state of American society at the turn of the millennium, people can often get away with questioning authority. The children's rights movement and the women's liberation movement and other "rights" movements have left twenty first century America somewhat confused about who has the right to say what to whom. In the litigious atmosphere of our day you are likely to end up in court if you dare to violate anyone's "rights" - including those who are under your authority - so even those who are in positions of authority are treading lightly in many instances. Many parents, for example, have found themselves in trouble in recent years for taking steps to discipline their children. Some have even gone to jail.

But however confused Americans may be about authority, there still is a structure of authority in place which can reign in those who get carried away with their freedoms (we still do have functioning police and judges and prisons); and there is still the supreme authority who is holding people responsible to submit to proper authorities.

And, of course, the confusion of our society and our age regarding the matter of authority is just a little "blip" on the radar screen in the flow of human history, because most societies in most periods of history have been much clearer than we are about who it is that answers to whom. When John the Baptist, for example, dared to criticize King Herod for taking his brother's wife for himself, King Herod simply had him imprisoned; and when the unfortunate day came that Herod made a rash promise to his stolen wife's daughter, who pleased him by her dancing, John the Baptist lost his head to the executioner - because Herod had that kind of authority!

Any confusion in our day and society regarding the matter of authority notwithstanding, the Lord is committed to the concept of authority, and is Himself the ultimate authority behind every legitimate lesser authority, so it is a wise move to show proper respect for those in positions of authority. Ultimately, in showing respect for those in positions of authority, we are showing respect for the authority of the Lord!

Are the lines of proper authority clearly drawn in your mind and life? Until we are seeing issues like that of authority in proper perspective in our lives, we are not yet fully benefitting from wisdom as we could and should be.

I. Benefitting from Wisdom 8:1

148

A. It Yields Interpretation 8:1a

"Who is like the wise man and who knows the interpretation of a matter?"

The wise man, as we have often been reminded in our studies of Ecclesiastes, is the man who does what he does in a skillful way. Wisdom, for example, was attributed to the artisans who constructed the tabernacle in the wilderness (as well as the temple of Solomon). Bezalel, the son of Uri and Oholiab, the son of Ahisamach, are named in Exodus 31:1-7 as men "filled with the Spirit of God in wisdom," and Huram-abi is described in II Chronicles 2:13 as a "skilled man, endowed with understanding."

Though it is quite obvious that wisdom comes in varying degrees, the truth about wise people generally is what we are told in the opening line of this chapter: The wise man knows "the interpretation" of a matter. He demonstrates his wisdom in the fact that he understands the issues involved in the matters which come before him - as Bezalel and Oholiab understood the issues involved in making things out of fabric and wood and metal in the construction of the tabernacle and all of its furnishings. Solomon himself demonstrated wisdom by his understanding of the many facets of life which he addressed in his lectures and his writings (I Kings 4:29-34).

Wisdom is tremendously beneficial to the person who is trying to get something accomplished, because his understanding of the issues involved enables him to do it well.

B. It Illumines the Face 8:1b

"A man's wisdom illumines him and causes his stern face to beam."

The illumination Solomon refers to in this verse is not only mental illumination but physical and facial illumination. We have all seen the look of puzzlement displayed on the face of a person who is not sure what to do in the circumstances he is facing. It is not the look we want to see on the face of our mechanic or our doctor, because it causes us to wonder if they know what they are doing as they try to address a challenge we have brought to them. A person's wisdom, by contrast, makes his face "shine" with a look of confidence and satisfaction in his work. It causes a change in outlook and even appearance because of the understanding and confidence it brings to the challenges of life.

We all enjoy seeing life's challenges handled well - and that is what wisdom makes possible for those who possess it. So let's take wisdom into the realm of authority and see how it would be wisest to deal with the authorities we come up against in our lives. The bumper sticker says we should question authority. What does wisdom say on the matter?

II. Cooperating with the King 8:2-4

A. Keeping the King's Command 8:2

149

"I say, 'Keep the command of the king because of the oath before God.'"

However those who are under authority may feel about it, those who are in authority (as illustrated by kings in eastern societies in ancient times) think authority is something to be heard and heeded! Kings didn't often make suggestions or requests. Kings were more likely to utter commands. Solomon's word is literally, "I say, keep the king's **mouth**" (*peh*), but what was likely to come out of the king's mouth was a command.

And what is true of kings is also true (in differing degrees) of the other authority figures in our lives. Did your parents ask you if you wanted to go to bed? Did your teachers ask you if you wanted to do another assignment? Do employers generally ask their employees to do one thing or another on the job? Do policemen and judges ask people if they want tickets or sentences? Do mayors and governors and presidents ask what people want them to do?

It is important for people who are under authority to do what they are commanded to do, both because it is the wise thing to do and because it is the right thing to do - "because of the oath before God." Solomon's reference to the "oath" before God probably refers to an oath of allegiance to a government and its governor, made in the name of God. I Chronicles 29:24 tells of all of the officials and mighty men, as well as all of King David's sons, pledging their submission to King Solomon. They were, in essence, taking an "oath before God" that they were going to cooperate with their new king.

As the book of Romans reminds us, kings are established by the Lord. Romans 13:1-2 sets forth Paul's challenge this way:

> Every person is to be in subjection to the governing authorities. For there is no authority except from God, and those which exist are established by God. [2] Therefore whoever resists authority has opposed the ordinance of God; and they who have opposed will receive condemnation upon themselves.

So, whether we formally take an oath to uphold government and its governors or not, we are responsible before the Lord Himself - who establishes governments and their governors - to "be in subjection to the governing authorities."

B. Recognizing the King's Importance 8:3a

"Do not be in a hurry to leave him."

The Scriptures record examples of the difficulty ancient peoples sometimes experienced in getting an audience with kings. Esther's uneasiness, for example, in making an uninvited appearance before King Xerxes - who was her own husband - is probably the most noteworthy example (Esther 4:11).

150

Just as it was important not to enter too hurriedly into the presence of a king, so it was very important not to leave too hastily as well. An audience with a king was to be seen as a privilege, so leaving hastily could easily be interpreted as insensitivity to the king's importance or, even worse, perhaps intrigue. When the Magi who came to Jerusalem looking for the newborn Jesus left Israel without checking back in with the king, as they were instructed to do, there were homes in Bethlehem which felt the king's wrath as their infant children were killed (Matthew 2:16)!

By application, whether we are talking about kings or presidents or governors or employers or teachers or parents, it is important that we treat every legitimate authority with respect - showing such common courtesies as respectful greetings and attentive interest in what they think and say. Even the way in which we leave an encounter with someone in authority is worth our careful consideration. Leaving a king's presence too hastily could result in trouble - especially for those leaving to do something the king might consider evil.

C. Recognizing the King's Authority 8:3b

"Do not join in an evil matter, for he will do whatever he pleases."

Doing anything a king considers "evil" is a dangerous activity, because a king has a great deal of power and authority at his command, and a king is free and far more able than the common man to "do whatever he pleases"! Solomon's father David was unfortunate enough to be considered an evildoer by Israel's King Saul, and there were numerous times when David nearly lost his life in his attempts to keep out of the king's path (or out of the path of his spear). Without the help of the Lord, David would probably have been destroyed by the angry monarch.

A king's ability to do whatever he chooses to do (within reasonable limits, of course) makes him a dangerous opponent, as many an unfortunate person has discovered. Even giving unsolicited advice to a king can be risky business.

D. Recognizing the King's Sovereignty 8:4

"Since the word of the king is authoritative, who will say to him, 'What are you doing?'"

Even when a king is wrong, he has such authority on his side that it is difficult for anyone to address the problem. His advisers can get him to consider their advice only as long as they can convince him that they are right. If he thinks they are wrong, he does just what he wants to do - even if it flies in the face of all the advice he has received.

Solomon's son Rehoboam provides an example. When he ascended Solomon's throne he was asked to lighten the people's load by reducing their taxes. When his father's counselors advised him to do as the people requested, he decided he wanted a "second opinion" from the younger men who grew up with him. Even though it lead to rebellion on the part of the people in which his kingdom was split between himself and a rival (Jeroboam), he chose to do what he wanted to do (I Kings 12:3-19)!

More than one royal adviser has learned the hard way that giving advice to a king can be a hazardous occupation. Even when they are wrong, kings often want to hear only what they want to hear! The prophet Micaiah was sent back to prison on a diet of bread and water for failing to say what Israel's King Ahab wanted to hear him say (I Kings 22:26,27)!

Because the actual truth is that kings only do what they please within divinely prescribed limits, and because kings sometimes do respond to questioning on the part of their subjects, there are some people who think this passage is not so much about the authority of human kings as it is about the authority of the "king of kings" - the Lord. It is certainly true that we need to heed the authority of the Lord more than the authority of any mere human king or human authority. But the fact that the passage sets the king in contrast to God in verse two seems evidence enough that it is Solomon's point that we need to submit to the human authorities in our lives as the better part of wisdom.

Wisdom enables those who have it to see things more clearly - like the importance of cooperating with life's authorities. Does our compliance with the authorities the Lord has allowed into our lives demonstrate a heart of wisdom?

It is a wise move to show proper respect for those in positions of authority. It is obviously the prudent thing to do, because it can keep us out of all kinds of trouble. And, beyond that, it is the right thing to do, because the Lord has commanded it in His word. Similar to Paul's challenge in Romans 13:1-2, quoted earlier, is Peter's challenge in I Peter 2:13-17:

> Submit yourselves for the Lord's sake to every human institution, whether to a king as the one in authority, [14] or to governors as sent by him for the punishment of evildoers and the praise of those who do right. [15] For such is the will of God that by doing right you may silence the ignorance of foolish men . . . [17] Honor all people, love the brotherhood, fear God, honor the king.

How wise are you in your response to authority - both human and divine?

152

Keeping Out of Trouble
Ecclesiastes 8:5-9

We all live out our days on earth in what someone has described as a "chain of command." Everyone is under the authority of someone else; and that person is under the authority of someone else; and on and on it goes throughout the human family - with all men ultimately responsible to the God and Creator of all. Solomon has already written of the human "chain of command" in Ecclesiastes 5:8.

Sometimes people get to the place where they want to "kick over the traces" and get out from under the authorities in their lives, but getting out from under authority is normally a dead-end experiment. Those who try it discover, sooner or later, that even if they succeed in getting out from under an immediate authority, there are other authorities who soon step in to take their place! The classic example is that of the young man who gets tired of being under the authority of his parents, so goes and joins the Marines; or the young woman who gets tired of living under the authority of her parents, so runs off and marries a man who makes her life more miserable than her parents ever could!

Mankind can't do better in life than to submit to life's authorities - and especially to the One who is highest in authority. Do you find it easy to submit to the authorities in your life? Or do you live with the notion that you have a better plan?

I. The Troubles of Life 8:5-6

While it is true that life on our sin-cursed earth is full of trouble, the Lord has cushioned the blow of many of life's troubles for those who submit to His plan.

A. The Avoidance of Trouble 8:5

"He who keeps a royal command experiences no trouble, for a wise heart knows the proper time and procedure."

Though Solomon doesn't use the word in his Hebrew original, the New American Standard Bible translators have written of a "**royal** command" in this verse because of the context of the preceding three verses (8:2-4) where the command of the king was in view.

The person who keeps a command and experiences no trouble may well be keeping the command of a king, because it is kings and others in places of high authority who are most likely to give commands. And it is kings and others in places of high authority who are able to cause trouble for those who fail to keep their commands.

As an example, when Solomon himself ascended to the throne of Israel, he commanded his older brother, Adonijah, who had just tried to have himself crowned king in Solomon's place: "Go to your house." (I Kings 1:53). The implication of the king's command was, "be sure you stay at home and mind your own business, or you will be in trouble." When Adonijah had the nerve, then, to employ Solomon's mother to ask that Abishag, the beautiful young woman who had been a nurse to King David in his last days, be given him as a wife, Solomon had reached his fill of his older brother's meddling, and sent the soldier Beniah to Adonijah to execute him (I Kings 2:25)!

It is obvious that Adonijah had very little sense of the "proper time and procedure" in his life. He was not very skilled at handling the issues of his life. So he was soon in serious trouble with Solomon. If he had been more sensitive to what Solomon considered the "proper time and procedure," he might have lived out his days to their normal conclusion, but his failure to "keep the royal command" cost him his life.

People who don't follow instructions well are irritating to people who have the authority to give instructions - whether kings or others in places of authority. So the wise person is the one who, when he hears the person in authority over him give a command, takes care to obey the command to the letter.

Of course, there is the distinct possibility that Solomon was not thinking about just a "royal command" but a divine command when he wrote this verse. Remember, the word "royal" has been added by the translators. It is even truer that "He who keeps a divine command experiences no trouble" - because the commands of the Lord are designed not to get us into trouble but to get us out of trouble - and to keep us out of trouble.

How are you at keeping out of trouble with those who are in authority because you are careful to keep their commands? Most importantly, how sensitive are you to the commands of the Lord?

B. The Response to Trouble 8:6

"For there is a proper time and procedure for every delight, though a man's trouble is heavy upon him."

An important part of wisdom is knowing "the proper time and procedure for every delight" in life. Adonijah, for example, was in pursuit of one of life's common "delights" in seeking a beautiful woman to be his wife, but his sense of timing was way off, which also threw off the procedure he chose in pursuit of his intended delight. He should have waited to pursue his delight at least until his "trouble [was not] heavy upon him."

Because life is full of trouble, the man who is wise needs to evaluate everything he does in terms of its timing and its procedure. If he chooses a time or a procedure in pursuit of his goals in life which happens to correspond with weighty problems, he is probably asking for trouble. If Adonijah should ever have asked for Abishag in marriage, he obviously should have known

154

better than to ask when he did! Having recently learned that Adonijah had tried to steal his kingdom, Solomon's needed no reminder that his brother was still around, and still meddling in his business! And because Solomon was preoccupied with the transition from his father's administration to his own, it was a serious blunder for Adonijah to ask for a favor so foreign to Solomon's frame of mind at the time. But, lacking wisdom, he didn't know the proper time and procedure for pursuing what he wanted, and he paid for his folly with his life!

How are you at avoiding the troubles of life by following the instructions you are given by the authorities in your life? Do you have a good sense of timing and procedure which keeps you out of the path of authorities who are preoccupied with troubles of their own?

II. The Uncertainties of Life 8:7-9

It is a part of our human condition that life is full of surprises. And what is true for mankind generally is equally true for those who are in authority.

A. Man and Uncertainty 8:7

Though mankind has increased greatly in his knowledge about many things in the world around him, knowledge of what is going to take place in the future is still almost entirely beyond his reach. Even the weatherman, with all of his sophisticated training and equipment, frequently fails to anticipate what is ahead on the weather scene. It is a fact of life that even people who are in places of "authority" have little or no control over future events.

1. The Uncertain "What" 8:7a

"If no one knows what will happen . . ."

What is around the next bend in our lives is always unknown to each one of us. Though we may think we know what is coming up, we never know until it gets to us what a day will bring forth. The book of James addresses this sense of uncertainty in James 4:13-15:

Come now, you who say, "Today or tomorrow we will go to such and such a city, and spend a year there and engage in business and make a profit." [14] Yet you do not know what your life will be like tomorrow. You are just a vapor that appears for a little while and then vanishes away. [15] Instead, you ought to say, "If the Lord wills, we will live and also do this or that."

Life on earth is full of uncertain events, so life is also full of uncertainties when it comes to the timing of those uncertain events.

2. The Uncertain "When" 8:7b

" . . . who can tell him when it will happen?"

Because we can never be certain about what will happen next in our lives, we must also be uncertain about when things will happen in our lives. It was my plan one Thursday afternoon to go to my study after lunch, check on the day's mail, then go visiting with one of our church's deacons at the home of one of our church families. But a phone call revealed that the people we were thinking about visiting weren't available, and it soon became evident that the Lord had other plans - which I learned about when someone called on the telephone needing some help in getting started along the spiritual path of life, after professing faith in the Lord with a counselor from clear across the country.

I could hardly have told you in advance **when** I would be talking with someone who had spiritual needs that Thursday afternoon, because I didn't know in advance that the person I ended up talking with even existed on the face of the earth!

The fact that our lives are full of uncertainties results from the fact that we have very little real authority over the affairs of our lives - not even if we are one of life's "authorities."

B. Man and Authority 8:8-9

1. Man's Lack of Authority 8:8

"No man has authority to restrain the wind with the wind, or authority over the day of death; and there is no discharge in the time of war, and evil will not deliver those who practice it."

No man (not even the king) has authority over the wind. Though we are well aware of the wind because of its impact upon our daily lives, we have no power or authority to play wind against wind to exercise control over the wind. We generally never give any thought to where the wind is coming from, let alone how to get it to go where we might like it to go.

And no man (not even the king) has authority over death. Though we all know that, apart from the Lord's intervention in our lives as a result of the return of Christ, we are going to keep our appointment with death, none of us knows when the time for that appointment is going to be. Even doctors often tell patients, whom they believe to have terminal illnesses, that they can expect to live for months or years, only to have them die in days or weeks - or the other way around.

Furthermore, no man (not even the king) has authority over war. Many a soldier has looked forward to the time when he thought he would be released from military duty, only to see his nation enter into conflict and find his military service extended. Many of my friends during high school and college days joined the military, then had difficulty getting out when they thought they would get out because of complications in connection with the Vietnamese War.

156

And Solomon's fourth observation - no man (not even the king) has authority over evil and its results. Many a person has thought that he could get himself ahead by engaging in some form of evil - only to discover that evil more often works the other way around. How many people, thinking that trafficking in illegal drugs will make them rich, instead end up in jail?

No matter how much we may want to be in authority over the affairs of our lives, we all have to live with very real limitations to our authority. Even those in places of highest authority among men live with limitations to their authority. And human authority is often exercised very poorly by those who have it.

2. Man's Abuse of Authority 8:9

"All this I have seen and applied my mind to every deed that has been done under the sun wherein a man has exercised authority over another man to his hurt."

Though Solomon had a great mind, and though he applied it diligently in his search for meaning in life, he labored under the handicap that his search was focused on an "under the sun" perspective. Leaving God out of the picture, Solomon saw inequities in his search for which the providence and sovereignty of God were not seen to be the counterbalances which they are. So Solomon observed that life can be very frustrating.

The realm of authority was one of the areas where Solomon experienced frustration. He, of course, exercised authority as Israel's king. He was surrounded by the normal array of servants as a part of his kingly administration. In addition, he was commander in chief of his nation's military forces. And he gathered large numbers of artisans and builders and slaves for the construction projects he engaged in - from the construction of his own dwelling and the temple of the Lord to the construction of a fleet of ships (I Kings 9:26). In addition, he had many occasions to see others in places of authority exercise their authority over those who answered to them.

In all of the human relations he oversaw as king of Israel, Solomon was well aware that people who have authority over others sometimes use their authority in ways which cause harm to those they oversee. His own father's insistence (against advice) on conducting a census of the people of Israel resulted in God's judgment upon the nation - an experience Solomon surely remembered (I Chronicles 21). So Solomon was well aware that human authority can be exercised to the harm of those who are under it.

That doesn't negate Solomon's earlier observation, though, that "He who keeps a royal command experiences no trouble." Though life is full of trouble and uncertainty and abuse, it still goes best for those who are wisely obedient to the God-appointed authorities in their lives.

True, human authorities are imperfect because, in addition to their inherent depravity, human authorities are faced with the uncertainties and limitations common to man. But it is by divine providence that human authorities are where they are, to help keep us out of trouble. So, though

157

there are authorities who sometimes add to our troubles, generally speaking the authorities in our lives help us avoid trouble.

People can't do better in life than to submit to its proper authorities - especially to the One highest in authority, the Lord. So how are you at submitting to the authorities which the Lord has placed in your life? Are you making the most of authority by submitting to the ultimate authority who is "above the sun" and who is committed to the well-being of those who trust in Him?

Judgment Day Someday
Ecclesiastes 8:10-13

We live in a world where justice is often more elusive than it should be. Though we seldom if ever know all of the relevant facts, it certainly appears at times that innocent people get "taken to the cleaners" in the courtrooms of earth, while people who are as guilty as the devil walk away from their crimes with hardly any consequence for their atrocities. I think, as an example, of the 1996 high profile trial of the Menendez brothers (Lyle and Erik) which resulted in a hung jury - though they had admitted to the shot-gun killing of their parents, Jose and Kitty Menendez.

The good news (for those who are seriously interested in justice) is that the courts of humanity do not have the final say when it comes to justice. There is an ultimate judge who is one day going to render judgment with regard to all of the affairs of human life with absolute justice - on the basis of His omniscience and omnipotence. The Lord will bring every act of mankind to justice in His good time.

Until that time comes, of course, we all need to be giving some very serious thought to what perfect justice is going to mean for us. If the truth, the whole truth, and nothing but the truth were known about our lives, would that be reason for encouragement or for dismay in the presence of the judge of the universe?

The day is coming when the truth, the whole truth, and nothing but the truth **will** be known - and it is going to be a solemn day for all who have committed wickedness, as Solomon is going to acknowledge in the verses before us in Ecclesiastes.

I. The Futile Way of the Wicked 8:10

While it often seems that the wicked are "getting away with murder" in our world, the fact is that their day of judgment is coming.

A. The Burial of the Wicked 8:10a

"So then, I have seen the wicked buried . . ."

Like everyone else on earth, people who give their lives over to doing what is "wicked" in the eyes of the Lord come finally to the day of death and (in most cases anyway) burial. As the author of Hebrews put is (9:27), "It is appointed for men to die once . . ."

There is a bumper sticker which says something to the effect that "God doesn't want me, and the devil won't have me, so I am going to live forever," but its message is far out of touch with reality. Every person alive, apart from the direct intervention of God, has an appointment to keep with death - including those who are "wicked"! Al Capone, for example, was "one mean man" - a man who sent many people to their deaths during the years of his reign over the mob scenes of

New York and Chicago. But, for all of his power over the lives of other men in the gangster world, he finally kept his own appointment with death, as a result of the syphilis he contracted through his wicked lifestyle.

Keep in mind, however, that it isn't only the worst of the wicked who keep that eventual appointment with death.

B. The Pretense of the Wicked 8:10b

Solomon's reference to the wicked he saw buried describes some of them as " . . . those who used to go in and out from the holy place . . ."

The wicked people of earth are not necessarily those who never have anything to do with the realm of religion. Solomon relates some of the wicked dead to the "holy place." The "holy place" is Solomon's reference to the temple in Jerusalem. As a technical term "holy place" applies to the front section of the temple building, an area accessible (according to the Mosaic law) only to the priests of Israel.

It isn't only those who appear to be absolutely godless whose lives are given over to wickedness. Sometimes it is those who frequent the place of worship - even those who provide leadership in worship - whose lives are committed to wickedness. In ancient Israel Nadab and Abihu, the sons of Aaron, committed wickedness by offering up "strange fire" before the Lord (Leviticus 10:1), so the Lord sent His own fire to wipe them out. The sons of Eli were infamous as wicked men in their role as priests of Israel (I Samuel 2:12), and the sons of Samuel didn't turn out much better (I Samuel 8:5). As we know, these corrupt "spiritual leaders" of ancient Israel have had wicked successors in places of leadership right down to our time.

It is one of the sad facts of life that people would commit their lives to wickedness, because there is nothing about wickedness which commends it to anyone.

C. The Obscurity of the Wicked 8:10c

Though wicked people sometimes become well-known in their time, like everyone else their time comes to an end, " . . . and they are soon forgotten in the city where they did thus. This too is futility."

Down through the years and centuries there have been many occasions to remember and even celebrate the lives of righteous people. In both the secular and spiritual realms we remember national and religious heroes, men and women whose lives have left a positive imprint on our world. But who cares to remember the Nadabs and Abihus - and Al Capones - of our world? Their lives fade away into practical oblivion - amounting to nothing more than the "futility" which Solomon has spoken of so often in this book.

Because wicked lives amount to so little of practical value in our world, we could wish that they might be quickly assigned to their rightful judgment - allowing life to move ahead to more important things. But there is a practical problem in man's ability to bring wickedness to judgment on our sin-cursed earth which makes this unlikely.

II. The Unrestrained Way of the Wicked 8:11

A. The Problem of Slow Justice 8:11a

Solomon saw that justice was sometimes elusive "Because the sentence against an evil deed is not executed quickly . . ."

One of the frustrations of the American judicial system - and apparently the judicial system of ancient Israel as well - is the fact that too much time can elapse between the committing of a crime and the time when the criminal is tried and sentenced for his crime. As a result, the human memory may sometimes be too short to associate the crime with the judgment.

I suggested ("tongue in cheek," of course) to the mayor of our town, during a discussion of the problem of gangs and graffiti that, if he authorized the police to shoot on site anyone caught painting graffiti, the word would probably get around town that painting graffiti was not the thing to do! He agreed that such an approach would probably help clean up the problem of graffiti, but said he didn't think we could get away with it in a democratic society. And because he was right, justice for many graffiti artists continues to come very slowly - if at all.

B. The Result of Slow Justice 8:11b

" . . . therefore the hearts of the sons of men among them are given fully to do evil."

When criminals are apprehended, it often takes so long before they are tried and sentenced - sometimes with a laughably light sentence in view of their crime - that the impact of their punishment is almost completely lost in the passing of time. So criminals themselves don't feel the impact of justice in their own lives when they commit a crime; and the watching society doesn't see the impact of justice executed against criminal activity; so many people continue down the path of evil without believing that evildoing has serious enough consequences to cause them to refrain from doing evil!

But, whether human justice makes the issue clear or not, the truth is that doing evil does have consequences in the bigger picture. You are aware, I hope, that human courts are not the only courts of justice - and not the final courts of justice.

III. The Outcome for the Wicked 8:12-13

A. The Hypothetical Long-lived Sinner 8:12a

161

"Although a sinner does evil a hundred times and may lengthen his life . . ."

God's plan is that people who do evil should be stopped in their evildoing by the power of human government. But it doesn't always work that way - at least not in a timely manner. Katherine Ann Power, for example, finally surrendered to legal authorities in 1993 after evading the law for the preceding 23 years since she drove the getaway car in a 1970 bank robbery in which a Boston policeman was killed.[24]

The general teaching of God's word is that people who commit themselves consistently to doing evil die young as a result of their evil behavior - and they often do. But we all know that there are exceptions to the general rules of society, and even to the generalities of the word of God, which can leave the thinking person confused about whether it really pays to do what is right or not. But Solomon assures us that it does!

B. The Reward of Those Who Fear God 8:12b

" . . . still I know that it will be well for those who fear God, who fear Him openly."

The truth is that, even in this life, things almost always go best for those who fear God - carefully living their lives in view of the day when they will stand before the Lord and give an account of the way in which they have lived.

The Bible is full of examples of the lives of men and women who lived their lives in the fear of God; people who feared God "openly" (i.e. publicly) - even against great pressure to do otherwise. Daniel is a classic example - kneeling in prayer by his open window, in spite of the command of the king that anyone caught praying during a thirty-day period to anyone other than the king himself would be thrown into a den of lions (Daniel 6:10)! And we know that it went well for Daniel - though his night with the lions must have been on the unpleasant side!

The bigger picture presented in Scripture assures us that, far beyond this life, it will continue to go well for those who fear God - and who fear Him openly. In fact, it will continue to go well for them eternally. But there is bad news for those who do not fear Him!

C. The Reward of Those Who Do Evil 8:13

"But it will not be well for the evil man and he will not lengthen his days like a shadow, because he does not fear God."

---

[24] Internet entry from TIME Magazine, (1995 TIME Inc. Magazine Company, Compact Publishing, Inc.).

162

Though there appear to be exceptions in time, the general truth is that those who refuse to fear the Lord - committing themselves openly to wicked ways - don't live well and don't live long. Al Capone, cited earlier, who lived his wicked life as a gangster - spent years of his life in prison, thus barely "living" even while alive, and died of syphilis at the age of 48.

Even those who live longer in their wicked ways will not, Solomon assures us, lengthen their days "like a shadow." His mention of a "shadow" creates an interesting mental picture. A shadow stretches out as the day comes to an end but, like life in the present age, a shadow is very insubstantial. It is certainly not to be compared favorably with the much brighter picture of eternity.

Those who refuse to let the Lord be master in their lives - refusing to live in view of their eventual appointment with death and with the judge of all men - will discover much too soon that life on earth is very brief. Life on earth is only a short introduction to eternity, and eternal issues. It is eternity which will forever demonstrate whether our earthly lives were lived well or not lived well.

Though wicked people may seem to get away with their wickedness, it is only a matter of time before they will be judged appropriately. The Lord will bring every act of mankind to justice in His good time.

What will be the result of the Lord's just dealings in your life? Are you living your life in the "fear of the Lord"? Are you consciously steering your course away from wickedness - not only because this is the best thing to do in time, but also because it is the best thing to do in view of the judgment of God which will position you for all of eternity?

163

Life's Puzzles
Ecclesiastes 8:14-17

The fact that our world is well-populated by philosophers and psychologists and a wide variety of religions, each with numerous and varied schools of opinion, is evidence that something very profound must be happening on our planet.

If life was simple, there would be more agreement about what is going on and what it all means. But we are faced with a dazzling array of opinions about what life is all about, because it isn't easy to understand!

Consider only the wide array of religious viewpoints which have been proposed in man's attempt to understand and explain life's mysteries (beyond, of course, the viewpoints of Judaism and Christianity as they are revealed in God's word). A short A-Z list includes Animism, Bahai, Buddhism, Hinduism, Humanism, Islam, New Age, Taoism, Unity and Zoroastrianism.

No matter how many ways man seeks to explore and explain the complexities of life, there will never be any exploration or explanation which answers all of the questions life raises because life is sometimes apparently unfair and is beyond man's ability to understand.

How do you deal with the complexities and profundities of life which you don't understand? We find Solomon wrestling with such things in the passage before us.

I. The Inequity of Life 8:14-15

Though children are born with the sense that things in life ought to be "fair," they normally don't get too far down the path of life before someone is telling them that life is not fair. And, because of the presence of sin in our world, life **isn't** fair.

A. Solomon's Observation of Inequity 8:14

1. Righteous Men Rewarded with Evil 8:14a

"There is futility which is done on the earth, that is, there are righteous men to whom it happens according to the deeds of the wicked."

Any thinking person will have to admit that there are many things in life on earth which seem rather vacuous. They seem to be like wind or breath in terms of their substance. So Solomon begins the passage describing that which takes place on earth as "futility." He has turned earlier in the book of Ecclesiastes to the endless cycles of nature to illustrate the futility/vanity of life on earth. There he considered the ongoing living and dying of the generations (1:4); the ongoing rising and setting of the sun (1:5); the circuitous patterns traveled by the wind (1:6); and the

164

circuitous hydrological cycle (water flow and evaporation and rain) (1:7).

Solomon's current illustration of life's futilities is an illustration he has cited earlier in the book (3:16; 7:15): that of bad things happening to good people and good things happening to bad people. We have all struggled with just such apparent inequities in life in our own experience. I think, for example, of a man who was a deacon in our church family who loved the Lord and sought to do what was right, but had to suffer for thirty years with a painful case of rheumatoid arthritis, fifteen of those years with a life-threatening case of kidney failure, plus other complications and pains, before dying at a relatively young age. And this is only one of many examples I might cite of bad things happening to a good person. And just to make matters worse, there are two sides to this puzzling coin.

2. Evil Men Rewarded with Good 8:14b

"On the other hand, there are evil men to whom it happens according to the deeds of the righteous. I say that this too is futility."

We all have known of people whose lives were committed to unwholesome habits and ungodly acts who have lived in apparent health and happiness far longer than it would seem someone with so little regard for decency and deity should live. Take, for example, the founder of the pornography publishing empire who has peddled his product and flaunted his immoral lifestyle for decades - living in evident luxury the whole time.

As Solomon looked at such apparent anomalies in his time he couldn't help but conclude that it just didn't seem fair. Like so many other things he observed in his life time, he declared such things "futility." His Hebrew word (*hebel*) can be translated by such words as "breath, breathing; exhalation, vapor, mist, darkness," so it speaks here of that which is vain and empty.

You have almost certainly seen such inequities in life. So where do we go from here?

B. Solomon's Commendation of Pleasure 8:15

"So I commended pleasure, for there is nothing good for a man under the sun except to eat and to drink and to be merry, and this will stand by him in his toils throughout the days of his life which God has given him under the sun."

As long as we are looking (as Solomon is, throughout most of the book of Ecclesiastes) at life as we find it "under the sun" (with God out of the picture), the best things in life are the things which bring the greatest pleasure. A good meal is something almost every person enjoys - with regularity if at all possible. A favorite drink is another thing which Solomon commends as bringing pleasure into life in a confusing world - and Solomon had no reservations about using alcoholic drinks (with moderation - Ecclesiastes 2:3). And a third thing which Solomon mentions as one of life's pleasures to be pursued is "being merry" - i.e. having a good laugh, probably with some close friends or associates.

We would all probably agree that we have derived a great deal of pleasure in a crazy world eating and drinking and enjoying merriment. And if we had nothing more important to think about in life, it wouldn't be a bad idea to focus our attention more fully on these diversions from life's problems.

As Solomon acknowledges in the final phrase of the fifteenth verse, life's toils really are lightened very consistently by the prospect of something good to eat or something refreshing to drink or a light-hearted exchange with some good friends or associates. Some of the most enjoyable experiences of a typical day take place during lunch and coffee breaks and at dinner parties.

Life's inequities are made more tolerable by its pleasures. Almost anyone can settle down more easily to the daily grind of life in a world which often doesn't make much sense if we can take a break every once in a while for something more enjoyable than puzzling over things which seem unfair.

One of the frustrations of puzzling over things which seem unfair is the fact that you can puzzle all you want and never come up with any very satisfying answers to the questions life's puzzling things raise.

II. The Inability to Understand Life 8:16-17

A. Solomon's Attempt to Know Wisdom 8:16

"When I gave my heart to know wisdom and to see the task which has been done on the earth (even though one should never sleep day or night) . . ."

There came a time in Solomon's life when he became very introspective. Exactly what it was that brought it on and when it took place no one can say for sure. But we do have enough information about Solomon that we can hazzard a guess.

Solomon started out his career as king of Israel with everything going his way. He was chosen by his famous and successful father (as well as the Lord Himself) from among the many sons of David to be successor on David's throne. His father's long and stable reign as king had seen the subjugation of all of the surrounding enemy nations; it had seen the organization of Israel's military and political and religious personnel into a smooth operation; and it had amassed a considerable amount of wealth with which to begin both his administration and the eventual construction of both the temple and some elaborate quarters for the king and his family.

And Solomon's comfortable place in life was advanced significantly through His worship of the Lord when, while he was offering sacrifices at a high place in Gibeon, the Lord appeared to him and said (I Kings 3:5): "Ask what you wish me to give you." Solomon's request for "an understanding heart to judge Your people to discern between good and evil" (I Kings 3:9) pleased the Lord greatly and resulted in the gift of wisdom for which Solomon became so well-known - not only in Israel but throughout the middle-eastern world! And the Lord granted Solomon the blessings of riches and honor on top of all the other blessings he enjoyed.

But Solomon's success apparently became the source of his undoing. Because he was so wealthy and influential, he began to acquire a large harem of wives and concubines (many of them apparently through political alliances with surrounding nations), and the Scriptures tell us (I Kings 11:4) that "his wives turned his heart away after other gods; and his heart was not wholly devoted to the LORD his God, as the heart of David his father had been."

So Solomon apparently became so spiritually disoriented at this point in his life that he became disillusioned with life and launched himself on the search for meaning and satisfaction in life which the book of Ecclesiastes is all about.

Solomon has told us, in the early pages of the book, what he now tells us again: that he gave his heart to know wisdom and to see the task which has been done on the earth. And he has made it evident, in the early pages of the book, that his search for wisdom was a very extensive search - a search which the last phrase of this verse indicates apparently even deprived him of sleep both night and day at some points. If you have ever gotten so completely engrossed in an interesting project that you didn't want to stop even for rest, you have experienced what Solomon apparently experienced. But Solomon's efforts didn't get him where he wanted to be.

B. Solomon's Acknowledgment of Failure 8:17

1. The Diligent Man's Inability to Discover 8:17a

" . . . and I saw every work of God, I concluded that man cannot discover the work which has been done under the sun."

All of Solomon's efforts to come to a full understanding of what life is really all about left him without discovering what he was looking for. He found life to be far more complex than he had imagined when he began his search. And though Solomon had the mind and the time and the resources to search more thoroughly than most people could ever search, he came to the conclusion (when all was said and done) that life was beyond his understanding.

Solomon's search was complicated, of course, by the fact he has so often written of before - that his investigation concerned only "the work which has been done under the sun." He was at a time in his life, as a result of his attention to pagan wives and their pagan religions, when the Lord was not the central factor He should have been in Solomon's search.

If you have had a time in your life when the Lord was not in His rightful place of centrality, you may have some first-hand knowledge of how frustrating it can be to try to understand the complexities of life without the help of life's Creator!

2. The Wise Man's Inability to Discover 8:17b

"Even though man should seek laboriously, he will not discover; and though the wise man should say, 'I know,' he cannot discover."

Moses explained the way it is in his final messages to the people of Israel in Deuteronomy 29:29: "The secret things belong to the Lord our God, but the things revealed belong to us and to our sons forever, that we may observe all the words of this law."

No matter how diligently a man - even the wisest of mere men - should search out an understanding of life's most difficult challenges, he will never be able to understand and explain them. There are things which the Lord has reserved to His own understanding but has not revealed to anyone among men. Interestingly, there were even some things in God's plan which Jesus Himself indicated had not been revealed to Him (Matthew 24:36)!

It wasn't Solomon's lack of wisdom which prevented Him from understanding life's complexities. Even the wisest of men have simply not been given all of the pieces of the puzzle! The apostle Paul wrote of the incomprehensible ways of the Lord in Romans 11:33-36:

Oh, the depth of the riches both of the wisdom and knowledge of God! How unsearchable are His judgments and unfathomable His ways! [34] For who has known the mind of the Lord, or who became His counselor? [35] Or who has first given to Him that it might be paid back to him again? [36] For from Him and through Him and to Him are all things. To Him be the glory forever. Amen.

Life's inequities are made tolerable by its pleasures, but its mysteries are beyond human understanding. Anyone who thinks he has a handle on all of life's complexities is simply deceiving himself - as any bend in the road may soon make abundantly clear.

Life is sometimes apparently unfair and is beyond man's ability to understand. But be encouraged that there is One who understands, and He has good things in store for those who place their trust in Him! Can you trust the Lord to perfect His purposes for your good even when life doesn't add up?

168

Making the Most of Earthly Life
Ecclesiastes 9:1-9

Christians enjoy a brighter prospect for the future than any other people on the face of the earth. Even if their lives on this earth are full of toil and trouble (as many have been, and many still are), those who know Jesus Christ as Savior look forward to a glorious future with eternal dimensions where, as Paul put it in I Corinthians 2:9, they anticipate:

> Things which eye has not seen and ear has not heard,
> And which have not entered the heart of man,
> All that God has prepared for those who love Him.

Paul quoted and adapted this verse, by the way, from Isaiah 64:4 where, in its original context, we find that even the ancient people of Israel who waited on the Lord lived with an expectancy which most of the world doesn't know anything about.

> For from days of old they have not heard or perceived by ear,
> Nor has the eye seen a God besides You,
> Who acts in behalf of the one who waits for Him.

As our study has often revealed, because Solomon wrote at a time when he was not "waiting on the Lord," the book of Ecclesiastes does not offer a very positive perspective on life. It was written from the viewpoint of the man who sees only things which are "under the sun"- with God out of the picture of human experience or, at best, only remotely involved.

If God is out of the picture of human experience, or only remotely involved, life takes on quite a different appearance than it does for those who see Him as a Savior and Lord and Friend and loving Provider. But, though Solomon was not as close to the Lord as he could and should have been when he wrote Ecclesiastes, he could still see that the Lord has destined man (under the sun) to enjoy life as much as he can on his way to the grave.

Recognizing the limitations of earthly life, do you also look for every opportunity to enjoy what the Lord has provided as fully as He enables you to do it?

I. The Sovereign Control of the Lord 9:1

"For I have taken all this to my heart and explain it that righteous men, wise men, and their deeds are in the hand of God. Man does not know whether it will be love or hatred; anything awaits him."

Solomon apparently did quite a bit of pondering the puzzles of life during the spiritual detour which resulted in his writing of the book of Ecclesiastes. His spiritual roots wouldn't allow him to dismiss the Lord entirely from the picture of human experience, but he certainly lost site of the

169

Lord as the "friend" He had been to his father David!

Solomon couldn't deny that God is the ultimate controller of all things. He could see that the best of men live out their lives with the hand of God on the controls in the final sense. Though a man might be "righteous" (i.e. conforming his life in thought, word and action to the will of God), his life is still lived within the limits of the controlling hand of God! Noah, for example, was a righteous man, but he had to build an ark to save himself and his family (and the animals) from the effects of the flood. And though a man might be "wise" (very skilled in understanding and handling the affairs of his life), his life is still lived within the limits of the controlling hand of God. Job, we are told, was among the wisest men of his day, but the Lord allowed difficulties to come into Job's life, and Job had no choice but to face them.

No matter how good a man might be, Solomon could see that life can be either extremely pleasant or extremely painful! Job is a man who walked with God, and who for many years enjoyed nothing but the best in life, then (without any understanding of why it happened) suddenly encountered nothing but the worst!

Why should life be so unpredictable? Why should its most predictable feature be that of its termination in death?

II. The Common Fate of All Men 9:2-6

A. The Classes of Men All Headed for the Same Fate 9:2

"It is the same for all. There is one fate for the righteous and for the wicked; for the good, for the clean and for the unclean; for the man who offers a sacrifice and for the one who does not sacrifice. As the good man is, so is the sinner; as the swearer is, so is the one who is afraid to swear."

As Solomon spells it all out in this verse, it doesn't matter who a person is or how a person lives, at the end of whatever life may bring there is always the same cold reality of death staring him in the face! Whether a person is righteous or wicked he will still die! Whether a person is clean or unclean (in either a physical sense or in a ceremonial sense) he will end up in the grave! Whether a person is faithful in offering sacrifices to the Lord or whether he never sacrifices to the Lord, he will still die! Whether a person is good or bad doesn't change the fact; the best of good people and the worst of bad people end up "six feet under"! And whether a person is one who binds himself by means of oaths or is afraid to take an oath, his life on earth will end with a funeral!

B. The Condition of Men All Headed for the Same Fate 9:3

"This is an evil in all that is done under the sun, that there is one fate for all men. Furthermore, the hearts of the sons of men are full of evil and insanity is in their hearts throughout their lives.

Afterwards they go to the dead."

We like to think that some people are good and some people are bad, but it is closer to reality to say that all people are bad and some people are very bad. As Paul sums it up in a series of Old Testament quotations in Romans 3:10 and following:

"There is none righteous, not even one;
[11] There is none who understands,
There is none who seeks for God;
[12] All have turned aside, together they have become useless;
There is none who does good,
There is not even one." (Etc., etc.)

Words like "evil" and "insanity" (madness) sound like harsh terms to use in a description of any person, but the reality is that an investigation of our inner hearts reveals that such words are an accurate description (in some measure, at least) of every person! The "righteous" King David, Solomon's own father, became guilty of adultery and murder because of the evil and insanity which were present in the depths of his heart!

C. The Hope of the Living as They Head for Their Fate 9:4-5a

1. The Hope of the Living 9:4

"For whoever is joined with all the living, there is hope; surely a live dog is better than a dead lion."

Looking only at life as we see it "under the sun" (apart from a meaningful relationship with the Lord), there is hope only as long as a person is alive. The "dog" in Jewish thought was a very lowly creature. Ancient Jews didn't treat dogs as domesticated house-pets, as modern Americans do. They saw them as wild scavengers (more like Americans see coyotes and wolves). It was, for example, dogs running loose in the streets of Jezreel which consumed the body of Queen Jezebel when she was thrown out of an upper story palace window to the street below and left there for only a short time (II Kings 9:5-37).

On the other hand, the "lion" in Jewish thought was the greatest and strongest of animals. When Jacob described his son Judah (in Genesis 49:9) as a "lion's whelp," he was describing him as the one who would exercise power and control over the other sons of the family as the source of Israel's kings. But as lowly as the dog was in Jewish thinking, and as lofty as the lion, there can be no doubt that the living dog has more going in his favor than the dead lion does! It is far better to be lowly, but alive, than to be mighty, but dead!

2. The Fate of the Living 9:5a

171

"For the living know they will die . . ."

There isn't a creature alive today (or in any other day) on our sin-cursed earth which, apart from the supernatural intervention of the Lord, will not one day experience the fate of all living things in the termination of its earthly life (in the form in which we know it today).

The thought of death is such an unhappy prospect, that we ignore it as long as we can. It is often difficult for families to get the senior members among them to make realistic preparations for their departure from this life, because people don't want to think about their departure. But no amount of ignoring the fact of death can keep it from occurring, because (as the author of the epistle to the Hebrews reminds us in 9:27) "It is appointed for men to die once." And once death occurs, apart from the power of the Lord the picture is pretty bleak!

D. The Hopelessness of the Dead 9:5b-6

" . . . but the dead do not know anything, nor have they any longer a reward, for their memory is forgotten. Indeed their love, their hate and their zeal have already perished, and they will no longer have a share in all that is done under the sun."

From all appearances, the person who is dead has ceased to exist. He can't tell you anything because he appears not to know anything. You can't do anything to make him feel better because he appears to have no feelings. And it isn't long before those who are dead play essentially no part in human life. Except for their closest of kin, most people never know that those who have died ever lived. And soon their closest of kin have died, so no one remembers them any longer - unless they happen to have been among the few who did something important enough to have been recorded in the written account of history. Most people who live on earth are forgotten completely just a short few years after they have died.

As warm and winsome as the love of the living can be in its impact on those who are near and dear, the love of those who have died soon fades into insignificance - almost non-existence. As powerful and painful as the hate of the living can be in its influence for ill and for harm, once a person has died his hatred generally fails to sustain its influence very long. As exciting and influential as the zeal of the living can be on those who feel its ability to motivate and accomplish things for good and for ill, the zeal of those who have died soon loses its impact altogether.

Death is the end of everything - or so it would appear from a merely earthly perspective (which is basically Solomon's perspective in the book of Ecclesiastes). So (looking at life "under the sun") anyone who is hoping to accomplish or enjoy or experience anything at all better make the most of the opportunities afforded by life while it lasts, because (at best) it won't last very long.

III. The Challenge to the Living 9:7-9

172

A. The Lord's Approval of the Acts of the Living 9:7

"Go then, eat your bread in happiness and drink your wine with a cheerful heart; for God has already approved your works."

In view of the approach of the "grim reaper," it would be wise for every person to make the most of the few days of life he is given to live on earth.

One of life's greatest pleasures is eating, so that is where Solomon takes us first. Bread, as the "staff of life," represents all that we enjoy as our food - and Solomon's advice is enjoy your food. Wine was the common drink of Solomon's day - a drink enjoyed with almost every meal, so Solomon advises that a man enjoy something to drink (and a glass of wine is well known for its ability to help create a cheerful heart).

We know, of course, that there are many things people do of which the Lord does not "approve" in the sense that He recommends them to His people. But He does approve our works in the sense that He is the One who has given us satisfying activities to fill our days, and He is pleased to see us busy about the things He has equipped us to do. The Lord enjoys seeing His creatures do what they were created to do; and He enjoys seeing them get satisfaction out of the things He has given for their satisfaction (e.g. food and drink and the pursuits of life). In fact, Solomon describes such things as the Lord's "reward" for His creatures.

B. The Lord's Reward for the Living 9:8-9

"Let your clothes be white all the time, and let not oil be lacking on your head. [9] Enjoy life with the woman whom you love all the days of your fleeting life which He has given to you under the sun; for this is your reward in life and in your toil in which you have labored under the sun."

White garments are a symbol of purity and ease; and oil is a symbol of joy and comfort. So it was Solomon's wish that each person live well and enjoy it.

One of life's greatest joys is that of a close relationship with a life-partner. So Solomon commends the joy of marriage as the gift of God which it is, and expresses the hope that each person might enjoy a happy and fulfilling relationship in marriage and family. This is one of life's greatest rewards, as Solomon observes, and it seldom lasts as long as people hope it will, because life is short, at best. There will be plenty of toil for each person in earthly life, so it is Solomon's encouragement that we each take advantage of the good things the Lord has provided for us to eat and drink and celebrate and enjoy as often as life will allow it. It is incumbent on those who live to recognize God's hand in allowing them to enjoy life's blessings as they make their way toward their inevitable appointment with death.

Do you live in recognition of the fact that the Lord, who has drawn the bounds of life on a

173

sin-cursed earth, wants His creatures to make the most of His gifts as long as we have life to do it? While it is true that none of us know what lies ahead - except that we will eventually die - the Lord wants His creatures to make the most of whatever may come their way. It is His intention that they should enjoy the normal pleasures of life - including food and drink and marriage and family. Should trouble come, as it might, it should be handled as well as possible. But there is no sense in borrowing trouble. So, living in view of God's sovereign control and in a manner which is pleasing to Him, make it your aim to make the most of earthly life!

174

Beyond Our Control
Ecclesiastes 9:10-12

Bob was a young man who appeared to have a great deal going for him. A member of the youth group in my home church, he was an apparently healthy young man, good looking and intelligent. He lettered in high school as a swimmer, and became quite an accomplished water polo player during college years. Following college he became an officer in the Air Force, serving in the field of military intelligence during the Viet Nam War era.

Things seemed to be going very well for Bob - until the day he and some of his military friends met for a party and, some time after lunch, he was found floating lifelessly in the pool. If any of my friends shouldn't have died in a swimming pool, Bob topped the list - but he drowned in the prime of life with everything seemingly going his way, and I learned the lesson by experience, as a junior college student, that life on earth is filled with surprises, even for those who give it the best they can.

You have noticed, haven't you, that life sometimes just doesn't turn out the way it seems it should? Sometimes people get their lives all messed up because they don't apply themselves to the opportunities which come their way. But there are other times when people who seem to be headed in the right direction end up shipwrecked somewhere along the shores of the "sea of life" after sailing through some stormy waters.

The fact that life on earth is unpredictable at best should challenge each of us to make the most of whatever it brings.

I. The Urgency of the Present 9:10

A. Solomon's Call to Diligence 9:10a

"Whatever your hand finds to do, do it with all your might . . ."

Because life is fleeting (as Solomon has just observed in verse nine), we seldom seem to have enough time to do all the things we think we would like to do. I have jokingly said that I am trying to make a deal with the Lord to let me take my library to heaven because, at the speed I read, I figure it will take me eternity to get it all read!

Anything we are going to get done during the brief lifetime we spend on this earth will have to be done now or the opportunity will soon be gone. So Solomon calls his readers to diligence - to do with all our might whatever it is we decide to do with the short span of time we call our lifetime. Life will soon be over, and the chance to do what we wanted to do will be gone.

B. Solomon's Reminder of Mortality 9:10b

" . . . for there is no activity or planning or knowledge or wisdom in Sheol where you are going."

Sheol is the place of the dead. Sheol is not the translation of a Hebrew word, but the transliteration of Solomon's word. Though its sixty-six occurrences in the Hebrew Bible are systematically transliterated "sheol" in the New American Standard Bible, it might be more helpful to our understanding to go back (in at least some of those passages) to the translation of the King James Bible - "the grave."

Solomon and other Old Testament saints didn't have the revelation we are given in the New Testament concerning life after death. He didn't live with the anticipation that "to be absent from the body" is "to be at home with the Lord" as we do (II Corinthians 5:8), so he looked at death as the end of life. He knew that people who are dead can no longer do the things they did when they were alive so, from his "under the sun" perspective in the book of Ecclesiastes, he treated death as if it were the end of all activity and planning and knowledge and wisdom. It seemed clear to him that dead people are not physically active; that they don't appear to have any knowledge; and that they don't make plans for the future.

If you think of life only "under the sun" - without God in the picture, as Solomon is thinking throughout most of the book of Ecclesiastes - human existence is very brief. It comes to an end with the death of the body. So you need to make the most of life while you have it, because the day will come when you will be gone, and everything you left undone will go undone forever - as far as you are concerned.

Are you making good use of the time and energies and resources and opportunities which you have today? You should, even if you are blessed to have an "above the sun" perspective, because they will soon be gone! You have no guarantee that you will be around to finish what you have started even as long as another day! As Jesus put it (John 9:4): "We must work the works of Him who sent Me as long as it is day; night is coming when no one can work."

As Christians who have the advantage of New Testament revelation, we know that the death of the physical body is not the end of all things. But keep in mind as well that, in terms of earthly life alone, physical death **is** the end of an experience in which even your finest effort is no guarantee of success.

II. The Uncertainty of the Present 9:11-12

While you probably have some plans in mind for your day, you need to be alert (as we all do) to the possibility that your plans will be altered, before the day is over, by circumstances you had no idea you would need to deal with as you mapped out your path for the day. "The best-made plans of mice and men oft' are g'ing awry" - as they say.

A. Life Has Few Guarantees 9:11

176

1. Its Surprises 9:11a

"I again saw under the sun that the race is not to the swift and the battle is not to the warriors, and neither is bread to the wise nor wealth to the discerning nor favor to men of ability;"

Life on our sin-cursed earth - especially life "under the sun" (without consideration for the Lord) - sometimes doesn't turn out the way we would like or the way we think it should. It would seem that "the race of life" would always turn out best for the person who can run the fastest - but there are times when it doesn't turn out that way at all! II Samuel 2:22-23, for example, tells of the death of the warrior Asahel, who could literally run faster than Abner (the military leader he was chasing on foot), when Abner killed him with a blow to the stomach with the butt end of his spear.

It would seem that the person most likely to succeed in battle would be the seasoned warrior, who has made preparation for battle the focus of his life, but there are times when battles against trained warriors are won by those who have little or no training in military matters. The uneven contest between the seasoned warrior Goliath of Philistia and the Israeli shepherd-boy David (I Samuel 17:41-49) is certainly a classic example!

It would seem that the person who is skilled in his ability to handle the issues of life would have no difficulty providing bread for his daily needs, but there are times when the wisest of men find themselves in the embarrassing position of lacking even their necessary bread. From the life of David again, there is the example of his stop, during flight from Saul, at the Tabernacle at Nob where he asked for bread to sustain himself and the men who were fleeing with him (I Samuel 21:1-3) - though he was a military commander in Israel's army and the son-in-law of Israel's king!

It would seem that the person who is discerning would have no difficulty turning his assets into significant wealth - but there are times when the most discerning among men come to their death with little or nothing to show for all their discernment! Jesus Himself, the most discerning person who ever walked the face of the earth, went through life with "nowhere to lay His head" (Matthew 8:20) and was buried in a borrowed tomb - after soldiers divided his few possessions among themselves at the foot of the cross where He was crucified (Matthew 27:57-60)!

It would seem that the person who has great abilities would easily find favor in the eyes of others because of his abilities - but there are times when those with great abilities are rejected and despised as if they didn't have any ability at all. Genesis 25:27, for example, uses the same word Solomon uses here for "men of ability" to describe Esau as a "skillful hunter" - but Esau's abilities as a hunter won him neither the favor of his mother nor the favor of the Lord (Genesis 25:28; Romans 9:13)!

Life simply does not always stack up the way we think it should. Even the native abilities each person has are no guarantee that he will excel in the things for which he appears to be well-

177

equipped - because native abilities are only one factor in the complex equation of life.

2. Its Certainties 9:11b

" . . . for time and chance overtake them all."

No matter how capable a person may be in one area of life or another, one of the factors in life's equation he has little or no control over is that of timing! I think, for example, of the evangelical leader who was distressed that he was dropped off at the airport a little too late to catch the flight he was scheduled for - until he learned that his scheduled flight was involved in a crash. The Lord had used the troubling delay in his arrival at the airport to save his life!

And no matter how capable a person may be in one area of life or another, there is a second factor in life's equation over which he has little or no control - the factor of chance. I was driving from Flagstaff to Phoenix in Arizona one mid-August day when a rain storm turned to hail, and iced up the road ahead of me, causing me to lose control of the car and hit the vehicle ahead of mine. I had to wonder what the chances were of an icy road in the summer in Arizona where heat is a more likely summer experience!

Whatever our abilities or disabilities in life, nothing is guaranteed to turn out the way it might seem it should. Whether we like it or not, there will always be factors of timing and chance, over which we have little or no control, which can and will make all the difference in the world in the way our lives turn out! Life is full of surprises, and sudden turns!

B. Life Has Some Sudden Turns 9:12

1. Its Timing 9:12a

"Moreover, man does not know his time"

Because time and chance are factors in life which are beyond our control, we can never be sure **when** events will take place or even **if** they will take place. The plans of man are always subject to the will of God - as James observed in James 4:13-15:

Come now, you who say, "Today or tomorrow we will go to such and such a city, and spend a year there and engage in business and make a profit." [14] Yet you do not know what your life will be like tomorrow. You are just a vapor that appears for a little while and then vanishes away. [15] Instead, you ought to say, "If the Lord wills, we will live and also do this or that."

2. Its Treacheries 9:12b

" . . . like fish caught in a treacherous net and birds trapped in a snare, so the sons of men are

178

ensnared at an evil time when it suddenly falls on them."

Leaving God out of the equation of human experience (which, by this point in the study of Ecclesiastes, we should have figured out is a very foolish thing to do), people are little more than the hapless victims of the circumstances of life. People who leave God out of their lives will find themselves faced with a life in which evil things happen to unsuspecting victims without any warning - like the trapped fish and birds Solomon cites in this verse. Because people have only one opportunity to make the most of the present, it is important for them to try to do their best. But it is important to take into account the fact that life, as we know it, is plagued with many uncertainties which may undermine even the best we can do! Life "under the sun" is filled with surprises, even for those who give it the best they can.

Can you seen, then, why it doesn't make good sense to try to live your life, as Solomon was trying to live his when he wrote the book of Ecclesiastes, with regard for only that which is "under the sun"? How much better to have the perspective of the apostle Paul who gave a challenge very similar to that which Solomon gives in this passage - but with the critical difference that he challenges us to look "above the sun": "Whatever you do, do your work heartily, as for the Lord rather than for men" (Colossians 3:23).

179

The Worth of Wisdom
Ecclesiastes 9:13-18

If you were to ask a group of young people what they would like to aim their lives toward in their adult years, you would get numerous responses. Some would probably respond with a general category they would like to fit into: famous or intelligent or powerful or wealthy. Others would name a specific job they would like to do: a basketball player or a computer programmer or a doctor or lawyer or teacher. But few, if any, would tell you that they would like most to be wise - even though it is wisdom which, more than anything else, could make them successful in whatever they eventually decide to do.

Wisdom is more valuable than many of the things people prize most highly in life. But wisdom isn't something we are likely to be taught to pursue anywhere except in the pages of God's word - and especially in the "wisdom literature" of God's word. If you have ever taken a course in wisdom it was probably a course you took, not necessarily by design, in the "school of hard knocks" - unless you have caught on to the fact that the Lord wants His people to learn to be wise by applying themselves diligently to the study and implementation of His word.

I. An Illustration of Wisdom 9:13-15

A. Solomon's Evaluation 9:13

"Also this I came to see as wisdom under the sun, and it impressed me."

The Scriptures describe ancient Israel's King Solomon as, apart from the Lord Jesus Christ Himself, the wisest man who ever lived (I Kings 3:12). But even Solomon knew more about wisdom as an academic matter than as a practical matter, because there are things he teaches as wisdom in his writings which we know he didn't put into practice in his own life. Solomon, for example, taught his son (in the well-known words of Proverbs 3:5-6) to "Trust in the Lord with all [his] heart," and not to "lean on [his] own understanding," and "in all [his] ways to acknowledge Him," - with the result that the Lord would "make [his] paths straight." Yet Solomon himself traveled some rather crooked paths in his life - for failing to fully trust in the Lord. His plural marriages to pagan wives are example enough!

But, in spite of some glaring failings in his life, Solomon did come to see some worldly wisdom ("wisdom under the sun" as he refers to it in verse thirteen). He was impressed by the superiority of wisdom over many of the things people are most likely to pursue in their lives - things like physical strength and human authority and military hardware (as he will tell us in verses sixteen through eighteen).

B. Solomon's Illustration 9:14-15

180

1. A Small City Under Siege 9:14

"There was a small city with few men in it and a great king came to it, surrounded it and constructed large siegeworks against it."

Ancient cities often built strong walls for protection against invaders. Some ancient cities were "city-states" - political units in and of themselves - with no one to look to for protection beyond themselves. But even cities which were a part of a larger nation were normally isolated enough from other cities in their nation that they needed walls for their security.

The small city with few men in it which Solomon cites as an example could easily have been one of the many cities we are familiar with from Biblical history - like Jericho, famous for its formidable walls, which the Lord brought down without any siege works!

Because ancient cities normally had strong walls, a standard procedure in conquering an ancient city was to build siege works - wooden structures or mounds of earth against the walls from which battering-rams could be brought into play to knock the walls down. When the walls could be breached, opposing armies could enter the city to defeat its citizens.

This is the scene Solomon describes in verse fourteen - a powerful king coming against the walls of a small city and its small army in what was likely to be certain defeat for the small city - except for the presence of a poor but wise man in the city.

2. A Poor Wise Man's Deliverance 9:15

"But there was found in it a poor wise man and he delivered the city by his wisdom. Yet no one remembered that poor man."

The Scriptures actually record a historical example of almost exactly the scene which Solomon describes (II Samuel 20:14-22). As noted earlier in our study, it was a scene where King David's top general, Joab, was pursing Sheba, a man who had attempted to incite a rebellion against David after the defeat and death of David's rebellious son Absalom. The only difference between the scene which took place in the life of David's general Joab and the scene which Solomon describes for us in Ecclesiastes is the fact that the "poor wise man" in the real story was a **woman**. The city in question, Abel Beth-maacah, was no match for the forces of King David under Joab as he besieged it and proceeded to tear down its walls. But a single wise woman in the city used her wisdom to deliver the city. No one even knows what her name was - so (as Solomon said it would be) she didn't receive much glory for the wise thing she did in saving the city from certain destruction - but she demonstrated Solomon's point. There is greater value in one person's wisdom than in the power of kings and generals and armies, if wisdom is put to use.

How are you at putting wisdom to use? Have you ever used wisdom in your own life to protect yourself or those you loved from certain ruin?

II. An Assessment of Wisdom 9:16-18

As noted earlier, wisdom doesn't generally receive the attention it deserves in the world around us. Its highest praises are found in the pages of Scripture, where life's greatest values are seen most clearly.

A. Solomon's Comparison of Wisdom and Strength 9:16

1. Wisdom's Superiority to Strength 9:16a

"So I said, 'Wisdom is better than strength.'"

Virtually everyone admires strength. But there are things an unusually strong person can't do by brute strength which even a weakling can accomplish by making use of just a little wisdom. A large rock, for example, which even a very strong man can't move, can be moved by someone with only average strength by putting a fulcrum and a lever to good use.

2. Wisdom's Connection with Social Status 9:16b

" But the wisdom of the poor man is despised and his words are not heeded."

Unfortunately, for all of its value, people who possess wisdom, but who can't excel in some of the qualities society thinks are important, often go unappreciated by society at large. America, at the turn of the millennium, is well populated by common people who have far more practical wisdom in the important issues of life than many of its wealthy leaders in the nation's capital. In some cases their voices and common sense approach to life can be heard on conservative radio talk shows day after day, but most of them will never be well-known or highly admired because of American society's badly skewed values. They aren't rich or famous enough to get national attention.

B. Solomon's Comparison of Wisdom and Authority 9:17

"The words of the wise heard in quietness are better than the shouting of a ruler among fools."

People who rise to prominence in the community or the country are often heard in the public arena, because of their position of authority and visibility. But for all the noise they make, and all the followers they gain, many are seriously lacking in terms of their fitness to rule. Totalitarian rulers have frequently been charismatic leaders, often in the public eye - in spite of glaring faults in their viewpoints and their policies.

Adolph Hitler is just one of many who could be cited as a leader whose voice came to be heard and heeded by millions of people - people whose willingness to follow such leadership demonstrated their lack of wisdom. If such a man had been replaced by the quiet voices of people far less charismatic, but more sensible, what a different world we might have known! Dietrich Bonhoffer, on the other hand, made his views known through print after Hitler's forces took him from his pulpit and placed him in prison (where he was finally executed) - but had Bonhoffer's views prevailed in Germany there would probably have been no World War II!

C. Solomon's Comparison of Wisdom and Weapons 9:18

"Wisdom is better than weapons of war, but one sinner destroys much good."

The person who has most profoundly impacted our world was the personification of wisdom - the Lord Jesus Christ. His life and teaching have influenced more people than the military might of any person who has ever lived - in any place or in any age on the face of the earth!

As Solomon observes in the final line of the chapter, there have been many times in history when one person who has committed himself to folly, has created all kinds of destruction. From the approximate time of Christ, King Herod the Great of Judea is a man who has gone down in history as a brutal and destructive leader - one of whom someone observed that it would be safer to be Herod's pig than to be his son (because of Herod's habit of murdering family members).

But all the destructive genius of any evil ruler who has ever lived has not been a match for the unparalleled wisdom which characterized the life of Jesus, wisdom which profoundly changed the course of human history - and is still changing it today, and will yet change it in the future! As someone has put it (in the American Tract Society tract "The Incomparable Christ"):

Jesus never marshaled an army, nor drafted a soldier, nor fired a gun; and yet no leader ever had more volunteers who have, under His orders, made more rebels stack arms and surrender without a shot fired.

Though wisdom isn't always valued as it should be - especially if it comes from someone without much social status, wisdom has greater worth than power, authority, or weapons. Wisdom is more valuable than many of the things people prize most highly in life. So do you value wisdom as much as you should?

183

Complications of Foolishness
Ecclesiastes 10:1-7

Do you know who in the Bible has a name which, in the Hebrew language, means "fool"? If not, you will find the answer in I Samuel 25:25 where his wife, named Abigail, spoke to David concerning him: "Please do not let my lord pay attention to this worthless man, Nabal, for as his name is, so is he. Nabal is his name and folly is with him; but I your maidservant did not see the young men of my lord whom you sent."

While Abigail's description of her husband as "this worthless man" sounds like a very harsh assessment for a wife to make, the truth is (as the story of Nabal's actions in I Samuel 25 shows) that Abigail was simply speaking the truth! The fact that one of Nabal's servants had said the same thing about Nabal to Abigail earlier the same day reveals that Nabal's foolishness was a matter of public record!

Nabal was a wealthy rancher who owned numerous animals (3,000 sheep and 1,000 goats) - animals which were sometimes prey for both animal predators and human thieves. So, when David and his army of men - on the run from the anger of Israel's jealous King Saul - ended up in the wilderness of Paran (the area where Nabal's servants kept his animals), David and his men became to Nabal's servants and animals (in the words of one of the servants - I Samuel 25:16) "a wall . . . both by night and by day."

When David learned that Nabal's servants were shearing his sheep - an occasion which was often accompanied by a time of festivity and food - he sent ten of his six hundred men to bear his respectful greetings, and to ask Nabal to share some of his food with him and his men. But Nabal responded negatively and very rudely - with the result that, had it not been for the intervention of Nabal's wife Abigail, an intelligent, gracious and attractive woman, David would have led his army against Nabal and wiped out every man on his ranch!

Nabal is just one of many examples of the truth that folly has great potential for disrupting things as they ought to be. Had Nabal responded appreciatively and generously to David's request, he might easily have become a special friend of the future king of Israel and found himself in good stead for it. But, as it was, his foolish response almost cost him both is fortune and his life - to say nothing of the grief David would have experienced if he had gone ahead with his angry intent.

Have you seen how folly can turn a placid scene into disaster? It often does (as almost any day's news report will illustrate), and it doesn't take a great deal of folly to do it.

I. The Impact of Foolishness 10:1-4

A. The Weight of Folly 10:1

184

"Dead flies make a perfumer's oil stink, so a little foolishness is weightier than wisdom and honor."

I know very little about the art of the perfumer . But it would make sense that the ingredients (including oil) which are used in making perfume would need to be treated with care and kept as pure as possible. So the perfumer would need to take precautions to keep anything out of his formula which might compromise the process - including flies, which can easily get trapped in liquids, bringing impurities with them - even if they only set down briefly. More likely, though, they will land, get trapped, and die in the liquid, where their dirty little bodies putrefy the product.

The problems caused by flies in the hot climates of middle-eastern desert countries were so well-known in ancient times that the Arabic peoples built one of their proverbs around the issue: "A fly is nothing, yet it produces loathsomeness" [25]

And so it is with folly in our lives. It doesn't take much folly to compromise an otherwise commendable life. Years and years of skillful performance in life have many times been virtually negated by the discovery of very little folly in a person's life. Some of America's best-known and, in some cases, most skillful leaders (including spiritual leaders) have seen promising careers come crashing down over single significant indiscretions! Richard Nixon's powerful political career and influence were undone as a result of the Watergate break-in. In the sports and acting world, O.J. Simpson's brilliant record was called into question by the events of one evening!

No amount of wisdom and honor can withstand just one significant incidence of folly, so a person can't be too careful to stay away from even the appearance of folly!

B. The Direction of Folly 10:2

"A wise man's heart directs him toward the right, but the foolish man's heart directs him toward the left."

It can be shown that the Scriptures sometimes treat that which is on the right hand as positive and that which is on the left hand as negative. In His Olivet Discourse teaching on the judgment of the nations, Jesus pictures those on God's right hand entering His kingdom while those on God's left hand are sent away into eternal fire (Matthew 25:31-33)!

But Solomon builds his own case in this verse by telling us that the wise man's heart directs him toward the right. The Bible speaks so highly of wisdom that, wherever it directs, the people of God ought to be heading in that direction. Wisdom is definitely heading in the right direction.

---

[25] Ginsburg, quoted in the *Liberty Bible Commentary* (Lynchburg, VA: The Old Time Gospel Hour, 1982), p. 1277.

Cf. Proverbs 1:33
  "But he who listens to me [wisdom personified] shall live securely
  And will be at ease from the dread of evil."

Cf. Proverbs 8:32-35
  "Now therefore, O sons, listen to me [wisdom personified],
  For blessed are they who keep my ways.
  [33] Heed instruction and be wise,
  And do not neglect it.
  [34] Blessed is the man who listens to me,
  Watching daily at my gates,
  Waiting at my doorposts.
  [35] For he who finds me finds life
  And obtains favor from the Lord."

If a wise man's heart is directing him toward the right, then the foolish man's heart, which directs him to the left, is directing him the wrong way! So which direction is your heart directing you? Are you following its direction to the right, to the building up of your eternal soul, or to the left, to its destruction? Unfortunately, if you are heading to the left it will probably become obvious to everyone who comes across your path.

C. The Demonstration of Folly 10:3

"Even when the fool walks along the road, his sense is lacking and he demonstrates to everyone that he is a fool."

The fool's behavior soon marks him so profoundly that he cannot conceal his folly, so it is evident to everyone who meets him that he is on the wrong path! For example, I hadn't been living in Tucson, Arizona very long before I met a man named Roger. He stopped by my study at the church building, and it was obvious from the time I first met him that he was not on the path to the right! He was always unkempt; he was almost always intoxicated; he was often foul-mouthed; he boasted of behavior that he should have been embarrassed to reveal; his conversation revealed that he had often heard the truth of the Gospel, but his behavior revealed that he had never embraced it.

Because Roger's behavior was so obviously and outrageously foolish - so often and for such a long period of time - my family came to recognize him, and could not drive past him walking along the road without commenting on the sadness of his condition. And because he sometimes arrived at the church building in his sad state during church services, people of our church came to recognize him as well. It is very sad to see people whose lives are so marked by folly that folly is on public display, like a billboard - for all who pass by to see.

Unfortunately, not all whose lives are marked by folly are people of no influence or status in

186

society.

D. The Response to Folly 10:4

"If the ruler's temper rises against you, do not abandon your position, because composure allays great offenses."

If the ruler's temper were rising for good cause, Solomon would be instructing us differently. He would be instructing us to do the wise thing - correct our own folly and submit to rightful authority. But the advice Solomon gives us clues us in to the fact that he has in mind a situation where the ruler's temper is rising without cause on our part. I worked, for example, during my early months as a seminary student, for a man who was often at odds with his employees, in very demonstrable ways, with very little cause. I remember watching him in amazement as he chewed out a new employee - a young boy - for failing to do something he hadn't yet been trained to do!

If we are unfortunate enough to find ourselves under the authority of a "ruler" - any authority figure in our lives - who has an unruly temper, Solomon's wise counsel is: don't panic - just because he/she may be in a state of apparent panic. A common response when someone in authority gets upset is to get out from under the unpleasant pressure of the situation by "abandoning" our "position" (running away from home; dropping out of a class; quitting the job; getting out of the marriage; etc.). But, rather than allowing someone's unruly temper to become our undoing, Solomon's advice is: maintain your composure, because composure in the face of an ugly temper "allays great offenses" (literally "quiets great sins").

How are you at dealing with foolishness? When it is seen in the life of someone who is in authority over you, can you maintain your composure in the face of folly long enough to see if the folly will settle down? And how about the folly in your own life? Are you mindful of the fact that it only takes a little folly to spoil an otherwise commendable life?

Because folly is so destructive, it ought to be eliminated. But the sad fact of life on a sin-cursed earth is that it is often exalted instead!

II. The Exaltation of Foolishness 10:5-7

A. The Seriousness of Exalted Folly 10:5

"There is an evil I have seen under the sun, like an error which goes forth from the ruler—"

Solomon again (as in verse 4) has in mind the behavior of people in authority - the realm in which, because he was a king, he himself lived and moved.

Because they are in positions of authority, rulers ought to be especially careful not to promote what is foolish. So many people can be adversely affected in the process! But, as he surveyed life "under the sun" - with the Lord out of the picture of human experience - Solomon witnessed as one of life's evils (an evil which even rulers are guilty of) the exaltation of folly in a variety of ways.

B. Illustrations of Exalted Folly 10:6-7

1. Folly Exalted Over Riches 10:6

" . . . folly is set in many exalted places while rich men sit in humble places."

From his earthly perspective, it seemed to Solomon that people who are rich should be acknowledged for their wealth by placing them in "exalted places." Though we know that not all rich people are good people or capable people, it is generally true that people who have significant wealth have done something well in life in order to obtain their wealth and/or to retain their wealth. So, if they have done well, it would seem that they should be recognized for their abilities by placing them in positions of influence and authority.

What Solomon saw happening - often enough that it merited his comment in this passage - was people who were foolish being exalted to places of influence over people who had earned his respect, because they had gained or retained wealth by their wise behavior. A modern example of such exalted folly which comes to mind was the elevation of Joycelyn Elders to authority as U.S. Surgeon General during the Clinton administration - until it became too embarrassing to retain her because she couldn't "keep her foot out of her mouth."

Though the Bible is clear in its witness that people who possess wealth are not to be trusted simply because they possess wealth (James 5:1-5, for example), it is also true that people who are foolish should not be exalted above people who are wealthy just to spite the wealthy!

2. Slavery Exalted Over Nobility 10:7

"I have seen slaves riding on horses and princes walking like slaves on the land."

It would have been a very rare thing in Solomon's day to find a slave riding on a horse or a prince walking like a slave. Slaves weren't likely to earn enough to own a horse, and their masters weren't likely to take the chance that putting them on a horse would make them soft and lazy - or arrogant and unruly. Princes, on the other hand, were likely to enjoy enough in terms of material benefit that they wouldn't need to walk like a slave, but could travel on animals or in horse-drawn conveyances.

So what Solomon tells us he saw - slaves on horses and princes on foot - was out of conformity with the social norms of his day, and any time social norms are set aside it is likely to be because something is amiss.

188

Solomon reiterates the truth of this verse in a similar verse in Proverbs 19:10: "Luxury is not fitting for a fool; Much less for a slave to rule over princes." Luxury is not fitting for a fool because luxury has to be managed well in order to be maintained, and a fool does not have the capacity to manage luxury. And it is not fitting for a slave to rule over princes, because ruling well requires skills which slaves have not normally had the opportunity to develop.

Under normal circumstances in Solomon's day, a "slave" did not receive many privileges in life - like education and wealth and independence. This tended to put slaves - whatever their inherent ability - in the lower ranks of society on a rather permanent basis. They could accumulate little or nothing of material wealth, they were not likely to receive much education, they had little opportunity to know and associate with people of influence, and they were often stuck with menial tasks for much of their life. As a result, they had little opportunity to become highly skilled at anything of importance.

Princes, on the other hand, enjoyed the best life had to offer. They grew up in royal dwellings, received educational advantages (often with specialized training to prepare them for leadership), enjoyed and learned to manage wealth, and associated with people of influence. Generally speaking they were exposed to every opportunity which would prepare them for significant leadership roles and positions of influence.

To take a slave, then, - totally unprepared for the decisions and trappings of royalty - and try to make him a ruler would be a very foolish thing to do. A palace, a royal robe, and a scepter don't qualify just anyone to be and perform well as a king! So to treat him as a king would be folly - just as it would be folly to treat a prince like a slave. And a little folly can lead people in the wrong direction - and even disrupt society.

We have probably all seen people who followed folly in the wrong direction to their harm or even destruction. And we have probably all seen disruption in society because of the folly of putting the wrong people in the wrong places! Such an act is folly, and folly has great potential for disrupting things as they ought to be.

It only takes a fly or two to ruin a great batch of perfume! So the person who is wise will make every effort to keep on the path which goes to the right, not the left (i.e. the wrong). Are you alert to the destructive potential of folly in our society? In your own life?

189

The Challenges of Chance and Conversation
Ecclesiastes 10:8-14

Because we never know what will be around the next corner, it makes good sense to take the corners of our lives with care.

I headed for our church building one evening, looking forward to practicing with the choir. I rounded a corner in the road to find a line of traffic on a road where there is little reason to expect congestion. It took much longer than normal to get to the traffic light ahead where I was going to make a right turn. When I got to the signal I was facing a forced right turn, because of an overturned vehicle in the intersection. No problem (for me) - a right turn was the turn I wanted to make. But when I made my right turn I discovered that I was in another line of backed up traffic - in another place where there is little reason to expect congestion. Creeping along slowly to the next signal, where I wanted to go straight, I was directed by police in the intersection to make a left turn, because there were emergency vehicles on the road just past the signal (where our church building was located). Taking a circuitous route, eventually coming back to the church building from the opposite direction (quite late, by now, for choir practice), I discovered that the emergency vehicles were there to fight a fire at our church building! So, needless to say, choir practice was cancelled.

In everything we do, and in all the things we say, we are constantly dealing with life's uncertainties, so we need wisdom to make the most of life's chances and conversations. How sensitive are you to your need for wisdom in the things you do and say?

I. The Challenges of Chance 10:8-9

A. The Chance Fall 10:8a

"He who digs a pit may fall into it . . ."

There are many reasons why a person might want to dig a pit. I used to dig them for fun as a child - to create "forts" and hideouts and places to play. But digging pits becomes a necessary part of life for those who make their living in landscaping and construction and warfare, and so forth.

Once a pit is dug it becomes a potential hazzard for anyone who does not treat it with adequate care. My father had occasion one evening to carry me, as a young child, from our house to the house of one of our neighbors. To save steps, he carried me across an empty lot next door instead of rounding the corner on the paved road - only to discover (too late - in the dark) that the lot next door contained several of the "forts" I had built with some of my neighborhood friends, so we fell into one of them, and then (as I recall) another one, cutting across the lot.

Though pits are sometimes necessary, they always create a certain amount of risk - even for

190

the person who dug them, if he isn't careful enough when he is around them!

B. The Chance Bite 10:8b

" . . . and a serpent may bite him who breaks through a wall."

Anytime we place our hands where we can't see all that surrounds them we are in danger of being injured. If you have never broken through a wall and been bitten by a serpent you got too close to without seeing it, you may have been bitten, or otherwise injured, by something beyond your vision which you touched and shouldn't have touched - like the cactus plant I touched one day when I was trying to clean weeds out from under some shrubs in the back yard.

It is just one of the facts of life that we sometimes need to reach beyond what we can see, and anytime we do we are in danger of reaching something we didn't want to reach. It is simply one of the chances we live with in life as we know it.

C. The Chance Crushing 10:9a

"He who quarries stones may be hurt by them . . ."

Working with stones, like many other kinds of work, has its occupational hazzards. Solomon pictures someone who is quarrying stones - digging up and moving large rocks, probably so they can be put to use in some other location (as when Solomon had his men quarry stones from the Judean wilderness to be used in the construction of the temple in Jerusalem). Who of us, while working around rocks, haven't had one roll over and mash a finger or a toe or bruise a shin - even though few if any of us have ever worked in a rock quarry.

There is almost nothing we do on earth which doesn't offer the potential of some kind of accident or injury - so working with rocks is just another illustration of the chances we all face from day to day as a part of life.

D. The Chance Striking 10:9b

" . . . and he who splits logs may be endangered by them."

Every time a woodsman swings his axe in an attempt to split a log, he faces a variety of possibilities. The log may be too solid to accept his axe head - causing it to turn with a twisting force or to bounce back toward him. The log may be too soft to keep his axe from plunging through unexpectedly and heading for his foot or his leg. The log may splinter and send pieces of wood flying his direction, endangering any part of his body they should strike.

Whatever we are doing in life - whether digging pits or reaching through broken walls or working with rocks or splitting logs (or any of a "million and one" other things) - there are

191

chances we take that things won't turn out the way we thought and hoped they would turn out.

None of us fully control the circumstances of our lives - no matter how much we would like to control them. But there are things we can do to improve the prospects and reduce the risks in trying to accomplish whatever it is that we are trying to accomplish. So it is the better part of wisdom to think ahead and try to anticipate the eventualities of our lives to the best of our ability.

II. The Advantages of Wisdom 10:10-11

A. The Wisdom of the Woodsman 10:10a

"If the axe is dull and he does not sharpen its edge, then he must exert more strength."

Anyone who has worked at cutting wood has probably discovered, in the process, that it makes quite a difference whether our tools are in good condition or not, and used correctly or not. You may have heard about the man who needed to cut some trees for fire wood and purchased a chain saw, which someone told him could be expected to cut several cords of wood in a day. When he wasn't able to cut as much as he thought he should, he took the saw back to the shop to ask why it didn't perform as it should - and was surprised at the sound the saw made when the proprietor started up the motor! And it is only a little more work to try to cut wood with a chain saw which isn't running than to try to cut wood with a chain saw which is running, but has a dull blade!

Some of us are so anxious to get the wood cut that we don't want to take the time to sit down and sharpen the axe. So we have to work twice as hard and take twice as long to do half as much work because we don't apply wisdom to the process - whatever it is in life we are trying to accomplish.

B. The Success of Wisdom 10:10b

"Wisdom has the advantage of giving success."

Wisdom is the skill which causes a person to think through all the issues involved and to address them properly in the process of doing whatever it is he or she is trying to do. As we have seen before in our study of Ecclesiastes, the word "wisdom" (*chokmah*) is the word which was used to describe Bezalel, the son of Uri, and Oholiab, the son of Ahisamach - the craftsmen who did, or who supervised, the work of constructing the tabernacle in the wilderness in the days of Moses. These men were chosen by the Lord because He had given them the "wisdom"(skill) "to make designs for working in gold and in silver and in bronze, and in the cutting of stones for settings and in the carving of wood, so as to perform in every inventive work" (Exodus 35:32-33).

Whether we are building a tabernacle in the wilderness of Judea, with all of its furnishings, or we are trying to choose the best path for ourselves in some area of life, or trying to provide good leadership for our families or our church or our community or our nation or our world - "wisdom has the advantage of giving success." So what is the level of our commitment to wisdom? How committed are we to doing what we do as well as it can be done?

If we want to be as successful as we can be, we have no other choice than to pursue wisdom, because wisdom is the pathway to success. Though there are other ways to do things (the woodsman **can** chop down a tree with a dull axe if he keeps at it long enough), the alternative to the way of wisdom will always be more difficult, and will always be less productive than it needs to be!

Solomon offers another illustration.

C. The Wisdom of the Charmer 10:11

"If the serpent bites before being charmed, there is no profit for the charmer."

There are certain movements which someone skilled in dealing with snakes can make which get the snake's attention and exert a measure of control over the snake's actions - or so I have heard (because I have very little experience at charming snakes). So if the snake handler fails to approach the snake with just the right movements, and the snake doesn't fall under his control soon enough in the process, the snake handler may get bitten - after which it may well be too late to care whether the snake gets charmed or not. One bite from a deadly cobra is all it takes to make a snake charmer's skills or lack of skills a moot point!

Because our lives bring us face to face with "the serpent of old, who is the devil and Satan" (Revelation 20:2), in a life and death contest, it is very important that we commit ourselves to the pursuit of God's wisdom. Without God's wisdom in our lives, our fall into the "pit" Solomon mentioned in verse eight could be the pit of hell! Without God's wisdom in our lives, the bite of the serpent Solomon mentioned in verse eight could become the bite of the "serpent of old" himself - with far greater reason for concern than just some medical concerns.

Though we can get through life with very little of God's wisdom, we won't do it with the satisfaction and success He wants to give us if we will only commit ourselves to pursuing His wisdom in everything we do - and in everything we say, which presents a challenge all its own.

III. The Challenges of Words 10:12-14a

The apostle James assures us that there is no area of our lives which is more difficult to keep fully in check than the words we speak. As he writes in James 3:2, "For we all stumble in many ways. If anyone does not stumble in what he says, he is a perfect man, able to bridle the whole body as well." Just as it is in our best interests to apply wisdom in other areas of our lives, if we want to be successful, so it is in our best interests to apply wisdom to the words we speak.

193

A. Words of the Wise Man 10:12a

"Words from the mouth of a wise man are gracious . . ."

God's goal for our lives is that, in everything we do, we be involved in the process of building people up. So, if we want our words to be wise words, they need to be words which build people up - "gracious words" (as Solomon puts it in this verse).

Jesus undoubtedly spoke gracious words, because the apostle John tells us that those who saw His glory saw "glory as of the only begotten from the Father, full of **grace** and truth" (John 1:14). Even the enemies of Jesus testified that no one ever spoke as He spoke - well-chosen words of truth which communicated without condemning.

Do you think people would characterize your words as the "gracious" words of wisdom? Hopefully they wouldn't characterize your words as the words of a fool - in view of the destructive force they have.

B. Words of the Fool 10:12b-14a

1. They Consume 10:12b

" . . . while the lips of a fool consume him;"

Not even the fool himself is safe from the destructive impact of his words. He speaks and his words not only "consume" but they "consume **him**." The man Nabal (whom we have met earlier in our study) is a man whose name (*nabal*) means "fool" (though it is a different word for "fool" than Solomon uses in this verse - *kesil*). Nabal was a man who, by the words he spoke to the servants of David (I Samuel 25), almost brought upon himself and his household a military style disaster. It was averted only because he had a wife whose words were gracious.

2. They Deteriorate 10:13

" . . . the beginning of his talking is folly and the end of it is wicked madness."

Some people see, as they speak, the negative effect their words are having and soften their words so they will not be so destructive and incendiary. But the fool starts out speaking his normal folly, sees the negative effect his words are having upon those who hear them, and turns his conversation in a downward direction rather than up. When Ahab, for example, was confronted by the prophet Micaiah - who first mocked the foolish king by telling him what he wanted to hear - Ahab flew into a fit of rage and sent the righteous prophet back to the dungeon on a diet of bread and water, as evidence of the wicked madness which filled his foolish heart!

3. They Multiply 10:14a

194

"Yet the fool multiplies words."

Solomon tells us, in Proverbs 15:2 that "The tongue of the wise makes knowledge acceptable, But the mouth of fools spouts folly." Because he likes to hear himself talk, convinced as he is that he is the only one who has anything worthwhile to say, once a fool gets his mouth going you can expect to wait a long time before anything or anyone can slow it down!

The words of a fool, for all their volume (both in terms of noise and number), will never bring any success because (as Solomon has assured us in verse ten) it is wisdom which "has the advantage of giving success."

Are our words wise words, as evidenced by their graciousness? They will have to be if we are going to enjoy a productive future - with all of the future's normal uncertainties.

IV. The Uncertainty of the Future 10:14b

"No man knows what will happen, and who can tell him what will come after him?"

It is only the Lord who is able to see around the next bend in the road of our lives. No matter how wise or foolish a man might be, life at best is uncertain - with both good and evil coming unannounced into the lives of both the good and the evil among men. Jesus told His disciples, in His "sermon on the Mount" (Matthew 5:45) that the Lord "causes His sun to rise on the evil and the good, and sends rain on the righteous and the unrighteous," so it may be either sunny or rainy on any one of us - whether wise or foolish, evil or good, righteous or unrighteous.

The uncertainties of life and the power of words make it imperative that we live as wisely as we can. We need wisdom to make the most of life's chances and conversations. Are the chances and the conversations of your life characterized by wisdom?

195

Whatever a Man Sows
Ecclesiastes 10:15-20

The apostle Paul stated a timeless principle which has broad significance in understanding the complexities of life when he wrote, in Galatians 6:7: "Do not be deceived, God is not mocked; for whatever a man sows, this he will also reap."

Paul had just stated, in Galatians 6:6, that "The one who is taught the word is to share all good things with the one who teaches him," so he was (among other things) encouraging Christians to sow their material blessings on behalf of their teachers in Christ. But he went on in Galatians 6:8 to broaden out the application of the verse when he said: "For the one who sows to his own flesh will from the flesh reap corruption, but the one who sows to the Spirit will from the Spirit reap eternal life."

Jesus Himself would be the clearest illustration of this truth in its broader application. How much sowing did Jesus do to His flesh (i.e. how much did he cater to fleshly desires and how much did He accumulate to Himself in terms of material things)? And how much did He sow to the Spirit (i.e. how much of His time and energies and abilities did He yield up to the Holy Spirit)? And what did He reap as a result? Because Jesus never sowed to the flesh, He left behind virtually no physical trace of His existence - no address; no estate; no physical family; not even a body in a tomb! But His Spirit-led life has transformed and is still transforming lives among the hundreds of millions of people who have followed Him, and who will worship Him forever as the recipients of the eternal life He gave them as His legacy!

We can play a major role in determining the outcome (reaping) of our lives if we will be careful about what we put into our lives (sowing) - whether we are thinking in terms of labor or leadership or diligence or luxury or the words we speak or any of a long list of other things. I mention labor and leadership and diligence and luxuries and the words we speak in the context of the things we sow because these are the things which Solomon addresses in the passage before us in Ecclesiastes - a passage which offers little in terms of a common theme from verse to verse except the thought that we generally reap what we sow, whatever we are doing in life.

Life's fortunes are influenced by many factors - most of which we can control. So what are the things you are sowing in your life going to bring in terms of the harvest - short term and long term? We would do well to think of the control we are exercising in a wide variety of responsibilities and opportunities in life - or we could find ourselves in the shoes of the fool mentioned in verse fifteen.

I. The Weariness of the Fool's Toil 10:15

"The toil of a fool so wearies him that he does not even know how to go to a city."

Toil has a way of causing weariness for anyone who engages in it, so you don't have to be a fool to become weary as a result of toil! But the toil of a "fool" is more wearisome than toil in general because he is a fool. Solomon's word for "fool" comes from a Hebrew verb (*kasal*) which means "to be or become stupid," so it (*kesil*) describes a "stupid fellow" or a "dullard." He is not mentally deficient by reason of his birth. Though he could do much better if he really wanted to, he has chosen to be stupid because that is his preference!

Northern Israel's King Ahab is probably a good example. He may well have been as bright and capable as any of the righteous kings of Judah, but his life amounted to little of lasting significance because he chose to leave the Lord out of his life - sowing foolish choices (e.g., his foolish choice of a wife, foolish worship, foolish wars) and reaping corrupt consequences.

In his commentary on Proverbs, Derek Kidner has commented on this particular kind of fool with the following observation:

> The root of his trouble is spiritual, not mental. He likes his folly, going back to it "like a dog that returns to his vomit" (26:11); he has no reverence for truth, preferring comfortable illusions . . . At bottom, what he is rejecting is the fear of the Lord (1:29): it is this that constitutes him a fool, and this that makes his complacency tragic; for "the careless ease of fools shall destroy them" (1:32).[26]

Because work is foreign to his mind-set, when he actually gets around to doing some work it wears him out so completely that he can't even get back to town! So picture a foolish farm-hand in Solomon's day, making his way out of town to spend a day of work on one of the many farms surrounding the cities of ancient Israel - then spending the night in the country because the work he did (which may have been precious little, at that) left him too little energy to make his way back into town!

Those who don't discipline themselves to work hard easily run out of steam when there is work to be done - even just a little work. And those in positions of leadership who don't discipline themselves to the demands of leadership don't lead any better than the foolish worker who wipes himself out by what he does.

II. The Results of Different Kinds of Leadership 10:16-17

A. The Woe of a Land with Young and Dissolute Leadership 10:16

"Woe to you, O land, whose king is a lad and whose princes feast in the morning."

The role of a king (or any person in leadership) makes demands which not everyone is qualified to carry out. Generally speaking, the responsibilities of leading a nation require skills which are learned best by those who have been around a few years to learn them. As we have

---

[26] Derek Kidner, *Proverbs* (London: Inter-Varsity Press, 1964), p. 40.

seen before, when Solomon followed his father David as king of Israel, he was very sensitive to the fact that he lacked the understanding his father had gained over his many years as king. So, when the Lord gave him the opportunity to ask for anything he would like to have, he pleased the Lord by asking for understanding to be a good leader of his nation.

Any nation is likely to find itself in trouble if it is lead by a king who is too young and inexperienced to understand the complexities of the issues his nation faces. When Judah installed seven-year-old King Jehoash (Joash) they were fortunate that he had righteous Jehoida, the priest, to instruct him (II Kings 11:17), or the nation could have been in for difficult days. Imagine how things would have gone for the nation if Solomon's imaginary scenario had been the order of the day in Jehoash's reign - if the king's greatest concern had been his breakfast menu, and he had gathered around him a group of seven-year-old playmates who joined him each morning at 8:30 for a royal breakfast feast in the palace banquet room.

B. The Blessing of a Land with Noble and Dignified Leadership 10:17

"Blessed are you, O land, whose king is of nobility and whose princes eat at the appropriate time—for strength and not for drunkenness."

The suggestion that a land ought to have a king who comes from nobility might sound a little too elitist for twenty-first century American ears. But the reality is that, in ancient times, the families of kings had the resources many other families lacked to provide training for the children of the family who were likely to ascend to the throne.

Because a young king might use the resources of his realm to satisfy his own desires, it would be far better for the nation to crown a king with a rich background of training and some practical experience, and to see him choose mature and experienced counselors with enough sense to regulate their diet of food, and other appetites, with the best interests of the nation in mind.

As it is with individuals, so it is with nations - that what is sown will determine what is reaped!

III. The Problems of Inattention to Duty 5:18

"Through indolence the rafters sag, and through slackness the house leaks."

The rafters which hold up any roof in the world are subject to the forces of gravity and the degenerative impact of entropy, so it becomes necessary from time to time to reinforce them or replace them to keep the roof in good shape. If sagging rafters are not tended when they need tending, it will be only a matter of time before the sagging opens leaks up in the roof (and probably the walls) - so it is important that things like rafters be watched for signs of trouble.

Of course, rafters are just one of a million and one examples of things in our lives which need

198

to be tended if we don't want trouble in our lives. Our communities, for example, are full of homes where the rafters are in good shape, but where the families who live beneath them are under pressures of other kinds which are threatening to destroy, or actually are destroying, the families and the individual members who make them up - all because of the indolence of those who should be exercising wise leadership for the family.

Life is full of issues where indolence needs to be addressed by diligence, or we can expect to reap the proverbial whirlwind as a result of our inattention to opportunity and to duty. Are you careful enough to do what needs to be done when it needs to be done that you are keeping yourself out of "deep weeds"?   And does your attention to duty allow enough time for enough pleasure to give your life a sense of proper balance?

IV. The Pleasures and Profits of Life 10:19

"Men prepare a meal for enjoyment, and wine makes life merry, and money is the answer to everything."

One of the gracious provisions the Lord has given to take some of the drudgery out of life on a sin-cursed earth is food - along with the benefit and the pleasure which comes out of both the physical nourishment and the social interaction a good meal often allows. Even a good meal eaten alone provides a reprieve from other activities in our lives - and a meal eaten in company with others often more than doubles the pleasure and the benefit of a good meal.

Solomon's comments about wine making life merry could easily be misunderstood in our day and age and society. Wine, of course, was a regular part of the diet of most of the people of Israel (as it has been down through the centuries for many of the people of earth). But in the days before distillation, wine didn't have near the alcohol content that modern wines can have. It did have enough alcohol, though, to serve as a stimulant - giving a feeling of relief and merriment to ease the tensions of the day. Even the many Christians today who do not use alcoholic beverages often enjoy the refreshment which comes from beverages with lesser stimulants than alcohol - especially caffeine. For many people, a glass of iced tea or a cup of hot tea or coffee or a soft drink with dinner adds a refreshing touch to a good meal.

Anything in life not improved by a good meal and a refreshing drink should be covered by Solomon's comment that "money is the answer to everything." Though money isn't the answer to everything, there are many people who seem to believe that it is, so Solomon is apparently playing along with their line of thinking. As the Quest Study Bible indicates in its note on this verse,

There may be a note of sarcasm in the Teacher's voice [in his comment about money being the answer for everything in verse 19]. Throughout this book he has taught that there is no answer for anything. On the other hand, though, lots of money would help anyone

199

searching for pleasure in an attempt to escape life's harsh realities."[27]

Most of us can see the humor in Tevya's song, "If I Were a Rich Man" in the musical "Fiddler on the Roof," when he whimsically asks the Lord if it would ruin His grand design for the universe to make him a rich man - instead of the poor man he is in the play. Even though the Scriptures warn us not to make money the supreme good in our pursuit of life, we are all aware that it doesn't hurt to have enough to meet our needs, and just a little more to afford a few pleasures in life.

Though few of us are gourmet chefs or financial "wizards," we can see the value of good food and drinks and a balanced checking account, with some savings on the side, to pursue such sources of enrichment in our lives! We can improve our lives and the lives of those around us in such practical matters as food and finances, and we can improve our lives by the careful use of our tongue as well.

V. The Illusiveness of Private Words 10:20

"Furthermore, in your bedchamber do not curse a king, and in your sleeping rooms do not curse a rich man, for a bird of the heavens will carry the sound and the winged creature will make the matter known."

The Bible warns us numerous times of the troubles our tongues can get us into. The book of Proverbs is full of pointed sayings about the tongue, and the book of James contains the classic New Testament passage on the subject in the opening twelve verses of the third chapter.

Solomon reminds us in this verse that even the words we speak in private places have a way of making their way out into the open. The words the wicked man Haman in the book of Esther, for example, shared in the privacy of his own home with his wife and close friends, came back to haunt him when he was discovered and confronted by King Xerxes - and his words were a part of the plot of the story which resulted in his death!

Though birds don't actually convey our private words to others, it might seem as if they do at times when words we have spoken come back to haunt us in the most inopportune times. When Israel's jealous King Saul was pursuing David, David was warned by his wife Michael (Saul's daughter) to save his life by fleeing from his home (I Samuel 19:11-17). When Saul sent men to capture David and found his bed occupied by a household idol and some goat's hair, Saul had some harsh words for Michael on the basis of what he surmised she must have said to her husband (as if the king had learned it from a "bird of the heavens").

Most of us have probably learned the hard way that ill-advised words can get us into a lot more trouble than we would like to be in. So we can't be too careful in the choice of our words -

---

[27] *The Quest Study Bible* (Grand Rapids, MI: The Zondervan Corporation, 1994), p. 923.

200

just as we can't be too careful in guarding the other things we sow in this life in view of the coming harvest we anticipate. The outcome of a person's life is influenced by whether he is foolish or not, serious or not, diligent or not, wealthy or not, and talkative or not. And, of course, each of these matters is largely in our hands!

Life's fortunes are influenced by many factors - most of which we can control. So what is your investment in life going to bring as your life's outcome? When you work, do you do your job like a fool or a wise person? When you lead, do you pursue your personal pleasure or the welfare of those in your care? Do you exercise diligence in maintaining the affairs of your life? Do you mix life's responsibilities with a healthy balance of pleasure? And are you careful, even in the privacy of your own home and room, to say nothing you wouldn't want to hear repeated in public?

In every area of our lives, what we sow in time will determine what we reap - all the way into eternity!

201

Succeeding in An Uncertain World
Ecclesiastes 11:1-6

The pages of human history are filled with the stories of people who made their lives count for good in spite of some difficult obstacles. The story of Abraham Lincoln has often been told. Lincoln once said, "I do the very best I know how - the very best I can; and I mean to keep doing so." His life is the best example of his own words -

1831- failed in business
1832 - defeated for legislature
1833 - again failed in business
1834 - elected to legislature
1835 - sweetheart died
1836 - had nervous breakdown
1838 - defeated for speaker
1840 - defeated for elector
1843 - defeated for congress
1846 - elected to Congress
1848 - defeated for Congress
1855 - defeated for Senate
1856 - defeated for Vice-President
1858 - defeated for Senate
1860 - ELECTED PRESIDENT.[28]

No one born into this life can ever be certain about what life will bring, so we are all faced daily with the challenge of making the most of the circumstances which we find before us - knowing (if we have an "above the sun" perspective) that the Lord is at work behind the scenes to reward those who seek to make the most of life's opportunities.

Success comes to those who, recognizing God's sovereignty, give life their best effort. Is this the approach you are taking in living out the years of your life? In spite of life's uncertainties, are you making the most of the opportunities which come your way each day?

As he nears the conclusion of his interesting search for meaning in life - a search which has focused primarily on life as we find it "under the sun" (without God at front and center, as He should be) - Solomon shares some of his thoughts on what it takes to be successful in an uncertain world.

I. Making Life's Investments 11:1-2

---

[28] Paul Lee Tan, *Encyclopedia of 7,700 Illustrations* (Rockville, MD: Assurance Publishers, 1979), p.1373, #6141.

202

A. Giving Generously 11:1

"Cast your bread on the surface of the waters, for you will find it after many days."

If you take a literal piece of bread and throw into the water, of course, it will become soggy and disintegrate and disappear - probably to be eaten by some creature of the waters. So Solomon is probably not thinking about literally casting bread into the water, but of taking your resources (pictured by bread, which Americans call the "staff of life") and spreading them around - whether as investments or as gifts.

Some interpreters have suggested that Solomon is thinking of the challenge, which was his, of sending resources to various places around the world by means of ocean-going vessels, and hoping to receive a good return on your goods in time. So the NASB Study Bible note on this verse advises: "Be adventurous, like those who accept the risks and reap the benefits of seaborne trade. Do not always play it safe."[29]

Whether you are investing your income or exercising philanthropy, the day will come when there will be some reward for what you have done! For example, take some money and invest it in a three-month Certificate of Deposit and, three months later, you will be entitled to your investment plus some interest - so it will come back to you in greater quantity than you invested. Or give some of your money away (or your time or energy or talent, etc.) to someone who is experiencing a need in their life, and you will deepen the ties that bind you together in this life and further their well-being and receive reward in heaven - whether you ever get your money back (or receive repayment in kind) or not!

No one who hopes to make their life count for good in the lives of others can do it by keeping to himself and keeping what he has to himself. It needs to be invested in others in some way in order to bring its maximum return.

B. Investing Broadly 11:2

"Divide your portion to seven, or even to eight, for you do not know what misfortune may occur on the earth."

The person who puts all of his "eggs" in the same basket is increasing the likelihood that he will run into difficulty and lose all of his "eggs." Whether we are talking about all of your money in the same investment, or concentrating all of your attention on a single person, or spending all of your time in a single activity, the likelihood of rich reward is diminished for those who don't build diversity into their lives.

It is wise to spread around what we have and what we do so that, if failure comes in one

---

[29] *NASB Study Bible* (Grand Rapids, MI: Zondervan Publishing House, 1999), p. 945.

investment or one area of our lives, we may be blessed with success in another. When Solomon suggests that you divide your portion to "seven, or even to eight," he is suggesting that you diversify your investments as broadly as you can so that you are protected (as much as possible) from the possibility that "misfortune may occur on the earth." A fire may wipe out your house; an accident may destroy your car; a thief may steal your jewelry; a scandal may take your bonds; a crash may evaporate your stocks - but all of these events are unlikely to happen at the same time!

No matter how carefully we try to guard against them, life is full of misfortunes which can undo what we are trying to accomplish in one or more areas of our lives, so it is in our best interests to have broad interests and broad contacts so that misfortune in one area of our lives doesn't finish us off!

II. Facing Life's Realities 11:3-4

A. Recognizing Predictables 11:3

"If the clouds are full, they pour out rain upon the earth; and whether a tree falls toward the south or toward the north, wherever the tree falls, there it lies."

A cloud can only contain so much moisture before it is inevitable that it is going to produce precipitation. So we need to plan for some rain in our lives when the clouds overhead reach the saturation point. Whether we are talking about the welcome rains which a farmer needs to water his crops, or the unwelcome rains which spoil a picnic or cause a flood - into each life some rain is going to fall, so we need to plan our lives with that eventuality in mind.

Every tree is eventually going to succumb to the process of deterioration and the force of gravity and come crashing down. We may be unsure whether it will fall toward the south or toward the north - but eventually it will fall, and once it falls there can be no undoing what has taken place. If it falls to the south, here's hoping that isn't where you built your house, because a falling tree is no respecter of persons - or of houses! "Wherever the tree falls, there it lies"! But if it falls south and crushes your house, you have some wood with which to begin rebuilding - so that is the thing to do.

Charles Ryrie's comment on this verse is: "There is an inevitable sequence and finality in many of life's events."[30] So we need to prepare, as best we can, for what is eventually going to happen, without allowing the possible to result in paralysis in our lives.

B. Avoiding Extreme Caution 11:4

---

[30] Charles Caldwell Ryrie, *Ryrie Study Bible,* Expanded Edition, (Chicago, IL: Moody Press, 1995), p. 1029.

204

"He who watches the wind will not sow and he who looks at the clouds will not reap."

Because of the possibility that it might be windy, the farmer might decide not to sow his crops. And because of the possibility that it might rain the farmer might decide not to harvest his crops. And so his life might be rendered unfruitful for his failure to do what he might have done if he wasn't paralyzed by the possibilities of the weather. Though I have never farmed, I observed the challenges farmers live with when I lived in Oregon and saw farmers - in a place where rains come frequently - try to decide when to do their haying. If a farmer cut his hay, and rain came while it was lying in the field, he could lose, or significantly diminish the quality of, his crop. But if he didn't cut his hay for fear that it might rain, he might never cut it - and have no hay to sell or feed to his livestock.

We cannot be successful in our lives if we aren't willing to face some of the risks which are built into our existence. Nothing we do in life will be without some element of risk, but the person who is unwilling to take some risks will end up doing nothing! Human beings have no other choice than to take some risks in this life where, "nothing ventured, nothing gained," because only the Lord knows all of the eventualities of our lives.

III. Dealing with Providence 11:5-6

A. Acknowledging Sovereignty 11:5

"Just as you do not know the path of the wind and how bones are formed in the womb of the pregnant woman, so you do not know the activity of God who makes all things."

There are many things which take place in life which are known only to the Lord - like the path of the wind, or how bones are formed in the womb of the pregnant woman. The providential dealings of the Lord, which encompass every facet of our lives, are beyond our knowledge and control. So we need to trust Him to do what is best for us, and then make the most of whatever it is that He does!

As Solomon challenged his son in the familiar words of Proverbs 3:5,6:

> Trust in the Lord with all your heart
> And do not lean on your own understanding.
> [6] In all your ways acknowledge Him,
> And He will make your paths straight.

And we have the comforting assurance of Paul's words in Romans 8:28:

> And we know that God causes all things to work together for good to those who love God, to those who are called according to His purpose.

205

So we need to live our lives with the awareness that all of life's uncertainties are under the control of the God who has demonstrated His love for us in sending His Son to die for us - in spite of our sinful condition (Romans 5:8)! So we can face each new day - uncertainties and all - with the assurance that, although life is uncertain, it is not without meaning. It does pay to do what we can do with the resources and abilities the Lord has placed in our hands, and then leave the results to the Lord.

B. Sowing Diligently 11:6

"Sow your seed in the morning and do not be idle in the evening, for you do not know whether morning or evening sowing will succeed, or whether both of them alike will be good."

Because the Lord has given us the morning hours, we need to find ways in which to use the morning hours to sow some of the seed He has placed in our hands - hoping that the seeds we sow in the morning will eventually result in a healthy crop. The person who sleeps away or wastes away the morning hours will definitely have nothing to show for the morning, so we need to get up and get busy with each new day, using our time so that it may result in success.

And, because the Lord has given us the evening hours, we also need to find ways in which to use the evening to sow some more of the seed that He has placed in our hands - hoping that both the seeds we sow during evening hours and the seeds we sowed earlier, during morning hours, will result in a healthy crop.

We never know what the efforts of any day or any hour of the day might bring forth in our lives, so it is the better part of wisdom to take all the hours the Lord gives to us and use them to the best of our abilities, in the hope that He will bless our efforts with the success which only He can give. It is good to try your hand at many things because no one but God knows what will be blessed.

On Abraham Lincoln's birthday one year an interesting cartoon appeared in a newspaper. It showed a small log cabin at the base of a mountain, and the White House at the top of the mountain. A ladder connected the two buildings. At the bottom of the cartoon were these words: "The ladder is still there."[31]

Success comes to those who, recognizing God's sovereignty, give life their best effort. Are you investing the effort required to make your life as successful as it can be? None of us have perfect bodies, but our bodies will only be the best they can be if we put them through the necessary paces, in terms of diet and rest and exercise, to keep them as fit as we can keep them. None of us have unlimited resources, but our resources will be maximized only if we put them to the best use we can put them to in our attempt to exercise wise stewardship for the honor of the

---

[31] Paul Lee Tan, *Encyclopedia of 7,700 Illustrations* (Rockville, MD: Assurance Publishers, 1979), p.1374, #6142.

206

Lord and the advancement of His cause. None of us have perfect minds, but our minds will only be the best they can be if we put them through the necessary paces in terms of education and stimulation - including education and stimulation in spiritual matters.

So the Lord is calling each one of us to do what we can to make the most of the opportunities He has set before us so that, for our benefit and His glory, we may be successful in our uncertain world.

207

Making the Most of Life
Ecclesiastes 11:7-10

One of the lies of our age - consistent with the evolutionary teaching that people are just animals, with no accountability to any higher being - is the lie that everyone is free to do whatever he wants to do. Because human beings are accountable to no one, the lie states, you are free to "do your own thing." The graffiti-painted walls and drive-by shootings and criminal behavior of modern gang culture are examples of people doing their own thing - as if what they do didn't matter to those around them.

As a result, much of what takes place in our world is characterized by silliness and selfishness and sadness and sin. The fad which has been pursued by many young people - turning to Gothic culture with its gloomy focus on death and dying, in a futile effort to find eternal love beyond the grave - serves as just one of many examples.

But our lives were not intended to be lived without purpose. The Lord is holding all people accountable for how they live their lives. So we, who recognize our accountability to the Lord for all we do in life, ought to live very differently from those around us who do not recognize their accountability to the Lord. Are we then, who claim fellowship with the God who walks in light (I John 1:5-7), clearly walking in the light of His person and His word?

I. Living In the Light 11:7-8

A. The Pleasantness of Light 11:7

"The light is pleasant, and it is good for the eyes to see the sun."

Keeping in mind the fact that Solomon has been attempting, in the book of Ecclesiastes, to find meaning in life "under the sun," it is significant that (as he nears the end of his search) he is encouraging us to look above and see the sun and enjoy the light!

There is hardly anyone who doesn't enjoy a sunny day. Clouds can be very interesting and can add a lot of beauty to the scenery - and they can bring a lot of benefit to the land if they bring rain with them - but days without any view of the sun can be rather dreary. After living for six years in America's Pacific Northwest, where it was not uncommon to go for months without ever seeing the sun because of the presence of rain clouds and rainy weather, it was refreshing to move to the American Southwest where there was seldom ever a week without some sunny days.

Light, which is the source of much of the life on our earth - and thus a symbol of life in the Scriptures, adds beauty and variety to earthly life, and treats the eyes to a dazzling array of views they could never enjoy without it, so "light is pleasant." It has been one of the ironies of recent years that many followers of the New Age Movement have such a fascination with crystals and the rays of light which they catch and deflect, without ever coming to know the Creator of the

208

light they worship in His place.

B. The Contrast to Light 11:8

1. Rejoicing in the Light 11:8a

"Indeed, if a man should live many years, let him rejoice in them all . . ."

Like light, with the benefits and the pleasures it brings, life itself is rich with potential for good in every person's experience.

Nearly everyone wants to live as long as they can - unless life brings them to a time of such intense and constant pain that it becomes too much to bear. Even then most people will do all they can to try to extend their days. I have heard people say they want to die, because life's problems have become too much, but I have seldom ever seen anyone stop eating and doing other things which can be done to prolong life. And such people can quickly change their outlook entirely when just a little hope for improvement is introduced into their experience.

The best our earthly adventure has to offer is a long life, full of things and experiences which give cause to rejoice. There is often a deep sense of satisfaction, even with the approach of death, for the person who has lived many years and can look back on a life of pleasant memories. But the best of human lives need to be lived in view of the inevitability of eventual death.

2. Remembering the Darkness 11:8b

" . . . and let him remember the days of darkness, for they will be many. Everything that is to come will be futility."

No one, in the present age, lives so well that his life goes on uninterrupted forever. As the author of the epistle to the Hebrews states it (Hebrews 9:27), " . . . it is appointed for men to die once and after this comes judgment." So the living need to give some thought to what will follow days of light and life!

Just as light is a symbol of life, so darkness is a symbol of death (and, perhaps, the difficulties which often lead to death). Because life is followed by death in the experience of every human being for whom God does not interrupt the process (and, so far, there have been only two - Enoch and Elijah - for whom the process has been interrupted), it makes sense to think ahead to the days of darkness which are going to follow the days of light and life we have to enjoy.

No matter how long we live, human life has always been followed by a much longer span of death. From an "under the sun" perspective, Solomon himself, who lived for sixty or seventy years, has now been dead for around three thousand years!

209

No matter how well we have lived, there is nothing that can prevent our earthly physical existence from deteriorating into futility. As Solomon has reminded us in Ecclesiastes before, earthly life is cyclical in nature. All the glory which belonged to Solomon during his earthly life fell prey to the principle he stated himself in 1:4: "A generation goes and a generation comes," and the principle he again stated in 3:2: there is "a time to give birth and a time to die."

So Solomon has brought us back to the theme of his book ("vanity of vanities, all is vanity") with the statement of verse 8: "everything that is to come will be futility." As Solomon continued to ponder life "under the sun" (i.e. without God in view), he could see only death and decay, with nothing beyond. So he concluded that it is important to make the most of the present while you have it to enjoy.

Though we, as Christians, have a much clearer view of the joys of life beyond the grave than Solomon did, it is still important that we seek to make the most of the present while we have it to enjoy! Are you taking the wonderful gift of life which God has given and living it to its fullest potential?

II. Reflecting on the Light 11:9-10

A. Making the Most of Light 11:9a-c

Because Solomon saw darkness ahead for those who live on earth, it was his challenge that those who enjoy the light of life should - as the American proverb has it - "make hay while the sun shines."

1. Rejoicing During Childhood 11:9a

"Rejoice, young man, during your childhood . . ."

Because childhood comes only once to human experience (in spite of all the talk of a "second childhood"), those who are blessed to be young ought to make the most of the benefits of being young. It is one of the sad facts of earthly life that children are often pressured to grow up too early - missing out on many of the joys which can only be experienced while they are young. And, in many times and places, children have been taken from their playrooms and sand boxes and sent to work at industrial jobs and in sweatshops which even adults shouldn't have to endure.

It is a happy thing when children are allowed to be children while they are young enough to enjoy childhood. It comes to an end soon enough without cutting it off prematurely! And what is true of childhood, is true as well of the years of youth.

2. Enjoying Young Manhood 11:9b

" . . . and let your heart be pleasant during the days of young manhood."

Like childhood, the days of youth offer opportunities for enjoyment which last for only a brief "window of opportunity." I recall, as a young man, going to "work" with my Dad (who was a banker at the time), and spending whole days exploring the beautiful California city of Carmel and its environs - flying model airplanes in the park; playing tetherball at a school playground; playing tree-tag or three-flies-up with a Frisbee at Carmel beach; collecting golf balls along the shoreline at the Pebble Beach Golf Course; swimming in the Carmel River; window shopping or exploring the quaint passageways between the shops in town.

All too soon the responsibilities of adulthood and the limitations of the aging process make youthful days only fond memories - if we have been blessed with the opportunity to create those memories while we were young enough to create them, which is what Solomon is encouraging us to do.

3. Experiencing Fulfillment 11:9c

"And follow the impulses of your heart and the desires of your eyes."

The impulses the heart of a young man wants to follow and the desires the eyes of a young man see to pursue are different from anything his heart and eyes will ever follow and see again as he grows older. So it is a blessing to be young enough and free enough to enjoy one's youth during the brief time it is available to be enjoyed. Mountains are never more climbable; rivers are never more swimmable; friends are never more available; challenges are never more achievable - than when a person is young.

Of course, some of the things young people think to pursue are not good things to pursue, so Solomon (looking for a moment above the sun) reminds us all of the truth of our accountability in the mist of it all.

B. Meditating on Accountability 11:9d

"Yet know that God will bring you to judgment for all these things."

Knowing the inclination of the human heart to turn toward what is evil, Solomon challenges us to keep in mind the fact that we will all have to answer to the Lord for everything we think and say and do.

The people of Israel were to live their lives within the boundaries of the Mosaic law - a law the Lord gave them to guide them in righteous ways, both for His glory and their own benefit. So children and young men do need to live their lives with the understanding that the Lord is aware of everything they do, and that He is going to call everyone to account before His throne of judgment.

This truth will be restated as a part of Solomon's conclusion to the book of Ecclesiastes in

12:13,14: "The conclusion, when all has been heard, is: fear God and keep His commandments, because this applies to every person. [14] For God will bring every act to judgment, everything which is hidden, whether it is good or evil."

The person who is wise will live his life in view of the fact that he will have to give account of everything he thinks and says and does to the Lord. But - with that sobering truth clearly in view - he will also make the most of the opportunities this life affords, while he is alive, to enjoy them. As a note in the NASB Study Bible puts it: "The prospect of divine praise or blame makes every detail of life significant rather than meaningless."[32]

C. Making the Most of Youth 11:10

Because people only have one opportunity to be young, it makes good sense to make the most of the blessings youth has to offer.

1. Avoiding Vexation and Pain 11:10a

"So, remove grief and anger from your heart and put away pain from your body"

Life is too short and too full of potential for good to allow vexation of the heart and pain in the body to play a bigger part than necessary. So Solomon's first challenge is "remove vexation from your heart." We have the power - and all the more so if we give the Lord His rightful place in our lives - to take control of vexing circumstances and rise above them, turning life's lemons into lemonade!

Consider, for example, what Joni Erickson Tada has done with vexations far more serious than most of us will ever have to deal with! As a quadriplegic, confined to a wheelchair since the diving accident she experienced in Chesapeake Bay which broke her neck, Joni has become an accomplished artist (painting with a brush held in her teeth), an author, a recording artist, a public speaker, and the founder and director of JAF Ministries (Joni and Friends) - a ministry which has had international impact in serving the needs of handicapped people and advancing the cause of Christ!

Human beings have the capacity to remove vexation from their hearts, and human beings often have the capacity to remove pain from their bodies. We have the ability to manage many physical pains by simply taking good care of our bodies - eating well and exercising well and resting well. And the Lord has blessed us with the help of many medications and medical professionals to help eliminate or control pains which won't go away without more help.

Life is too short to live unnecessarily with vexations and pains we don't have to endure. The days will come when pain and problems are harder to control - and it will come much too soon!

---

[32] *NASB Study Bible (*Grand Rapids, MI: Zondervan Publishing House, 1999), p. 945.

212

2. Acknowledging Life's Brevity 11:10b

" . . . because childhood and the prime of life are fleeting."

As Solomon will show us in the classic passage describing the aging process which begins the final chapter of Ecclesiastes, the days of childhood and youth will be followed all too soon by what he refers to as "the evil days" - those days preceding death which are characterized by diminished pleasure and diminished control over the affairs of our lives.

So Solomon's challenge is: make the most of the days of your youth, and do whatever you can to control vexation and pain for as long as possible, so that you can live your life for all it is worth! Because earthly life is brief and God will call all men to account for how it is used, we need to make the most of life and, especially, of youth.

Human life is precious - a sacred trust from the Lord - so we ought to use it as well as we can. Childhood and youth are brief at best - so we need to enjoy them and develop their potential as fully as we possibly can (and help our children and grand children and great grandchildren to do the same).

The Lord is holding all people accountable for how they live their lives. What will result from the Lord's review of your life? Are you making the most of life's opportunities - when and while they are available?

Section Four:
Solomon's Conclusion
and Solution
to Life's Futility

12:1-14

214

Give of Your Best
Ecclesiastes 12:1-8

Abigail Van Buren included "A Senior Citizen's Lament," written by an anonymous author, in her "Dear Abby" column some years ago:

Thought I'd let my doctor check me
"Cause I didn't feel quite right."
All those aches and pains annoyed me,
And I couldn't sleep at night.
He could find no real disorder, but he wouldn't let it rest.
What with Medicare and Blue Cross, it wouldn't hurt to do some tests.
To the hospital he sent me, though I didn't feel that bad.
He arranged for them to give me every test that could be had.
I was fluoroscoped and cystoscoped, my aging frame displayed,
Stripped upon an ice-cold table while my gizzards were X-rayed.
I was checked for worms and parasites, for fungus and the crud,
While they pierced me with long needles taking samples of my blood.
Doctors came to check me over, probed and pushed and poked around,
And to make sure I was living, they wired me for sound.
They have finally concluded: (their results have filled a page)
What I have will someday kill me, my affliction is OLD AGE.

And so it is, or all-too-soon will be, for each and every one of us - barring the return of Jesus to spare us the experiences which are common to man. Time passes with what seems like increasing speed (as each succeeding year becomes a smaller fraction of the whole), bringing every human being who lives into old age a growing list of complications. The results of aging make life challenging and make it increasingly difficult to serve the Lord in all the ways we might like to serve Him.

And so, as he brings us nearer to the conclusion of Ecclesiastes, which has recorded his search for meaning in life "under the sun," Solomon is about to conclude that life's meaning makes the most sense to those who seek it "above the sun" by giving their lives in service to the Lord. And the sooner the better!

It is important to begin serving the Lord early in life, before the complications of aging restrict service, culminating in death. As you look back over your life, are you satisfied that you have made the most of its opportunities - and that you have (as the old song puts it so well) given "your best to the Master?" It isn't a challenge any of us should put off for a later day!

I. Solomon's Challenge to Youth 12:1

A. The Challenge Stated 12:1a

"Remember also your Creator in the days of your youth . . ."

Solomon has just challenged young people to "rejoice . . . during childhood" and to "let [their] heart be pleasant during the days of young manhood" (11:9). But he has also cautioned that God needs to be taken into consideration, because "God will bring you to judgment for all these things."

And Solomon has just reminded us all that "childhood and the prime of life are fleeting" (11:10). So it is important - even imperative (for those who want to get the most out of their lives) - that young people begin while they are still young to "remember [their] Creator."

To "remember . . . your Creator" will involve more than simply thinking about Him. It will involve thinking about Him with a view to allowing Him to have the place of preeminence which He deserves in our lives - as Solomon will make abundantly clear before he is finished with this book.

To "remember . . . your Creator," Solomon will conclude (v. 13), means to "fear God and keep His commandments." And the reason Solomon will give for fearing God and keeping His commandments is (v. 14) that "God will bring every act to judgment, everything which is hidden, whether it is good or evil." So are you living your life, at whatever stage you have attained, in view of your accountability to the Lord? You can't start living life that way any too soon!

B. The Reason Stated 12:1b

" . . . before the evil days come and the years draw near when you will say, 'I have no delight in them.'"

It is possible for young people to do as Solomon has advised in the final verses of chapter 11: to "rejoice . . . during childhood" and "let [their] heart be pleasant during the days of young manhood." It is possible for young people (11:10) to "remove vexation from [their] heart and put away pain from [their] body." But the time comes much too soon when the responsibilities of life make it more challenging to "rejoice" and the aging of the body makes it more challenging to "put away pain."

I arrived at camp one week, when I was in my mid-twenties, to learn that each of the counselors were expected to take charge of a skill during the "skill hour" each day. One of the skills which hadn't yet been claimed involved the trampoline, so I signed up to oversee the skill hour for the trampoline - never having had any extensive trampoline experience. Because I thought it would be wise to develop a few skills of my own which I could teach, I spent a few hours the first day or two of camp getting acquainted with the process - only to discover that, for the rest of the week, every muscle in my body (including muscles I didn't know I had) was in pain from the workout!

216

If you haven't discovered it yet, you will discover it before too long - that increasing age brings more than opportunity. It brings as well a growing list of aches and pains which lead to what Solomon aptly describes as "the evil days." Many times now I have heard aging saints make the observation that "the golden years are not all that golden."

II. Solomon's Description of Aging 12:2-7

A. His Summary of Physical Decline 12:2

" . . . before the sun and the light, the moon and the stars are darkened, and clouds return after the rain;"

With the passing of time the sun, which shone so brightly during the days of childhood, doesn't shine as brightly as it used to shine. With the passing of time it takes more light to enable us to do what we once could do with less light. With the passing of time the glory of a moonlit night and a starry sky is not as glorious as it used to be - partly because we simply can't see as well as we used to see, and partly because darkness is a little more threatening than it used to be.

During childhood there may have been an occasional "storm" to weather, but it probably didn't last long or take much of a toll. I had a hernia surgery when I was five years old, but it didn't slow me down long, and it had virtually no long-term impact for ill in my life. But with the passing of time many people discover that they are just getting past one of the storms of life when - before the clouds have even fully cleared - their life begins to cloud up again for another storm! An aging church member, who as a young man had made a sizeable fortune working hard as a plaster contractor, told me when I met him late in his life that there was virtually no physical malady which he had not had. And I saw the "storms" continue to roll across the horizon of his life until they finally sent him to his grave!

B. His Description of Physical Decline 12:3-5

1. Weakened Arms 12:3

" . . . in the day that the watchmen of the house tremble . . ."

The "watchmen" of the house are the hands and arms - those body parts which reach out to deal with virtually everything which threatens our physical well-being. In childhood and youth they become stronger and more useful. But with the arrival of advanced age they lose their strength and agility and begin to tremble - until a simple task, like picking up a glass of water, can become the occasion for a shower!

2. Bowed Legs 12:3

" . . . and mighty men stoop . . ."

The "mighty men" of the body are the legs - including the largest and strongest muscles and bones in the body. Think of the times when you have needed more strength for a task and have figured out a way to use the strength of your legs to do what other muscles in your body couldn't do alone - like pushing a stalled car. Many an older person appears to have spent years riding a horse, as the leg bones begin to bow in the aging process.

3. Missing Teeth 12:3

" . . . the grinding ones stand idle because they are few . . ."

The "grinding ones" are the teeth we used as children and young people to chew thousands and thousands of meals - along with chewing gum and other things we perhaps shouldn't have been chewing - without ever giving the process a second thought. But when teeth begin to cause pain and to "defect" from the body, older people sometimes find themselves reduced to a soft diet because they no longer have the "hardware" needed to eat a good steak - or even a peanut butter sandwich!

4. Dimmed Vision 12:3

" . . . and those who look through windows grow dim;"

Vision is one of the ways in which we size up the circumstances of the world around us, so it comes as an unpleasant surprise, with the passing of time, that we can't as easily see many things we used to see without any problem. When I turned fifty and got my bifocals, I told the optometrist that it was nice to be able to see again - but it didn't take long to realize that there is nothing like original equipment!

5. Diminished Hearing 12:4

" . . .and the doors on the street are shut as the sound of the grinding mill is low . . ."

It is a sad day when, in order to hear something which makes as much noise as a grinding mill, we have to open the door. I spent just one week-end with impaired hearing, resulting from impacted wax in one ear, and came away very thankful that my problem could be easily corrected. I don't know how many older people I have known who have gone to great expense to purchase the latest in hearing aid technology, only to set their hearing aides aside with the complaint that they didn't really "do the trick."

6. Sleeplessness 12:4

" . . . and one will arise at the sound of the bird . . ."

It isn't the **sound** of the bird which causes those in advanced age to arise from the sleep of the night - because the chances are that they can't hear the sound of the bird. But Solomon reminds us that the passing of the years may well find us up at the crack of dawn - when the birds begin to welcome the new day with their songs - because advanced age has robbed us of the ability to sleep soundly as well as we once could sleep (perhaps because of aching bones).

7. Weakened Voice 12:4

" . . . and all the daughters of song will sing softly."

The "daughters of song" - the vocal chords - which once sang with volume and control, begin to lose their elasticity with the passing of the years. So we all too soon discover that we not only can't sing what we once sang, in terms of range and strength, but we may not be able to sing at all (or only softly at best).

8. Fear of Heights and Travels 12:5

"Furthermore, men are afraid of a high place and of terrors on the road . . ."

The passing of the years begin to make a person think more seriously about what could happen if they get up too high in the air, or what complications could arise if they decide to take a trip. Many people who began their early retirement years traveling extensively across the country, and even around the world, to see things they hadn't seen before, get to the place where they are fearful or even unable to drive themselves to a nearby doctor's appointment!

9. Greying Hair 12:5

" . . . the almond tree blossoms . . ."

When almond trees blossom, they bear light-colored flowers - similar in color to the "medicare blond" tint which is so common among the older members of society (and which became predominant among the hairs on my own head at a fairly early age).

10. Awkward Gait 12:5

" . . . the grasshopper drags himself along . . ."

Grasshoppers can be quite impressive when they jump and fly through the air - but if you have ever watched a grasshopper walk he may have reminded you somewhat of your grandfather in his senior years.

11. Sexual Impotence 12:5

219

" . . . and the caperberry is ineffective."

The caperberry was used among the people of Israel as an aphrodisiac (a sexual stimulant) - but there eventually comes a time in life for many of the aged when even the caperberry can't do what it used to do.

12. Physical Death 12:5

"For man goes to his eternal home while mourners go about in the street."

When all the indignities which tend to accompany aging have taken their toll in our lives, the final indignity of death will send us beyond this life into eternity, leaving behind only memories in the minds of those who care enough to grieve our passing by attending our funeral and making their way to the grave-side service - if there is one.

C. His Summary of Physical Death 12:6-7

"Remember Him before the silver cord is broken and the golden bowl is crushed, the pitcher by the well is shattered and the wheel at the cistern is crushed; [7] then the dust will return to the earth as it was, and the spirit will return to God who gave it."

Because the verses preceding these have contained images which could be easily identified as the parts of the body, many Bible students have attempted to align each of the images we find in verses six and seven with some part of the body. The "silver cord" has been viewed as the spinal cord; the "golden bowl" as the skull; and the "pitcher by the well" and the "wheel at the cistern" as a variety of things - harder to pin down.

It is probably best to see Solomon's message as a description of the general condition of brokenness which comes with the advancing of age. A "silver cord" is a thing of beauty - just as youth is a thing of beauty - but once the cord is broken it can never be restored to its original condition. A golden bowl is an attractive and valuable treasure - like youth is - but once it has been crushed it will never be the same again. The pitcher by the well and the wheel at the cistern are useful tools for capturing water (which, like youth, is a precious commodity) - but a shattered pitcher can never be restored to its original condition, and a crushed wheel may need to be replaced with a newer model.

When aging has taken its full toll, ending in death, there is nothing left behind on earth except the well-worn body which, without life, will soon return to the dust of which the original man, Adam, was made when God created him. Very encouraging, isn't it? Well, not really! But it is realistic.

III. Solomon's Summation of Life 12:8

220

"Vanity of vanities," says the Preacher, "all is vanity!"

For those who are seeking meaning in life "under the sun," as Solomon was in the writing of this book, the story ends at the graveyard and is not a happy ending.

"Vanity of vanities . . . all is vanity." Breath, emptiness, nothingness is what human life amounts to if you leave the Lord out of the picture. So don't leave the Lord out of the picture! And the sooner you get Him clearly in focus in your life, the better it will be!

It is important to begin serving the Lord early in life, before the complications of aging restrict service, culminating in death. So Solomon challenged young people to give the Lord their youthful years, because aging will all too soon begin taking its toll, ending in death.

Are you doing all you can to give the Lord the best you have to give Him in terms of service? Howard B. Grose wrote Solomon's challenge in the words of a hymn which has been familiar to earlier generations:

Give of your best to the Master,
Give of the strength of your youth;
Throw your soul's fresh, glowing ardor
Into the battle for truth.
Jesus has set the example -
Dauntless was He, young and brave;
Give Him your loyal devotion,
Give Him the best that you have.

Give of your best to the Master,
Give Him first place in your heart;
Give Him first place in your service,
Consecrate ev'ry part.
Give and to you shall be given -
God His beloved Son gave;
Gratefully seeking to serve Him,
Give Him the best that you have.

221

Solomon on Writing
Ecclesiastes 12:9-12

You have probably had the experience which I have had with some books. You pick the book up and look it over or begin to read it and realize, in the process, that it isn't worth your time.

The world today is full of books. And new books are being produced at such a rapid rate that there is no chance anyone will ever read them all. It would not even be possible today, if someone who was a fast reader gave his whole time to the task, to read all of the books being written in just the English language. In fact, it is generally agreed today that it isn't even possible to keep up with all of the worthy writings in just one area of study. There is no chance that anyone today could possibly read all that is being written in the field of the arts or biology or cooking or medicine or theology.

As we know, there is a lot of benefit to be found in the world of books - good books. But, since no one can read all of the books which are good, we will have to make some choices in the reading that we do. A pastor friend offered his thoughts concerning the pastor's library in a seminar for pastors , suggesting that since you can't read everything, and since there is so much good material waiting to be read, you should read only the very best. That would probably mean reading very little of the latest in order to leave time for the very best.

Because there is so much reading material available in our day, it would be helpful to have some of the Lord's thoughts about what is worth reading. And it just happens that, like many other topics of practical relevance in the Christian's life, the Bible speaks to the subject of worthy reading material. And the person whom God used to share some of His wisdom on the subject was a very likely source: the wise and prolific author, King Solomon.

Because he was an author himself, King Solomon was sensitive to the challenge of writing well. And he was also sensitive to the fact that, when it comes to the best in reading material, there is only one final source of that which is true and best. The Lord is the ultimate source of all wise words.

I. A Survey of Solomon's Writings 12:9-10

A. Solomon's Writing Accomplishments 12:9

We are blessed to have three Bible books which were written by Solomon - along with Psalms 72 and 127. His writings have come to us as inspired truth which the Lord specially and even uniquely prepared him to communicate.

1. His Wisdom 12:9a

222

"In addition to being a wise man . . ."

You will recall that, in Solomon's life as a young king of Israel, there came a time when, in one of his dreams, he was offered an amazing choice by the Lord. It is recorded in I Kings 3:4: "Ask what you wish me to give you." If you were given such an offer by the Lord, what would you choose?

As we have seen before, Solomon pleased the Lord with the request which is recorded in I Kings 3:9: "So give Your servant an understanding heart to judge Your people to discern between good and evil. For who is able to judge this great people of Yours?"

The Lord was pleased to give to Solomon that which he requested - along with many other blessings in his life, including wisdom. So Solomon became very well-informed and very wise in applying his knowledge to the practical issues of everyday life. He is identified in Scripture (I Kings 3:12;10:23) as the wisest man who has ever lived (apart, of course, from the God/man Jesus).

Solomon was a "wise man" in a fuller sense than any other mere human who has ever deserved that title - in terms of the wisdom he stated and recorded. As we know from our study of Ecclesiastes, of course, he did not always demonstrate his great wisdom in the way he conducted his own life. But Solomon did put his wisdom to work for the benefit of others.

2. His Teachings 12:9b

" . . . the Preacher also taught the people knowledge."

"The Preacher," as the opening verses of Ecclesiastes revealed (1:1,2,12), is the title Solomon used of himself in the book or Ecclesiastes. Like other national leaders, Solomon used his position as king as a "bully pulpit."

As we have noted before, the Bible tells us of some of the teaching that Solomon did in his day in I Kings 4:30-34:

Solomon's wisdom surpassed the wisdom of all the sons of the east and all the wisdom of Egypt. [31] For he was wiser than all men, than Ethan the Ezrahite, Heman, Calcol and Darda, the sons of Mahol; and his fame was known in all the surrounding nations. [32] He also spoke 3,000 proverbs, and his songs were 1,005. [33] He spoke of trees, from the cedar that is in Lebanon even to the hyssop that grows on the wall; he spoke also of animals and birds and creeping things and fish. [34] Men came from all peoples to hear the wisdom of Solomon, from all the kings of the earth who had heard of his wisdom.

Solomon was knowledgeable on many subjects, but we still look back today on Solomon as a man who specialized in the spiritual wisdom of the proverbs.

3. His Proverbs 12:9c

" . . . and he pondered, searched out and arranged many proverbs."

As we just read in I Kings 4:32, Solomon "spoke 3,000 proverbs" - i.e. wisdom sayings (as in our Biblical book of Proverbs, which contains, at best, only around two tenths of Solomon's total collection).

Anyone who has carefully studied the Proverbs of Scripture can readily appreciate the statement that Solomon "pondered . . . many proverbs." By their nature, proverbs are the kind of literary material which deserves and requires some pondering. This is the case even for the student, and so it would be even more true for the author. Consider, for example, the wisdom of Proverbs 10:2:

> Ill-gotten gains do not profit [Oh they don't? What about the mafia?]
> But righteousness delivers from death. [Oh really? What about Christian martyrs?]

Because Solomon's proverbs are statements of truth in a general sense, they are worthy of inclusion in the Scriptures; but because there are exceptions to many of the truths they teach, they will require some pondering.

The proverbs include many sayings of an apparently controversial nature, or a categorical nature, which required Solomon to "search [them] out" - to do some research. Take, as an example, Proverbs 10:27: "The fear of the Lord prolongs life, But the years of the wicked will be shortened." The relationship between a person's attitude toward the Lord and their longevity in life is the kind of relationship we might expect to see George Barna research in our day, but Solomon must have "searched out" the relationship in his day in order to write such a proverb.

B. Solomon's Writing Aim 12:10

1. His Search for Words 12:10a

"The Preacher sought to find delightful words . . ."

Solomon's word choices were such "delightful" choices that many of his proverbs stick in our minds yet today - nearly three thousand years after they were written. His words are well chosen and, in many cases, picturesque. Take, as an example, Proverbs 11:22: "As a ring of gold in a swine's snout So is a beautiful woman who lacks discretion." Or Proverbs 13:24: "He who withholds his rod hates his son, But he who loves him disciplines him diligently." Or Proverbs 14:12: "There is a way which seems right to a man, But its end is the way of death." Or Proverbs 15:1: "A gentle answer turns away wrath, But a harsh word stirs up anger." Or Proverbs 25:11: "Like apples of gold in settings of silver Is a word spoken in right circumstances." And there are many more examples.

224

After Solomon worked hard at finding delightful words, he sought to record them with accuracy.

2. His Selection of Words 12:10b

" . . . and to write words of truth correctly."

Most writings dating back as far as Solomon's time were discarded long ago because they had no lasting relevance. But because Solomon wrote words of truth, and because he did it with such care and skill, there are many people who read his book of Proverbs at least once every year, and some people even read it once every month. Years ago I heard Bill Gothard (founder of the Principles in Basic Youth Conflicts/Basic Life Principles seminar) suggest to his large audience that they read one chapter of Proverbs every day - the chapter corresponding to the day's date - as an aid to growing in wisdom, and many people have taken his advice.

Solomon was a very skilled author. And, as an author, he had some keen insights into the value and the nature of written communication.

II. A Survey of Other Writings 12:11-12

Solomon's work as an author placed him as only one among many. But it gave him insight into the world of written literature, qualifying him as a literary critic.

A. Solomon's Evaluation of Writing 12:11

Because wisdom literature was Solomon's specialty, he was alert to the benefits of wise words.

1. The Effect of Wise Words 12:11a

"The words of wise men are like goads . . ."

The "words of wise men" are words which arise out of the minds of people blessed with skill in their speech. This is the idea behind Solomon's common Old Testament word for "wise" (*chakam*). And the skill with which the words of wise men are chosen causes their words to have a profound and lasting impact. Think, for example, of the impact God's own wise words in the Ten Commandments have had on human society - both Jewish and non-Jewish; or of the impact the words of Psalm 23 have had; or of the impact the words of John 3:16 have had.

Solomon compares the impact of well-chosen words to the effect of a "goad." A "goad" was a stick with a pointed end (a cattle prod), used to control and direct animals. Like a "goad," the words of wise men prod those who read them to wise action. The author of Hebrews tells us, in Hebrews 4:12, that this is what the wise words of Scripture do: "For the word of God is living

225

and active and sharper than any two-edged sword, and piercing as far as the division of soul and spirit, of both joints and marrow, and able to judge the thoughts and intentions of the heart." Are you exposing yourself to the words of wise men (and especially the words of God) so that you will feel their impact in your life?

2. The Collection of Wise Words 2:11b

" . . . and masters of these collections are like well-driven nails;"

People who are well-versed in the collected words of "wise men" find their lives stabilized - as if the wise words they have become familiar with were nails driven in to hold their lives in place. People who are knowledgeable in any area of life experience a strengthening and stabilizing effect as a result of their knowledge. Generally speaking (though there are exceptions), educated people are more productive in life than non-educated people. And, of course, people who are well-informed in spiritual matters tend to be more productive in life and in human relations than people who are not well-informed in spiritual matters.

Truth stabilizes people and builds them up! Any area of truth will build people up, because all truth is God's truth.

3. The Source of Wise Words 12:11c

" . . . they are given by one Shepherd."

For the ancient people of Israel (as for the church today) there was only One person who could be finally and fully identified as the "one Shepherd." As the familiar words of the twenty-third Psalm state it, "the LORD is [that] shepherd." The Lord is the giver of every good and perfect gift (as James tells us, 1:18), and that includes the gift of truth.

Though we are most likely to associate the Lord with spiritual truth, the fact is that the Lord is the originator of truth in any and every dimension of life. As the Creator, He brought our world and our universe into being and solidly established them on the basis of what we sometimes call "natural laws" - probably a poor choice of terminology, arising out the humanistic emphasis of the Renaissance era. What we call "natural laws" are not "natural" at all, in terms of their origin. They have a supernatural origin. The facts of astronomy were established by the Lord. The laws of chemistry are His laws. The details of botany and zoology were designed by Him. Gravity is God's idea. Entropy came into existence by the Lord's decree. The theory of relativity may have been discovered by Einstein, but it originated with God!

Solomon realized that, though he was classed among men as a "wise man," and though he established a solid reputation as a teacher of truth and an author who wrote with skill, anything he knew or said or wrote that was worth knowing or saying or writing was given to Him by "the Shepherd"- the Lord God.

226

Words of truth - because they are God's truth - will act like "goads" to prod us into profitable action. And, when we make the effort to collect them and master them, they will act like well-driven nails - providing stability and solidity in our lives. But we need to be aware that not all words, and not all spoken words, and not all written words are words of truth.

B. Solomon's Warning About Writing 12:12

1. The Endless Writing of Books 12:12a

"But beyond this, my son, be warned: the writing of many books is endless"

We began this chapter thinking briefly about the endless parade of books coming off the presses in just our day and our own language. Add to that all of the books which have been written down through the ages, and all of the languages in which they have been written, and Solomon's point is very well taken. And with the advent of desk-top publishing the number is not going to be decreasing any time soon. Books are here to stay. So you can keep as busy at reading and studying as you want to.

2. The Impact of Devotion to Books 12:12b

" . . . and excessive devotion to books is wearying to the body."

I have spent entire days on the end of a shovel, or in other kinds of physical labor, and I know how tired a body can get by the end of a day. But I have also spent entire days (and nights, in a few cases) laboring over the books, and I know that you can get just about as tired by "excessive devotion to books." Lengthy study can create a serious case of weary eyes and an aching head!

Books are one of the blessings of life, but you can easily get too much of a good thing, even in the world of books. So we need to be discerning in our choices of reading material. If, as it has been said, "what you think is what you are, " we need to give careful attention to who and what is guiding our thinking.

As Solomon pondered the voluminous writings of men, including his own, he realized that God is the source of all truth. The Lord is the ultimate source of all words that are wise. The beauty of the words which Solomon and other Bible authors wrote is that they were wise words, designed to apply the wisdom of God to the issues of daily life, and to make us better people for having read them.

Do you place enough emphasis on God's truth as you choose what you will read from the inexhaustible supply of written material available?

If you and I are into the pursuit of only knowledge, we will be fair game for anything that comes off the presses of our world. You can use the check-out counter newspapers to increase

227

your knowledge. But if you and I are into the pursuit of truth and wisdom, there is a lot in print which won't need to concern us.

Given the fact that we can't read everything without wearing ourselves out trying, we need to read that which is the best so we will derive the good we can derive out of the reading we do. And never forget that, even after two thousand years (and much longer, for some parts) the Bible is the best there is.

Are you faithfully reading His book? And, if you are, are you wisely using His book to guide your life? And, because there is so much good literature available, are you making good use of the other good books available today to prod you on to greater stability and service for the Lord?

228

Solomon's Conclusion
Ecclesiastes 12:13-14

The book of Ecclesiastes has taken us for quite a trip with its author, King Solomon, as he went on a search for meaning in life.

Solomon began his reign as king of Israel in a very promising way. He was blessed with the "understanding heart to judge [God's] people to discern between good and evil" (I Kings 3:5) which he requested of the Lord. And he was a blessed, as well, with great wisdom and great wealth and great influence.

But Solomon mishandled the wisdom the Lord gave to him when he allowed the other gifts the Lord gave to distract him from single-hearted devotion to the Lord. So the time came when, having multiplied wives and wealth to himself, Solomon turned aside from the worship of the Lord to the worship of the foreign "gods" of his many wives. He got so far away from the Lord in his excesses that he began to lose sight of the purpose of his life, so he set out on the search for meaning in life which has been recorded for our examination in the book of Ecclesiastes.

As our earlier studies in Ecclesiastes have shown us, Solomon's search for meaning in life took him far and wide. Chapter two told of his exploration of pleasure and laughter and wine and folly in search of satisfaction. It records his construction projects and agricultural projects (including vineyards and gardens and parks and pools to water a forest of trees). It tells of his accumulation of male and female slaves and flocks and herds and silver and gold and other treasures. It tells of his acquisition of male and female singers, and the many women who became a part of his life as wives and concubines. But it does not tell us much about satisfaction he found in his search, because his search was conducted (for the most part) "under the sun" - i.e. apart from the consideration of the Lord and the spiritual realities which the Lord has commanded His people to make central in their lives.

So the book of Ecclesiastes would be a sad and empty record of an ambitious but fruitless search for satisfaction in life if it did not include the final chapter, with Solomon's conclusions regarding his search. The opening verse of the twelfth chapter of Ecclesiastes, however, rounded an important corner with its admonition for young readers to "remember also your Creator in the days of your youth."

Satisfaction in this life cannot be found by considering only what is "under the sun," because above and beyond the sun is the God who has created us to live in view of our accountability to Him! He has designed us with what has been described as a "God-shaped vacuum," which causes every person to ponder the eternal. And He has revealed Himself in His world and in His written word and His Living Word (Jesus), so that every person on earth can be held accountable before Him. On the coming day of judgment the Lord will call every person to account for their performance in terms of fearing Him and obeying His commandments.

229

Will the Lord's review of your life in the final judgment reveal that you have lived in fear of Him as your final judge? And will it show that your fear of God has lead you to live in obedience to the commands He has recorded in His word?

I. Solomon's Concluding Challenge 12:13

A. The Challenge Stated 12:13a

"The conclusion, when all has been heard, is: fear God and keep His commandments . . ."

By this final chapter of the book, "when all has been heard," we have heard quite a lot!

In addition to the summary of Solomon's many paths in pursuit of meaning in life (recorded in chapter two), Solomon has analyzed and philosophized about many, many different things in the other chapters of Ecclesiastes. He has written about changing times (3:1-11); life's good gifts (3:12-13); future judgment (3:14-21); the problem of oppression (4:1-3); the challenges of work (4:4-12); political success (4:13-16); false worship (5:1-7); and the list goes on and on.

But, after all the searching any person can do in pursuit of meaning in earthly life, we come face to face, sooner or later, with the God who made us! And coming face to face with the Lord, Solomon calls upon all people to do two things:

1. Fear God

Many people are very uncomfortable with the notion that God is a God to be feared. After all, He has revealed Himself as a God of love! "God is love," the Apostle John has written, not once but twice in his first epistle (I John 4:8 and 4:16). Why should a God of love be feared?

Some people have even suggested that the God of the Old Testament is a God to be feared, but the God of the New Testament has revealed Himself as a God of love, so New Testament saints shouldn't fear the Lord. It is an interesting thought, but (of course) the God of the Old Testament and the God of the New Testament are one and the same, unchanging God! And, besides that, the New Testament teaches that God's people should fear Him, just as the Old Testament does! I Peter 1:17 contains the challenge: "If you address as Father the One who impartially judges according to each one's work, conduct yourselves in fear during the time of your stay on earth."

So God is a God to be feared in every age; and God is also a God to be obeyed!

2. Keep His Commandments

Since the Garden of Eden, the Lord has been faithful to communicate with His human creatures. And in every age He has given commandments to be obeyed. The books of the

230

Mosaic Law contain hundreds of commands, many of them intended specifically for His chosen people, the Jews, living under the Law. But some of them, like the Ten Commandments, are applicable to all people in all times!

Though we do not live today under many of the commandments of the Law, there are plenty of commandments for us to obey as well. In addition to commandments from the Old Testament which are repeated in the New Testament for saints in this age of grace, there are many New Testament commandments for God's people to obey!

It won't do to argue that what Solomon is saying about fearing God and obeying His commandments applies just to Old Testament saints or to "Gentiles" or to the unsaved, because Solomon assures us that **everyone** needs to fear the Lord and obey His commandments!

B. The Challenge Directed 12:13b

" . . . because this applies to every person."

There isn't a person on earth who should not live out his life in fear of the Lord - because of what He is capable of doing in the lives of those who choose to cross Him.

In the Old Testament era, Nadab and Abihu should have feared what the Lord might do if they dishonored Him by offering strange fire before Him on His altar. But they didn't fear the Lord (Leviticus 10:1-2), so they were judged by fire which fell out of heaven and consumed them!

In the New Testament era, Ananias and Sapphira should have feared what the Lord might do if they attempted to deceive their church family. They made it appear that they had honored the Lord by giving all of the proceeds of the sale of their property as a gift to God (as Joseph/Barnabas had done). But they didn't fear the Lord, secretly and deceptively holding back a portion of the proceeds of their sale (Acts 5:1-2,5,10). So they dropped dead before Peter when he questioned them about their integrity!

In the coming Tribulation era, people ought to fear the Lord enough to listen carefully and respectfully to the two witnesses the Lord is going to send to prophesy His word among the people - but they won't fear the Lord. So even as they are celebrating the death of the two witnesses at the hands of the beast, the two witnesses will be raised to life and taken up into heaven (Revelation 11:11-13), while a tenth of the city of Jerusalem will be killed in the great earthquake which the Lord will send as His instrument of judgment!

In every age and place the Lord ought to be feared and obeyed by all people, but when He isn't, there will be some serious consequences!

II. Solomon's Concluding Explanation 12:14

231

A. The Fact of the Lord's Judgment 12:14a

"For God will bring every act to judgment . . ."

Though He is a God of love, the Lord is also a God to be feared - because He is the God who will serve as judge of every man. And judges, as their title suggests, have the authority to impose judgment! So a judge is someone before whom anyone who has done wrong ought to be afraid of the judgment which can come to wrongdoers. And, as the Bible clearly teaches, we have all done wrong! As Romans 3:23 assures us, "all have sinned and fall short of the glory of God."

I have been in courtrooms several times (always, thankfully, to deal with the problems of someone other than myself), and I have always had the distinct impression that the judge is not someone any thinking person would trifle with. From the initial "all rise," at which everyone in the room stands in honor of the judge, until the final bang of the gavel and the pronouncement of the judge's decision, everyone in a courtroom who is "hitting on all of his cylinders" is very respectful of the judge because of his authority and ability to make life difficult for anyone who doesn't. I was in a courtroom one day when a lawyer entered the court dressed in a shirt and tie but not a coat, and I heard the judge sternly remind him that he had better not appear again without the proper attire or he would not be allowed in the courtroom - and the lawyer's response (though lawyers project authority themselves) was "Yes Sir, I am sorry, Sir."

God is to be feared because, as judge of the universe, He has the power and authority to pronounce any form of judgment He chooses to pronounce. And He has the authority to pronounce judgment on anyone He chooses - including the authority to send a soul to eternal hell! And even for those who know that they will never be assigned to hell, because they enjoy a saving relationship with the Lord through Jesus Christ, God is to be feared because He can bring judgment of various kinds into His people's lives in both the present and the future.

An example of the Lord's temporal judgment upon believers is the weakness and sickness and even death which plagued some of the Corinthian saints as a result of their abuse of the Lord's Supper (I Corinthians 11:29,30). And an example of the Lord's future judgment is the loss of rewards which will affect every believer in some measure for eternity - as revealed at the Judgment Seat of Christ (I Corinthians 3:10-15). As Paul assured the Corinthian saints (II Corinthians 5:10): "For we must all appear before the judgment seat of Christ, so that each one may be recompensed for his deeds in the body, according to what he has done, whether good or bad."

The comprehensiveness of the Lord's judgment is addressed in the final phrase of the book.

B. The Basis of the Lord's Judgment 12:14b

" . . . everything which is hidden, whether it is good or evil."

232

We are not too surprised that the Lord would bring judgment upon the sins people have sinned openly. I Corinthians 6:9-10 tells us, for example that "neither fornicators, nor idolaters, nor adulterers, nor effeminate, nor homosexuals, [10] nor thieves, nor the covetous, nor drunkards, nor revilers, nor swindlers, will inherit the kingdom of God."

But Solomon assures us that the Lord's judgment is going to extend even to "everything which is hidden, whether it is good or evil"! Not even the deed done in darkness will escape the notice of the Lord as He exercises judgment upon humanity! Not even the words whispered in secret will escape the notice of the Lord as He exercises judgment! Not even the thoughts of our minds will escape the notice of the Lord as He exercises judgment.

The Psalmist David expressed his amazement at the comprehensiveness of the Lord's knowledge in Psalm 139:1-6:

O Lord, You have searched me and known me.
[2] You know when I sit down and when I rise up;
You understand my thought from afar.
[3] You scrutinize my path and my lying down,
And are intimately acquainted with all my ways.
[4] Even before there is a word on my tongue,
Behold, O Lord, You know it all.
[5] You have enclosed me behind and before,
And laid Your hand upon me.
[6] Such knowledge is too wonderful for me;
It is too high, I cannot attain to it.

Solomon's search for meaning in life ends with the finding that every person needs to live in fear of and obedience to the Lord in order to avoid divine judgment. The Lord will call every person to account as to whether they have feared Him and obeyed His commandments. It was Solomon's failure to fear and obey the Lord that resulted in the sense of futility which caused him to go searching for meaning in his life. It isn't possible to live life only "under the sun" and experience life at its fullest. Not until we are factoring into our lives all that we can know of God's perspective from "above the sun" will earthly life make as much sense as it can make. And factoring in God's "above the sun" perspective will require us to live in view of our accountability to Him as our judge.

Living life to its fullest will require us to conform our lives - in everything we think, and say, and do - to the instructions God has revealed in His word. Though there are bound to be things we won't understand as we make our way through life (because our world is cursed by sin), as we conform our lives to the revealed will of God, we will discover (as Paul expressed it so well in Romans 12:2) that the will of God is "that which is good and acceptable and perfect."

To what extent are you experiencing "that which is good and acceptable and perfect" in your life? Will God's appraisal of your life show you to have lived in fear of and obedience to Him?

233

Are you experiencing what Jesus said He wants His people to experience (John10:10) - "that they may have life, and have it abundantly"?

234

Bibliography

A. Books

Humanist Manifestos I and II, Buffalo, NY: Prometheus Books, 1973

Kaiser, Walter C., Jr., *Ecclesiastes, Total Life*, Chicago, IL: Moody Press, 1979

Kidner, Derek. *Proverbs*. London: Inter-Varsity Press, 1964

Leupold, H.C., *Exposition of Ecclesiastes*, Grand Rapids, MI: Baker Book House, 1952

McDowell, Josh, *The Resurrection Factor*, San Bernardino, CA: Here's Life Publishers, 1981

Preiffer, Charles F. and Harrison, Everett F., *The Wycliffe Bible Commentary*, Chicago, IL: Moody Press, 1962

Stedman, Ray C., *Is This All There Is to Life?*, Grand Rapids, MI.: Discovery House Publishers, Copyright 1999 by Elaine Stedman.

Tan, Paul Lee, *Encyclopedia of 7,700 Illustrations*, Rockville, MD: Assurance Publishers, 1979

B. Books: Multiple Volume

Keil and Delitzsch, *Old Testament Commentaries*, Grand Rapids, MI: Associated Publishers and Authors, 1861

Falwell, Jerry, Ex. Ed., *Liberty Bible Commentary*, Lynchburg, VA: The Old Time Gospel Hour, 1982

Henry, Matthew, *Matthew Henry's Commentary*, New York: Fleming H. Revell, Co., No copyright date

C. Dictionaries, Concordances, and Lexicons

Brown, Francis; Driver, S.R.; and Briggs, Charles A., *A Hebrew and English Lexicon of the Old Testament*, Oxford: Clarendon Press, 1907

Holladay, William L., Ed., *A Concise Hebrew and Aramaic Lexicon of the Old Testament*, Grand Rapids, MI: Wm. B. Eerdmans, 1971

235

Tragelles, Samuel P., translator. *Gesenius' Hebrew-Chaldee Lexicon to the Old Testament*, Grand Rapids, MI: Wm. B. Eerdmans Publishing Company, 1949

D. Bibles

The Quest Study Bible, The Zondervan Corporation, Grand Rapids, MI, 1994

NASB Study Bible, Zondervan Publishing House, Grand Rapids, MI, 1999

Radmacher, Earl D., Gen. Ed., *Nelson Study Bible*, Nashville, TN: Thomas Nelson Publishers, 1997

Ryrie, Charles Caldwell. *Ryrie Study Bible* (Expanded Edition), Moody Press, Chicago, IL, 1995

E. Computer Resources

Thompson Chain Bible Software, Colorado Springs, CO: NavPress

Wordsearch 8, Wordsearchbible.com, Austin, Texas, 2008